USAGE

*William Fay
Central Catholic
EM 1-0437*

COMPOSITION AND MECHANICS

Handbook
of English

▸ BOOK ONE

JOHN E. WARRINER
Head of the English Department,
Garden City High School, Garden
City, Long Island, New York

The English Workshop Series

HARCOURT, BRACE AND COMPANY

NEW YORK   CHICAGO

[j · 10 · 53]

ENGLISH WORKSHOP SERIES

WARRINER'S HANDBOOK OF ENGLISH: 1
(Grades Nine and Ten)

WARRINER'S HANDBOOK OF ENGLISH: 2
(Grades Eleven and Twelve)

ENGLISH WORKSHOP: GRADE NINE

ENGLISH WORKSHOP: GRADE TEN

ENGLISH WORKSHOP: GRADE ELEVEN

ENGLISH WORKSHOP: GRADE TWELVE

PREFACE

The *Handbook of English* is a basic teaching text for ninth and tenth grade classes. It was written for teachers who prefer to use their own methods of motivating composition and are therefore indifferent to the elaborate motivation found in the usual textbook. These teachers, it is believed, want a textbook which will state clearly and illustrate fully the rules and conventions of standard English usage. They want a book with enough practice material to fix those rules and conventions firmly in their students' speech and writing. They want a book which will help them teach the essentials of grammar-usage, display the necessary forms of composition, and act as a reference handbook for individual student use. The *Handbook of English* is that kind of book.

In both the ninth and tenth grades, the teaching situation requires abundant teaching materials and an arrangement of those materials which will permit easy reference. In the typical ninth grade class, students are drawn together from a variety of schools with no uniform English instruction. To bring them to a common level, the teacher usually feels that a complete reteaching of grammar-usage is necessary. In the tenth grade class, students arrive with greatly varying degrees of mastery of language essentials. One student may be weak in sentence sense, another in pronoun usage. But each student requires for his special weakness a full text explanation, a wealth of examples and practice material. Thus, the full teaching equipment in the *Handbook of English* makes it a valuable teaching tool for either ninth or tenth grade classes.

The full text explanations set this book apart from handbooks used in colleges and the later years of high school. It differs from these advanced handbooks in another important respect. It is not concerned, as they are, with advanced refinements of style and usage. Specifically, for instance, it does not contain materials on parallelism, subordination, writing the research paper. Its objective is limited: to establish knowledge of essentials which the average student in ninth and tenth grades can reasonably be expected to grasp and apply.

The handbook organization has the great advantage of highlighting essential rules and usages. They are set out from the surrounding text by boldface type and by numbers and letters. This arrangement has the further advantage of aiding review and relearning. The number-letter identification, together with the unusually complete index, will make it easy for student and teacher to find their way through the book. During the second year of use, the student may be expected to make reference use of this book with greatly increased ease and effectiveness. Complete coverage of usage problems enhances the value of the book as a reference tool. The student will find here a clear answer to any question of written or oral English which is likely to confront him.

The strongest motive in the preparation of the *Handbook of English* was the desire to create a book that would fit any course of study. The goal was a completely flexible teaching tool adaptable to any course of study or to any individual classroom. With the exception that the usage chapters require a certain knowledge of the grammar presented in the beginning chapters, all chapters and sections of the book are independent. They may be used as the needs of a particular class may dictate. The book does not impose a method or a sequence.

The *Handbook of English* may be used in the ninth grade alone or in the tenth grade alone. More profitably, it may be started in the ninth grade and carried over to the tenth grade. The student will be far more efficient in using the book a second year through greater familiarity with the arrangement and location of materials.

The division of materials by grades will depend upon the local teaching situation and must be left to the individual teacher, who will select those chapters or sections which his students need immediately, leaving others for later treatment. Similarly, teachers will select the materials they wish to teach to all students, leaving other matters for the individual to look up for himself as he needs them.

As a means of orderly arrangement, the grammar is presented separately from the usage. This is not to imply that grammar can be separated from usage in practice. The only valid reason for teaching grammar at all is to enable students to apply it to specific usage problems. However, it is an axiom of the "grammar approach" to good English that grammar cannot be successfully applied until it has been learned. A thorough review of grammatical relationships and terms, as provided in the first three chapters, is, therefore, a natural approach to the functional chapters which follow. Diagramming is included in the grammar chapters and used for illus-

trative purposes elsewhere because many teachers
find it useful in making word relationships clear.
The diagrams, however, are an accessory and not an
integral part of the teaching method. They may be
ignored if the teacher desires.

Two aspects of the book require special mention.
The first is the wealth of illustrative sentences.
The aim was to supply enough different applications
of rules and usages to make it likely that among them
the student will find a parallel to his own faulty sentence. The second aspect is the quantity of practice exercises. The book answers the common complaint that English texts do not contain enough drills.
Omission of space-consuming, detailed materials for
motivation of oral and written activities has permitted the inclusion in this book of a vast amount of
drill material. The subject matter of the drill paragraphs is interesting to ninth and tenth graders.
There is enough practice material to permit allocation
between ninth and tenth grades.

However, for the teacher who wants additional
drill materials, correlated workbooks are provided.
The handbook and the workbooks together are
known as the *English Workshop Series*. Within this
series there is a workbook for each high school grade.
The terminology and the statement of rules is uniform throughout the series. The workbooks provide extra drill at those points where it is likely to
be needed most.

The chapters on composition are meant to be exact guides with very definite directions to help
students learn the steps in building a paragraph and
planning a longer composition. All of the basic skills
of composition — outlining, organizing ideas, using

the library — are fully presented. A special study of diacritical marks is a part of the section on the dictionary. The chapter on the writing of letters contains the important conventions to be observed in informal and business correspondence. In all these composition chapters, the usual elaborate textbook motivation has been omitted, leaving more space for basic skills and forms.

The making of this *Handbook of English* has taken many years, and the several drafts have been put to the test of classroom use. A great deal of effort has gone into writing precise, accurate, and lucid exposition which the average student can readily understand. The author is keenly aware of the help given him by his students in this effort. He is also indebted to the following classroom teachers for their careful line-by-line reading of proofs: Miss Frances Barrett, Dearborn, Michigan; Mr. Joseph Blumenthal, Mackenzie High School, Detroit, Michigan; Miss Grace Chapman, Des Plaines, Illinois; Miss Lois Dilley, Rockford, Illinois; Miss Frances Hueston, Portland, Maine; Miss Mary Hutchison, Toledo, Ohio; Dr. A. Barnett Langdale, Erasmus Hall High School, Brooklyn, New York; Miss Frances Magdenz, Waukesha, Wisconsin; Miss Madeline Pfeiffer, Pittsfield, Massachusetts; Miss Catherine Sullivan, Rochester, New York. Miss Helen Mahar, librarian of the Garden City High School, Garden City, Long Island, gave valuable suggestions for the chapter "Using the Library." The author is also deeply indebted to his wife for her effective collaboration at every stage in the making of this book.

J. E. W.

CONTENTS

I. THE WORD

SPOTTING THE PARTS OF SPEECH

How much time you should spend working on Chapter 1 will depend on how well you remember the grammar you have learned so far in school. Do you know the names of words? Words are the materials you work with in your study of language. It is just as necessary to know their names as it is to know the name of anything else you wish to talk about.

Words are named according to the work they do in the sentence. There are eight kinds of work to be done in the sentence. The words that perform these eight kinds of work are called the *parts of speech*. The names of the eight parts of speech are:

noun	adverb
pronoun	preposition
adjective	conjunction
verb	interjection

As a result of your study of this chapter, you should know the eight kinds of work that words may do in a sentence so well that you can name the part of speech of almost any word in any sentence. You will be able to "spot the parts of speech."

THE NOUN

1a. A *noun* is a word used to name a person, place, or thing.

Your own name is a noun. The name of your home town is a noun. *Book* is a noun. The names of things which you cannot touch or see are nouns; for instance, *strength, happiness, emotion, thought, meaning, width.* Although these words do not name objects, they do name qualities or ideas. The name of a quality or an idea is just as truly a noun as the name of anything which has size and shape.

EXERCISE 1. There are 25 nouns in the following paragraph. Make a list of them.

1. A hurricane would not have left the room in so big a jumble. 2. From the door to the long window opposite and from the fireplace in the left wall to the piano on the other side, lay a collection of junk impossible to imagine. 3. The scene spoke of haste, of sudden departure, of great carelessness. 4. Black pieces of broken records, deflated footballs, battered hockey sticks, banners and pennants, books, rugs, and chairs were strewn about the floor.

EXERCISE 2. There are 25 nouns in the following paragraph. Make a list of them.

1. Every object was broken, even the furniture. 2. The lamp appeared to have dived frightened from the table and splintered into bits on the hearth. 3. Stuffing pulled from pillows added to the general disorder. 4. Books, their leaves torn, their bindings cracked, sprawled as in their final agony. 5. And clothes — unrecognizable at first glance — filled every space not otherwise occupied. 6. There were the separate legs of a pair of trousers, a sleeve violently ripped from its shirt, and a soiled uniform. 7. Over the forlorn heaps climbed a fine collection of mismated shoes.

EXERCISE 3. How many nouns can you spot in the following paragraph? Do not be misled by words which may be used as nouns in one place but as some other part of speech in another place.

1. A lamp, once tall and proud, lay twisted and shattered across a corner of the floor. 2. Pictures of athletes sitting in staring rows had been thrown into the pile, their frames splintered and their glasses in pieces. 3. The door to the closet hung open, revealing stark emptiness. 4. Articles had been hurled into the room, leaving the shelves bare. 5. The bright hues of a hundred neckties added color to the scene as the warm rays of the sun played upon them. 6. Jagged pieces of a jigsaw puzzle challenged me to try to fit them together, but the clean-up job which faced me was puzzling enough and at the time required a greater effort than I knew I could manage. 7. Quietly I reached for the doorknob. 8. I would shut the ugly sight from view. 9. The knob came off in my hand!

THE PROPER NOUN

Nouns may be divided into several classes. However, it is important for you to learn only one of these classes, the *proper noun*. *A proper noun names a particular person, place, or thing.* Ability to recognize proper nouns is important because they must be capitalized. Examine the following proper nouns.[1]

NAMES OF PARTICULAR PLACES: Europe, New York, Radio City, Main Street

NAMES OF PARTICULAR PERSONS: Franklin Delano Roosevelt, Thomas Edison, Captain Kelley

NAMES OF PARTICULAR THINGS: Empire State Building, Statue of Liberty, Field Museum, the *Queen Mary* (ship), the *Zephyr* (train), Atlantic Ocean

[1] Further study of proper nouns will be found under Capitalization, pages 373-84.

THE PRONOUN

1b. A *pronoun* is a word used in place of a noun.

You ask your teacher, "Is there any *ink* there?" Your teacher looks into the empty ink bottle and replies, "No, *it* is all gone." In place of the noun *ink*, the teacher has used the pronoun *it*.

A friend says to you, "I am looking for *Harry*. Have you seen *him?*" Here your friend has used the pronoun *him* in place of the proper noun *Harry*.

EXERCISE 4. By filling in the blanks in the following sentences orally, show what pronouns you would use in referring to the italicized nouns. Do not write in this book.

1. The *books* are on the library table. Please bring —— to me.
2. *Mary* and *Harold* are going to bring *Betty* and *Jean*. —— will arrive before lunch.
3. The principal wanted to see *Fred* and *John*. He asked —— to come to his office.
4. I asked *Jim*, "Will —— please help me?"
5. Wondering whether the pen belonged to *Jack*, I asked ——, "Is this *pen* ——?"
6. "No," he replied, "—— is not ——."

The words with which you filled in the blanks are all pronouns because, as you see, they are used in place of the nouns to which they refer.

Study the following list of pronouns.[2] Those words which are starred are not always pronouns.

---

[2] More complete discussion of pronouns will be found on pages 126–52, where such matters as person and case are taught. The purpose of the discussion above is merely to help students to *identify* pronouns.

Sometimes they are *adjectives*, the kind of words which you will study next.

I	this*	any*
you	that*	both*
he	these*	few*
she	those*	many*
it	my	much*
we	mine	more*
they	your	most*
me	yours	several*
him	our	some*
her	ours	one*
us	his	someone (anyone,
them	hers	everyone, etc.)
who	their	none
whom	theirs	other*
whose	each*	another*
which*	either*	everybody (somebody,
what*	neither*	anybody, etc.)
myself (himself, themselves, etc.)	all*	

THE ADJECTIVE

1c. An *adjective* is a word used to modify a noun or pronoun.

Modify means to change. In grammar, to modify a word means to change the meaning of the word by making the meaning more definite. Adjectives, then, are words used to *make the meaning* of nouns or pronouns more definite. An adjective may modify a noun or pronoun by telling *what kind* it is. For example: *green* dress; *tall* building; *great* beauty; *strong* man; he is *fat*. An adjective may point out *which one;* for example: *this* box, *these* pencils, the *approaching* train, the *wrecked* car. An adjective may tell *how many;* for example: *many* players, *few* lessons, *three* dollars. The commonest adjectives are the little words *a, an,* and *the.* They are frequently called *articles.*

An adjective is not always placed next to the word it modifies. It may be separated from the word it modifies by other words.

The *boys* were very *tired.*
The *box* seems much too *heavy.*

An adjective modifying a pronoun is almost always separated from the pronoun.

She looks *happy.*
They are *late.*

EXERCISE 5. In the following paragraph the adjectives (except *a, an,* and *the*) are printed in italics. Make a list of the adjectives and after each one write the word it modifies.

1. *Three young* soldiers in *full field* equipment turned into the *vacant* lot on our block as I passed by. 2. Their helmets were *battered* saucepans, and their packs were *gunny* sacks, but it was the *serious* expressions on their *grimy* faces and their *militaristic* walk that caught my attention. 3. I set up an *observation* post behind the *big* oak on the corner. 4. Suddenly each unshouldered his *wooden* rifle and, holding it in *both* hands, stooped over like a *skulking* Indian and disappeared into the ground. 5. I was so *curious* that I followed unthinkingly. 6. I had no more than entered the lot when I was halted by the *high-pitched* cries of the *alert* defenders, "Bang! bang! bang! Ratatatat! Ratatat! Uh-uh-uh-uh-uh!" and before I could turn around, the enemy had swarmed out of the *hidden* dugout and captured me.

EXERCISE 6. Copy the following sentences, supplying adjectives in the blank spaces. Try to supply meaningful, interesting adjectives. Read the paragraph through before you copy it.

Late in the afternoon we had our first view of Osborne's camp. It lay in a —— valley between two lines of —— hills. The river was a —— band of light cutting through the center of the camp. From our —— position we could see only the —— tops of the —— cabins and the —— line of the flagpole rising through the —— foliage. A —— column of —— smoke rose straight up in the —— air. The —— sound of the —— bell urged us on down the —— road ahead. The view was a —— prospect after a —— day of hiking.

EXERCISE 7. Write a paragraph, about a page in length, describing some scene familiar to you. Underline the adjectives once and the words they modify twice. Try to have at least ten adjectives in your paragraph. Be sure that your adjectives are not all of the same kind. Use some that tell *what kind,* some that tell *how many,* and some that tell *which one.*

PRONOUN OR ADJECTIVE

Now that you understand what an adjective is, you should be able to tell whether such words as *this, which,* etc. (the starred words in the list on page 5), are used as adjectives or pronouns. In the first sentence in each pair below, the words are used as pronouns to *take the place of* nouns. In the second sentence they are used as adjectives to *modify* nouns. Tell what nouns are modified.

1. The blue pen is better than *this.* (pronoun)
   The blue pen is better than *this* pen. (adjective)

2. I want *that*. (pronoun)
   I want *that* box. (adjective)
3. We found *many*. (pronoun)
   We found *many* shells. (adjective)

EXERCISE 8. Study the italicized words in these sentences. Make two columns on your paper, labeling one column *pronouns*, the other *adjectives*. List the italicized words in the proper column. How the word is used tells you what kind of word it is. Before each word, write the number of the sentence in which it appears.

1. Your brother insists that *this* gun is loaded.
2. *That* is the gun *which* he says is not loaded.
3. *Which* gun will you use in the rifle match?
4. *Both* are old, and *neither* is in good condition.
5. *All* guns are dangerous, but *some* are more dangerous than others.
6. There are *several* guns in my collection, but *all* are useless now.
7. *Those* weapons in *this* collection were collected by Mr. Sayles.
8. *Many* were used for hunting, but *this* was used in the Civil War.
9. *Each* of these pistols is older than the *other* guns.
10. *Few* collectors know *more* about guns than Mr. Sayles.

EXERCISE 9. The following words may be used as either pronouns or adjectives. Write a pair of sentences for each word. In the first sentence of each pair use the word as a pronoun; in the second, as an adjective.

1. this	4. either	7. much
2. each	5. several	8. other
3. any	6. both	9. what

EXERCISE 10. Write a paragraph about a page in length, including in it nouns, pronouns, and adjectives. Double-space your paragraph; write over each example what part of speech it is.

THE VERB

1d. A verb is a word which expresses action or state of being.

THE ACTION VERB

You will have little difficulty recognizing verbs which express action, provided you realize that verbs like *think* and *believe* are action verbs even though the action cannot be seen. Typical examples are: I *run*, he *plays*, they *fight*, you *make*, they *reply*, I *think*, we *know*, etc.

THE STATE-OF-BEING VERB

Verbs which express state of being are not so easy to understand. Let's tackle these verbs first. Study the following italicized examples.

1. Fred *is* lazy.
2. You *look* tired.
3. Arnold *seemed* angry.
4. Jane *appeared* excited.
5. Henry *feels* sick.

You see that these verbs do not express action. They help to describe a condition or state of being.

The following are the most commonly used state-of-being verbs: *be, become, seem, grow, appear, look, feel, smell, taste, remain, sound, stay.*[3]

---

[3] State-of-being verbs are sometimes called *copulative* verbs or *linking* verbs.

THE VERB "TO BE"

The commonest verb in any language is a state-of-being verb. This is the verb *to be*. Below is a list of the many forms of this verb.

am	have been	could be (can be,
are	has been	may be, might
is	had been	be, must be,
was	shall be	should be)
were	will be	could have been
be	shall have been	(can have been,
being	will have been	etc.)

A state-of-being verb is usually used with other words which fill out or complete its meaning. See how the state-of-being verbs in the following sentences need other words to fill out their meaning.

1. John is . . .
   John is *the winner*.
2. We might have been . . .
   We might have been *the winners*.
3. You look . . .
   You look *tired*.
4. He seems . . .
   He seems *well*.
5. I feel . . .
   I feel *strong*.

VERBS OF MORE THAN ONE WORD—
THE VERB PHRASE

Verbs frequently consist of several words which together express the action or state of being of a noun or pronoun.

1. The boys *had been playing* football.
2. A large ship *was lying* in the harbor.

3. Very few people *would enjoy* such a long journey.
4. For weeks Jean *had asked* for more allowance.
5. We *were building* a house.
6. This *has been* a rainy month.

Verbs of more than one word are called *verb phrases*.[4]

EXERCISE 11. Study the italicized words in this paragraph. They are verbs or verb phrases. Tell whether each one expresses action or state of being.

1. "Early to bed and early to rise" *is* good advice for a high school student. 2. If you *do* your homework when you *feel* sleepy, you *will make* mistakes in it. 3. Problems which *seem* hard late at night *look* easy in the morning when you *are* wide awake. 4. *Set* the alarm clock so that it *will awaken* you early. 5. You *will discover* how much more work you *can finish* in one hour before breakfast than you *could have done* at bedtime; furthermore, if you *stay* awake too late at night, you *will become* sleepy in school the next day. 6. Your homework *will have been done* poorly, and you *will sleep* through your classes. 7. You *will miss* important explanations about the next assignment, and the work *will seem* harder than ever.

EXERCISE 12. In the following paragraph there are 23 verbs and verb phrases. Write them in a column on your paper. Be sure to include all the words in a verb phrase, especially when the parts of the phrase are separated by other words. The word *not* in a phrase such as *could not see* is not a verb. The verb phrase is *could see*.

1. Ruth waited hopefully for Bob in the center of the hall. 2. She clutched her books in one hand, scratched a

---

[4] You will find further treatment of verb phrases on pages 29 and 34.

mosquito bite with the other, and hoped Bob would stop.
3. Bob, the new senior in Room 31, strolled down the
corridor, looked at Ruth, hesitated, and walked on.
4. Tears of desperation came to Ruth's eyes. 5. Nice
dates were scarce lately. 6. Though Bob, she felt sure,
would be a swell date, he had not asked her yet. 7. Maybe,
thought Ruth, I could ask him. 8. After all, he is the
new one around here, and I am a senior too. 9. Ruth
summoned her courage, raced down the hall, breathlessly
accosted Bob and said, "Hi, Bob. How about the dance
Friday? Will you come with me?"

EXERCISE 13.   From the following paragraph
select the verbs.   Write them in a column on your
paper.   Be sure to include *all* the parts of any verb
phrase.

1. At first we could not discover the cause of the fight.
2. It seemed as though all the dogs on our block were in it.
3. They snarled, growled, barked, and leaped around in a
circle until we could hardly tell big dogs from little dogs.
4. Flashes of black, tan, and white were mixed with rust
and a nondescript gray. 5. Suddenly a fawn-colored nose
appeared, and then a dirty tan and white pup emerged
triumphant from the noisy pack and tore across the street
with a huge bone in his teeth. 6. He was followed at
once by a string of dogs. 7. Although the sounds of the
fight could have been heard throughout the neighborhood,
the chase was breathlessly quiet. 8. You might have
thought they were playing a game if their quiet serious-
ness had not shown that this was an animal struggle for
food.

EXERCISE 14.   Write a paragraph of 150 words
or more relating an incident which happened in one
of your classes recently.   Underline all the verbs and

verb phrases. You can make your paragraph interesting by choosing vivid, lively verbs.

THE ADVERB

1e. An *adverb* is a word used to modify a verb, an adjective, or another adverb.

ADVERBS MODIFYING VERBS

Just as there are words which modify nouns and pronouns (adjectives), there are words which modify verbs. For example, the verb *walk* may be modified by such words as *slowly, rapidly, awkwardly, gracefully*, etc. The verb *jump* may be modified by *fast, high, far, suddenly*, etc. *A word which modifies a verb is an adverb.*

EXERCISE 15. There are 12 adverbs in the following sentences. Make a list of them. After each write the verb which it modifies.

1. The swarthy man came swiftly around the corner. 2. A monkey, which was dressed in a striped playsuit, followed timidly. 3. Tony turned smilingly to his pet and gestured hopefully to him. 4. The monkey danced quickly and gracefully; he jumped nimbly into the air and landed neatly on the organ grinder's shoulder. 5. Tony set him on the ground where the monkey performed happily in front of an ever-growing crowd of children who laughed delightedly as the little animal minced toward them and begged slyly, confidently, for pennies.

Adverbs, in modifying verbs, usually tell one of four things about the action of the verb. They may tell *when* the action was done; they may tell *where* it was done; they may tell *how* it was done; they may tell *to what extent* it was done.

1. Jim swam *then*. (The adverb *then* tells *when* Jim swam)
2. Jim swam *there*. (The adverb *there* tells *where* Jim swam)
3. Jim swam *rapidly*. (The adverb *rapidly* tells *how* Jim swam)
4. Jim swam *far*. (The adverb *far* tells *to what extent* Jim swam)

EXERCISE 16. Give three adverb modifiers for each of the following verbs.

| fled | pushed | rowed | spoke |
| moved | lifted | gathered | stopped |

EXERCISE 17. Make a list of all the adverbs in the following paragraph. After each write the verb it modifies. Include all parts of a verb phrase. Then state whether the adverb tells *when, where, how,* or *to what extent* the action is performed.

1. Betsy, the wheezy locomotive, puffed slowly, noisily, toward the station. 2. As the train approached its destination, the whistle blew long and shrilly. 3. A few hardy passengers waited patiently there; they had resigned themselves to the fact that Black Betsy was now finally making her last run; that tomorrow she would be guided quietly into the yards to live the rest of her life among the old wrecks who, it's said, grumble darkly in the quiet gloom of the deserted shed, and mutter throatily as to the fate of these new-fangled electric trains.

ADVERBS MODIFYING ADJECTIVES

You should be able to name the part of speech of every word in this sentence except *very:*

We followed a very narrow road.

If you will ask yourself just what *very* does in the sentence, you will probably find that it modifies *narrow*. It tells how narrow the road was. You know that *narrow* is an adjective because it modifies the noun *road*. *Very* modifies an adjective. *A word which modifies an adjective is an adverb.*

EXERCISE 18. In each of the following sentences there is an adverb modifying an adjective. List these adverbs on your paper and after each one write the adjective which it modifies.

1. The very sad camel named Gloomy gazed out from his cage.
2. He saw a surprisingly small boy struggling to climb up to the railing.
3. An extremely dirty little girl helped the boy to see.
4. He got a fairly good hold on the railing.
5. He stared with startlingly blue eyes at the camel.
6. Gloomy stared back with an amazingly snobbish expression.
7. Then a rather surprised look came over the camel's face.
8. He peered at the spotlessly clean sweater the boy wore.
9. It was extremely fluffy camel's hair!
10. Gloomy, who was somewhat sad, almost smiled.

EXERCISE 19. Use each of the following adverbs in a sentence, making the adverbs modify adjectives. Underline the modified adjectives.

too	rather	unusually
very	more	spotlessly
extremely	widely	brilliantly

ADVERBS MODIFYING OTHER ADVERBS

You have learned that an adverb may modify a verb or it may modify an adjective. *Some adverbs modify other adverbs.* There is an example of this in the following sentence:

Father drove the car *rather* skillfully.

From your study of the parts of speech, you can spot *skillfully* as an adverb modifying the verb *drove*, telling *how* Father drove. You can also see that *rather* modifies the adverb *skillfully*, telling *how* skillfully. Here then is an adverb modifying another adverb. *An adverb is a word used to modify a verb, an adjective, or another adverb.*

Caution: As you may have discovered, many adverbs end in *-ly.* But do not make the mistake of thinking that all words ending in *-ly* are adverbs. For instance, the following words are adjectives: *costly, lovely, friendly, deadly.*

EXERCISE 20. There are 20 adverbs in the following paragraph. Make a list of them. After each write the word which the adverb modifies and tell whether this word is a verb, an adjective, or another adverb.

1. I had plenty of very good reasons for doubting Alec's stories about the dog he formerly owned. 2. Alec told the stories so well that all of us greatly enjoyed listening to them. 3. He told them rather convincingly and, I suppose, fooled many people. 4. According to Alec, his dog Skipper possessed an unusually keen sense of smell. 5. When something was lost around the house, Skipper, who would usually be put on the scent, would manage somehow to find the lost article. 6. Then Alec decided to put this trait to some more practical use. 7. He played a lot of golf during the summer and frequently

suffered the annoyance of having to hunt for a lost ball.
8. One day it suddenly occurred to him to use Skipper
to hunt the missing balls. 9. He rubbed each ball in an
extremely smelly bone-dust fertilizer which his father had
recently spread over the front yard. 10. Anything which
had come into contact with the fertilizer was very attractive to Skipper. 11. Alec took Skipper with him on his
daily round of golf, and never did the dog fail to recover
a lost ball. 12. "Sometime," Alec would add seriously,
"I will tell you about the way he used to caddie for me."

EXERCISE 21. Use each of the following adverbs in a sentence. Draw an arrow from the adverb
to the word it modifies.

quickly	happily	tomorrow	now	out
often	rather	very	too	again

EXERCISE 22. The following words may be used
as either adjectives or adverbs. Write a pair of sentences for each word. In the first sentence use the
word as an *adjective;* in the second, as an *adverb.*

EXAMPLES Spelling drill is a *daily* occurrence.
Our English class meets *daily.*

weekly	more	late
high	fast	

EXERCISE 23. Write a paragraph vividly describing a scene at a football game or some other
athletic event. Get action as well as excitement
into your word picture. When you have finished,
underline all adjectives and adverbs. Note how important these parts of speech are in making a good
description.

REVIEW EXERCISE A. List the 35 italicized
words in the following paragraph. After each word

tell what part of speech it is. In a third column write down the word modified by each italicized adjective and adverb. Treat the underlined phrase as one word.

1. One of *our favorite games* when *I* was a boy was a vicious little *pastime* known as "duck on a rock." 2. I do not remember the *rules* of the game *now,* nor do I recall *very clearly* what the object of *it was.* 3. What is still very vivid to me is *my mental picture* of the game in progress. 4. On *summer* evenings after the arc lights had come on and people <u>*were sauntering*</u> out to *their* front porches and yards, the boys would gather at the corner for a game of "duck." 5. The wide, unpaved street, illuminated by the hanging street lamp, *provided* an excellent playground. 6. There was no danger from cars; only an occasional horse-drawn carriage disturbed us. 7. I *remember* how we respected the older boys — the ones in long pants. 8. *They managed* the game, using us youngsters as extras, laughing at *us* and praising us as we strove to play our parts manfully. 9. *Each* boy had to equip himself with a rock big enough to carry an impact, yet small enough to be rolled *easily* along the ground. 10. There was a great deal of throwing of rocks and hopping out of their way, as I recall, and many a lad *dropped* out of the game with a sore toe or a *bruised* shin. 11. The game was, theoretically at least, played on the ground, but rocks do bounce. 12. On a *large* boulder at either side of the street sat a smaller rock — the duck. 13. The enemy, from the *opposite* curb, tried to dislodge it by throwing rocks. 14. By the same means we tried to defend our duck and to dislodge *theirs.* 15. What happened when *ours* fell defeated in the dust or what rewards we won upon dislodging their duck, I have no *idea.* 16. The game usually lasted until the younger boys were called *home* to bed, and the older boys wandered *off* to find *more adult* amusements.

THE PREPOSITION

1f. A word used to show the relation of a noun or pronoun to some other word in the sentence is a *preposition*.

In the following sentences the prepositions are italicized. They show the relation to each other of the words in boldface type. In Sentence 1, for instance, the preposition *on* shows the relation of *rugs* to *floor*.

1. The **rugs** *on* the living room **floor** are beautiful.
2. The **boys** *in* the **boat** are good sailors.
3. The **seat** *behind* **me** is vacant.
4. We **left** *before* **dawn**.
5. Jerry **is working** *with* his **father**.

1g. A group of words beginning with a preposition and ending with a noun or pronoun is a *prepositional phrase*.

These four groups of words are prepositional phrases:

of the **story**   *in* the **house**
on the **train**   *from* **him**

Following is a list of words commonly used as prepositions:

SIMPLE PREPOSITIONS

aboard	among	between
about	around	beyond
above	at	but (*meaning* except)
across	before	by
after	behind	concerning
against	below	down
along	beneath	during
amid	beside, besides	except

for	over	underneath
from	past	until
in	since	unto
into	through	up
like	throughout	upon
of	to	with
off	toward, towards	within
on	under	without

Caution: Do not confuse prepositions with adverbs. In the sentence *The men walked down the hill,* *down* is a preposition. It shows the relationship between *walked* and *hill.* *Down the hill* is the prepositional phrase. But in the sentence *I fell down,* *down* is an adverb, telling where I fell.

EXERCISE 24. Use the following words as prepositions in sentences. Underline the phrase which each preposition introduces. Be able to tell between which words the preposition shows relationship.

in	like	with	at	across
on	over	during	by	for

Use the following words as adverbs in sentences.

over	in	under
across	around	down

THE CONJUNCTION

Study the use of the words in boldface type in the following sentences:

Mary **and** her sister wanted to go home, **but** they had no way to get there.

Homework must be done at home **or** in study hall.

You should observe that each of these words joins parts of the sentence together. In the first sentence, *and* joins *Mary* and *her sister;* *but* joins the first idea, *wanted to go home,* to the second idea, *they had no way to get there.* In the second sentence, *or* joins the two ideas as to where homework must be done.

1h. A word which joins together words and groups of words is a *conjunction*.

There are three kinds of conjunctions: *co-ordinating* conjunctions, *correlative* conjunctions, and *subordinating* conjunctions.

Co-ordinating conjunctions. The co-ordinating conjunctions are *and, but, or,* and *nor.*

Correlative conjunctions. Some conjunctions are used in pairs. Examples of these are: *either . . . or; neither . . . nor; both . . . and; not only . . . but also.* Study the *pairs* of conjunctions in the following sentences. Conjunctions of this kind, which are used in pairs, are called *correlative conjunctions.*

1. *Either* the president of the Student Council *or* the principal will take charge of our meeting.
2. *Neither* the treasurer *nor* the secretary could remember who had paid dues.
3. *Both* the freshmen *and* the sophomores wanted to give a dance.
4. *Not only* hot dogs and hamburgers were sold at the snack bar, *but also* candy and ice cream.

Subordinating conjunctions will be studied later in connection with subordinate clauses. See page 81.

EXERCISE 25. List the co-ordinating and correlative conjunctions in the following paragraphs.

1. Baseball and track are probably the most popular spring sports in our schools and colleges. 2. One is largely a team sport, but in the other, runners, jumpers, and weight men perform as individuals. 3. Team play among the members of a track team is not possible except in the relays, but co-operation among the players on a baseball team is of supreme importance. 4. In both baseball and track, however, the success of the team depends on every player's doing his part.

5. Lacrosse is a spring team sport popular in some sections of our country, but quite unknown in others. 6. This is somewhat strange; it is the only completely American sport we have. 7. It was played originally by the Indians and was adopted from them by the early French explorers in Canada. 8. Once a very brutal game used by the Indians in training for war, lacrosse today has been "civilized" and is played by both schools and colleges.

9. The lacrosse ball must be not only caught but also carried and thrown only with the crosse, or stick. 10. There is always danger of injury from a wild swing of the crosse, and helmets with metal face guards provide head and face protection. 11. The crosse itself is a rawhide net supported by a wooden handle. 12. In both lacrosse and hockey the object of the game is the same — to put the ball into the goal-crease at the end of the field. 13. The playing field is about the size of a football field; there is considerable running, and the game is physically strenuous. 14. In neither the East nor the West is lacrosse regarded very generally as a major sport, but it may some day rival baseball and track in popularity.

THE INTERJECTION

There are a few words which are used as exclamations to show strong feeling, such as anger, surprise, excitement, etc. Examples of these are *Oh! Heavens!*

Ah! Shucks! Ouch! Yea Team! These words are usually followed by an exclamation mark.

1i. Words expressing emotion and having no grammatical relation to other words in the sentence are *interjections.*

EXERCISE 26. Make a list of 10 interjections other than those given above.

DETERMINING PARTS OF SPEECH

1j. What part of speech a word is depends on how the word is used.

In the following sentences you will see that one word is used as three different parts of speech.

What part of speech is *play* in each sentence?

1. On Fridays the girls *play* games during gym period.
2. The seniors gave a *play* in assembly.
3. The children's *play* hour came in the middle of the morning.

EXERCISE 27. Number in a column on your paper from 1 to 15. Study the use of each of the italicized words in the following sentences. On your paper after the proper number write the part of speech of the word. Be prepared to explain to the class why the word is that part of speech. For example, in the first sentence *light* is a noun. It is the name of something.

1. We were blinded by the *light*.
2. Please *light* the fire.
3. The box looked heavy, but it was really very *light*.
4. This year we are studying *plane* geometry.

5. One of the boys in the shop will *plane* these boards for you.
6. A small *plane* circled overhead.
7. He has an *air* of self-confidence.
8. The chairman will *air* the grievances of the strikers.
9. An *air* gun can be very dangerous.
10. He never has *any* money.
11. I don't care for *any*, thank you.
12. She has just gone *out*.
13. She went *out* the back door.
14. I shall *room* at the Whites' home.
15. The *room* is a large one.

REVIEW EXERCISE B. Write three sentences for each of the following words, using the word as a different part of speech in each sentence. At the end of the sentence write the part of speech.

    stone   mail   water   store   star

REVIEW EXERCISE C. Now that you have learned eight parts of speech, you should be able to classify every word in the following paragraph. Arrange the 30 italicized words in columns, leaving a space between the columns. After each word write what part of speech it is. The underlined expression is regarded as one word. You should be able to tell why, and you should make a score of 100%.

1. I *had looked forward* a long time *to my first visit* to Washington. 2. *Everyone* had told me the *sights* I should see, *and* I had a *rather long list in* my hand as I *walked from* the Union Station. 3. *There* and *then* my list was forgotten because *almost immediately I* saw the dome of the Capitol in the *distance* and *headed toward* it. 4. *This* building was not the *top* item on my list, *but* it was as *good* a place as *any* for the start of a tour *like mine*.

REVIEW EXERCISE D. Arrange the 25 italicized words in columns on your paper, leaving a space between the columns. After each word write what part of speech it is.

1. The building *with* a *central* dome and large wings on *either* side *looks* somewhat like ours in the *state* capital at home, *but* it is *very* much *larger*. 2. I *had wandered* about aimlessly *for* an hour when I found a *guide* who *was showing* a group of sightseers *around*. 3. *This* conducted tour looked like a good way for *me* to see the important *places*, *and* I joined the crowd. 4. *Soon we* were *so* tired from walking and standing that it was a pleasure to get away and sit for a while on the *rear steps*, from which we could look *up* beautiful Pennsylvania Avenue.

REVIEW EXERCISE E. Arrange the 25 italicized words in columns on your paper, leaving a space between the columns. After each word write what part of speech it is.

1. The "Memphis Belle" was a *famous* flying fortress. 2. *Her* crew *flew* her *on* twenty-five missions *over* Germany *and then* brought her back to America. 3. On the last flight over enemy territory, the *plane carried*, in addition to her crew, a *camera* man *who* took colored pictures of the trip. 4. From *these* pictures and *others* taken by *Army* photographers, the Signal Corps made a wonderful *motion* picture. 5. The picture showed *clearly* what a *very* great *undertaking* a bombing *raid* is.

6. The target was a large industrial city, *but* not all the planes went *there*. 7. The raiders were *cleverly* divided into groups; *each* group flew in a different direction. 8. When the enemy detected the *approach* of raiders, they didn't know which was the main group, and *so* they had to try to stop all three of them. 9. One group of 300 planes carried no bombs at all. 10. *It* was a decoy.

2. THE SENTENCE

SUBJECT AND PREDICATE, SINGLE-WORD MODIFIERS

Most of your thinking, a very large part of your writing, and a smaller part of your speaking are done in sentence form. The sentence is the basic unit of expression. No matter whether you write a book of a thousand pages or a simple explanation of why you were absent from school recently, you will do it by means of sentences. Your purpose now is to understand the structure of a sentence so that you can write good sentences with ease.

2a. A *sentence* is a group of words containing a verb and its subject and expressing a complete thought.

The sentence is used chiefly in written expression. In our ordinary speech — our conversations with friends, our practical exchange of ideas on the athletic field, etc. — we do not use sentences very regularly. For example, you meet someone in the corridor after class.

"Hello, Joe. Going home?"

"Yes. Coming?"

"No. Cafeteria. See you tonight."

In this conversation, which is perfectly good *colloquial* English, there is, strictly speaking, not even one sentence. Your *thoughts* are complete, but your *expression* of them is incomplete because you and Joe are in a hurry. How unnatural the hurried conversation would sound if it were carried on in sentences.

"Hello, Joe. Are you going home?"

"Yes, I am. Are you coming?"

"No. I'm going to the cafeteria. I'll see you to-night."

These are your thoughts, but so far as you and Joe are concerned, you have expressed them in the first example quite adequately. However, when you are writing a careful explanation or an important letter, when you are trying to be convincing on paper or to state clearly what you know in an examination, you want to be as clear in your writing as you are in your thoughts. At such times you are careful to express your thoughts completely. To do this you make sure to write in sentences. At such times each group of words you use is a completely expressed thought. It begins with a capital letter and ends with a period (or, of course, a question mark or an exclamation point.)

SUBJECT AND PREDICATE

2b. A sentence consists of two parts: the *subject* and the *predicate*. The *subject* of the sentence is that part about which something is being said. The *predicate* is that part which says something about the subject.

Subject   Predicate
The largest planes | are not the most efficient.

Predicate   Subject
Strong and weatherbeaten and happy were | the returning campers.

Subject   Predicate
The old trapper | was telling one story after another.

EXERCISE 1. In the following sentences tell what the subject is and what the predicate is. If your teacher directs you to copy the sentences onto your paper, draw one line under the complete subject and two lines under the complete predicate. Bear in mind that, as in the second example above, the subject may come *after* the predicate. Do not write in this book.

1. Frances sang three songs at our concert.
2. A tall, gray-haired man attracted our attention.
3. All around us rose the snow-capped peaks.
4. The light drizzle became a downpour in the afternoon.
5. Many of your best friends will be waiting for you.
6. The new automobiles are faster and safer.
7. Freddie threw off his coat and began to work.
8. In the water was a large diving raft.
9. Jerry received a pen and pencil set as a birthday gift.
10. The king of France treated his subjects with indifference.

EXERCISE 2. Using the following subjects, add predicates to them to make a complete sentence in each case. Make your sentences interesting, colorful, vivid.

1. Our little brown and white spaniel
2. The blazing roof
3. A severe electrical storm
4. The varsity football squad
5. A new blue dress
6. The neighborhood brats
7. Sparkling jewels
8. Today's best-selling novel
9. Three sailors and a marine
10. Gun flashes

EXERCISE 3. Using the following predicates, add subjects to them so that you will have a complete sentence in each case.

1. . . . . . leaped into action.
2. . . . . . stood glumly on the sidelines.
3. . . . . . was wearing a bright red slack suit.
4. In the back of the room stood . . . . .
5. . . . . . pounded violently on the front door.
6. . . . . . danced gracefully across the stage.
7. . . . . . played his best.
8. . . . . . sneaked through the darkened rooms.
9. . . . . . landed a right hook on his jaw.
10. Around the corner at breakneck speed swung . . . . .

THE COMPLETE PREDICATE AND THE VERB

You have learned that the predicate of a sentence is that part which says something about the subject. This part is really the *complete predicate*. Within the complete predicate there is always a word (or group of words) which is the "heart" of the predicate, the key word or words in the predicate.

2c. The principal word or group of words in the complete predicate is called the *simple predicate* or, more commonly, the *verb*.

EXAMPLE A squadron of Army planes *flew* low over the school.

[Complete predicate: *flew low over the school;* verb: *flew.*]

EXAMPLE Several curious students **were standing** outside the door.

[Complete predicate: *were standing outside the door;* verb: *were standing.*]

THE VERB PHRASE

A verb is often more than one word. A verb of more than one word is a *verb phrase*. The following are examples of verb phrases: *am going, will be, has seen, has been seen, did send, would have been.* In the following sentences, the complete predicate is italicized, and the verb is printed in boldface type. Study the sentences carefully so that you will be able to pick out the verb in the sentences in the next exercise.

1. The principal **spoke** *to us this morning about our conduct.*
2. He **had entered** *the auditorium slowly and solemnly.*
3. Nearly everyone in the room **expected** *a scolding.*
4. The quiet tension **was felt** *by everyone.*
5. The president of our student council **arose** *stiffly from his seat.*
6. His serious expression **was** *an unmistakable warning.*
7. We **gave** *the flag salute mechanically.*
8. The council president **introduced** *the principal.*
9. The students in the crowded room **leaned** *forward.*
10. *Slowly toward the edge of the stage* **walked** *our usually good-natured principal.*

EXERCISE 4. Number in a column on your paper from 1 to 20. Find the verb in each of the following sentences and write it after the proper number on your paper. If you find a verb phrase, be sure to include all its parts.

1. Six o'clock is the busiest time of day for the gateman at the Main Street crossing.
2. Four express trains go through the village within a space of ten minutes.
3. The traffic on Main Street becomes very heavy at this time.
4. Pete puts the gates down at six o'clock.
5. Three minutes later he raises them.
6. They are lowered a second time at 6:06.

7. Two flyers thunder by in a cloud of smoke and cinders.
8. Once again up go the gates.
9. At 6:10 Pete cranks them down again for the *Cannon-ball.*
10. By this time dozens of cars are waiting.
11. Their drivers understand the situation.
12. They accept the delay calmly.
13. By 6:10 every day Pete is suffering from the jitters.
14. Beside the lines of traffic stand two perspiring police-men.
15. Forward under their direction move the lines of traffic.
16. Some of the drivers tease Pete good-naturedly.
17. They accuse him of making them late for supper.
18. Their teasing never bothers Pete.
19. The drivers appreciate the importance of Pete's job.
20. The new highway bridge over the tracks will put Pete out of his job.

THE COMPLETE SUBJECT AND THE SIMPLE SUBJECT

As you know, the subject of a sentence is that part about which something is being said. This part is really the *complete subject.* The principal word in the complete subject is called the *simple subject.*

2d. The *simple* subject is a word naming the person, place, thing, or idea about which something is being said.

EXAMPLE   *A heavy red **truck*** swung around the corner.
[Complete subject: *A heavy red truck;* simple subject: *truck.*]

In naming the subject, consider proper nouns as one word.

EXAMPLE   *The **Empire State Building** in New York* is the tallest skyscraper in the world.

[Complete subject: *The Empire State Building in New York;* simple subject: *Empire State Building.*]

Caution: Remember that *noun* and *subject* do not mean the same thing. A *noun* is the name of a person, place, or thing. *Subject* is the name of a part of a sentence; it is usually a noun or pronoun.

Throughout the rest of this book the word **subject** *will be used to mean the* **simple subject**.

HOW TO FIND THE SUBJECT
OF A SENTENCE

Because the subject may appear at almost any point in the sentence, you will find it easier to locate the subject if you will pick out the verb first. For instance:

The hero of the expedition led his men to safety.

The verb is *led*. Now ask yourself, "Who or what led?" Your answer is *hero;* hence *hero* is the subject. In the sentence:

In the middle of the morning came the mail.

the verb is *came*. Ask yourself, "who or what came?" Your answer is *mail;* hence *mail* is the subject.

The best way to find the subject of a sentence is to find the verb first and then ask yourself, "Who or what . . . . . ?"

EXERCISE 5. Number on your paper from 1 to 10. Write the verb and the subject of each of the following sentences after the proper number on your paper. Select the verb first.

1. A creaking sound startled me.
2. From out of the darkened hallway came a blinding flash.
3. The brilliant beam moved quickly.
4. It picked out the stairway at once.
5. To my ears came a muffled cry.
6. This unexpected sound indicated more than one visitor.
7. A few cautious footsteps on the stairs were followed by a dull thud.
8. The suspense became too much for me.
9. With a shout I leaped from my hiding place.
10. The hall lights revealed nothing.

EXERCISE 6. Number in a column from 1 to 10. In each sentence select the verb and the subject and copy them on your paper after the proper number.

1. A tall boy almost always has an advantage.
2. A few extra inches may make a lot of difference in a basketball game.
3. Height is of especial advantage under the basket.
4. Shots from beneath the basket are hard for a short player.
5. Long arms are a great help in retrieving the ball from the backboard.
6. The player with long arms and legs has an advantage in tennis too.
7. Some tall, long-legged boys are clumsy in their movements.
8. A short and fast athlete runs rings around them.
9. Certain positions on a baseball team are played better by a short, heavy-set boy.
10. Most famous catchers have been stocky in build.

THE SUBJECT IN AN UNUSUAL POSITION

There are two kinds of sentences whose word order you must change when you wish to find the verb and its subject. These are (1) sentences which begin with the words *there* or *here,* and (2) sentences which ask a question.

1. *Sentences which begin with* **there** *or* **here:**

EXAMPLE There were many reasons for leaving early.

To find the subject in this kind of sentence, drop the first word and move the verb to where it is needed to make sense. Then the sentence will read *Many reasons for leaving early were* . . . . . The verb is *were,* and the subject is *reasons.*

2. *Sentences which ask a question:*

EXAMPLE What were you doing?

A question should be changed into a statement: *You were doing what.* Now you can see that *were doing* is the verb, and *you* is the subject.

The words in a verb phrase may be separated from one another by other words. In the sentence *Did he help you?* the verb is *did help.* The subject *he* separates the parts of the verb phrase.

Other examples of verb phrases separated in this way are:

	Verb Phrase
Where have you been?	have been
Does he expect you?	does expect
Have you been playing football?	have been playing
Will your father be coming soon?	will be coming

EXERCISE 7. Number in a column from 1 to 10. Select the verb and the subject in each of the following sentences and write them after the proper number on your paper. Rearrange the sentences if necessary. Select the verb first. Be sure to write down all parts of a verb phrase.

1. There are ten boys in the class.
2. Where is the teacher of this class?
3. Where were you going?
4. There will be a pep rally this evening.
5. There is no reason for your taking such au attitude.
6. Did John take your book?
7. There are two strange books in my locker.
8. Where did he spend his summer vacation?
9. Are there any voters in favor of this plan?
10. Here are a few arguments against your idea.

SENTENCES IN WHICH THE SUBJECT IS UNDERSTOOD

Whenever you make a request of someone or command someone, you usually leave out of your sentence the subject, which is the word *you*.

EXAMPLES   Please bring me that pen.
            Go home at once!

In the first sentence the verb is *bring*. Who is to do the bringing? What the sentence means is "*You* please bring me that pen." In the second sentence, the verb is *go*. Who is to go? "*You* go home at once." Hence the subject in both sentences is *you*, even though the word does not appear in the sentence. A subject of this kind is an *understood subject*.

COMPOUND SUBJECTS AND VERBS

2e. When the subject consists of two or more connected words, it is called a *compound subject*. The commonest connecting words are *and*, *or*.

EXAMPLE   *James* and his *sister* *have gone* to a new school.
           [Verb: *have gone;* compound subject: *James* (and) *sister*.]

2f. When the verb consists of two or more verbs joined by a connecting word, it is called a *compound verb*.

EXAMPLE On our fishing trip *we **paddled*** more than a hundred miles and ***caught*** dozens of fish. [Compound verb: *paddled* (and) *caught;* subject: *we.*]

EXERCISE 8. Write 3 sentences containing a compound subject, 3 containing a compound verb, and 3 containing both a compound subject and a compound verb.

2g. The subject is never in a phrase.

A sentence in which the subject is followed by a phrase may be confusing. A phrase is a group of closely related words. For example, *in the morning, of the soldiers, by the river, with my friends* — all are phrases. Here is a sentence in which the subject is followed by a phrase.

EXAMPLE One *of these boys* will be elected.

You see, at once, that the verb is *will be elected.* When you ask, "Who will be elected?" you are likely to make the mistake of answering *boys.* However, that is not what the sentence says. The sentence says, "*One* of these boys will be elected." The subject is *one.* You notice that *boys* is part of the phrase *of these boys.* If you will remember that words in phrases cannot be subjects, you will increase your accuracy in identifying subjects.

EXERCISE 9. Number on your paper from 1 to 10. Write down the verb and before it the subject of each sentence. If the subject of the sentence is understood, write down *you* as the subject.

EXAMPLES (1) Unfortunately there is no acceptable excuse for your actions.

(2) The boys and girls work hard at their studies and play hard at their games.

(1) excuse   is

(2) boys   girls   work   play

1. There will be plenty of time later.
2. Is the old gentleman really expecting you?
3. Please bring your violin.
4. The new student and her mother called on the principal.
5. Where have you and Betty been sitting?
6. Both of these shoes are mine.
7. There are many vacant desks in Room 5.
8. How many people have you told this to?
9. Leave at once and go back to your class!
10. Will neither of those covers fit this box?

EXERCISE 10. Write the following:

3 sentences in which the subject precedes the verb

2 sentences in which the subject follows the verb

2 sentences in which the subject is followed by a prepositional phrase

2 sentences containing a verb phrase

1 sentence in which the subject is understood

2h. A sentence expresses a complete thought.

You have just learned that a sentence contains a verb and its subject. This does not mean that all groups of words containing a verb and its subject are sentences. To be a sentence such groups of words must also express a *complete thought.*

In *when he was in high school* there are a verb and its subject — the verb is *was;* the subject is *he.* Yet the group of words is not a sentence because it does not express a complete thought. It is a fragment, a part of a sentence. Contrast: *He played varsity football when he was in high school.* Now you have a complete thought, a *sentence.*

EXERCISE 11. Some of the following groups of words are sentences and some are sentence fragments.[1] Number on a sheet of paper from 1 to 20. Read each group of words thoughtfully. (Reading aloud will be better than reading silently.) If it is a sentence, put an *S* beside the corresponding number on your paper. If it is not a sentence, write an *F* for fragment. Ask yourself whether the group of words has a verb and its subject and *whether it expresses a complete thought.*

1. On the afternoon train.
2. Leaving the rest of us stranded.
3. I don't remember him very well.
4. My favorite radio programs.
5. The teachers held a meeting.
6. No one could understand the speaker.
7. Which my father made for me.
8. In the front of the room sat our headmaster.
9. If you want to go with us.
10. You ought to think before you speak.
11. Riding in the back part of the truck with boxes, crates, and baskets.
12. You will receive your reports tomorrow.
13. While the President was speaking on the radio.
14. After I had finished my homework last night.

[1] Further treatment of sentence fragments will be found in Chapter IV "Writing Complete Sentences."

15. As Walker stepped into the room and everyone turned to greet him.
16. If you will be patient, you will get what you want.
17. With four children of her own and two nephews to care for.
18. A committee was appointed to study the problem.
19. Day after day and night after night.
20. Please give me another day for this assignment.

EXERCISE 12. Number on your paper from 1 to 20. Read each of the following groups of words aloud. If the group of words has a verb and its subject and expresses a complete thought, write *S* for sentence after the corresponding number on your paper. If it is not a sentence, write *F* for fragment.

1. Whom we have always liked.
2. George agreed to do the work for me.
3. He gets much better marks than I do.
4. As the crowd roared its disapproval.
5. Both of my brothers were in the Army.
6. Lifting the heavy boxes onto a truck.
7. Which the family objected to.
8. If you will leave your name and address.
9. She offered to do the work for nothing.
10. Mother refused to give us her permission.
11. Have you ever been here before?
12. Expecting a victory, the crowd was disappointed.
13. During the Christmas vacation last year.
14. If the weather should be stormy.
15. Singing college songs around the piano all evening, we had a good time.
16. The reason for her leaving was a mystery.
17. Where we put our tent.
18. I disagreed with the decision of the judges.
19. On the new playground behind our school.
20. As though he had not a care in the world.

EXERCISE 13. There were 10 sentence fragments in the preceding exercise. Write these on your paper and, by adding to them, make each one a complete sentence. The words you add may be placed before or after the fragment.

2i. Sentences may be classified according to their purpose.[2]

There are four kinds of sentences: (1) declarative, (2) imperative, (3) interrogative, (4) exclamatory.

(1) A sentence which merely makes a statement is a *declarative* sentence. Its purpose is to *declare* something. Most of the sentences you use are declarative.

EXAMPLES At the end of the day everyone was exhausted.
I told my brother to do his own homework.

(2) A sentence which gives a command or makes a request is an *imperative* sentence.

EXAMPLES Raise your right hand.
Please bring your literature books to class.

(3) A sentence which asks a question is an *interrogative* sentence. To *interrogate* means to *ask*. An interrogative sentence is followed by a question mark.

EXAMPLES Where have you been?
Isn't he tall?

(4) A sentence which expresses strong feeling is an *exclamatory* sentence. It exclaims. A declarative, imperative, or interrogative sentence may be spoken in such a way that it will be exclamatory. Then it should be followed by an exclamation mark.

[2] Classification of sentences according to *structure* is taught in connection with the study of modifying clauses on pages 86-89.

EXAMPLES That is enough! [Declarative becomes exclamatory.]

Bend over! [Imperative becomes exclamatory.]

Isn't he tall! [Interrogative becomes exclamatory.]

EXERCISE 14. Classify the sentences in Exercise 9 according to the four kinds you have just learned.

EXERCISE 15. Write 3 sentences which could be read as declarative, interrogative, or exclamatory, according to the speaker's purpose. For instance, look at the following sentence:

Johnny's coming. [declarative]
Johnny's coming! [exclamatory]
Johnny's coming? [interrogative]

DIAGRAMMING SENTENCES

Many students find that they can understand sentence parts better when they use a diagram. A diagram is a means of arranging a sentence in a kind of picture form. The picture shows clearly how the various parts of the sentence fit together and how they are related. You may find diagramming useful to you, and for that reason this book contains an explanation of how to diagram each of the parts of a sentence.

The first thing to do in making a diagram is to draw a straight horizontal line on your paper. Somewhere to the left of the center of the line draw a short vertical line crossing the horizontal one. This vertical line is the dividing point between the complete subject and the complete predicate of your sentence. The subject and all words that relate to it (in other words, the complete subject) go to the left of this vertical line; the verb and all words that relate to it (in other words, the complete predicate) go to the right.

1. *Diagramming the subject and the verb:*
On the horizontal line to the right you place the verb. To the left you place the subject.

subject	verb

2. *Diagramming the understood subject:*
For an understood subject use the word *you* in parentheses as the subject in your diagram.

EXAMPLE Please go at once.   (you) | go

3. *Diagramming modifying words:*
Modifiers of the subject and the verb (adjectives and adverbs) are written on slanting lines connected to the subject or verb.

EXAMPLE An ancient jalopy rattled noisily by.

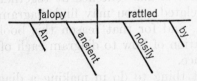

4. *Diagramming compound subjects and verbs:*
When you have a sentence with a compound subject or a compound verb, diagram it as in the following example.

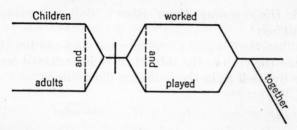

Notice in the above diagram how the word *together*, modifying both parts of the compound verb, is diagrammed so that it clearly is related to both parts. The same method is used when a word modifies both parts of a compound subject.

5. *Diagramming here, there, and **where** as modifiers:*

When the words *here*, *there*, and *where* are modifiers of the verb, diagram them as in the following illustrations.

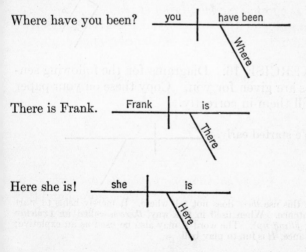

Where have you been?

There is Frank.

Here she is!

6. Diagramming **there** *when it does not modify anything:* [3]

When *there* begins a sentence but does not modify either the verb or the subject, it is diagrammed on a line by itself as in the following illustrations.

There were six boys.

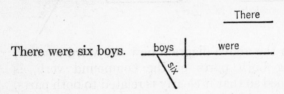

7. Diagramming a modifier of a modifier:

A word which modifies another modifier is diagrammed like *very* in the following illustration.

We walked very slowly.

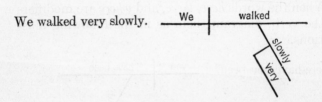

EXERCISE 16. Diagrams for the following sentences are given for you. Copy these on your paper and fill them in correctly.

1. We started early.

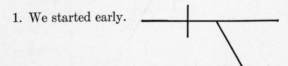

[3] In this use *there* does not tell where. It merely helps to start the sentence. When used in this way, *there* is called an *expletive* (Latin, *filling up*). The word *it* may also be used as an expletive; for instance, *It* is fun to play ball.

2. Our train traveled rapidly.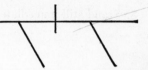

3. The workmen left early.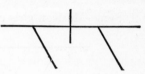

4. A small package came today.

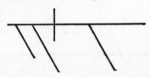

5. Both girls studied late.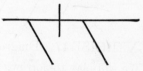

6. Our neighbors arose early today and went away.

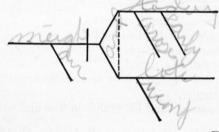

7. There was a loud explosion.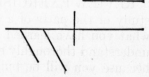

8. Stand still immediately.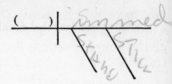

9. Some Mexican girls came here today.

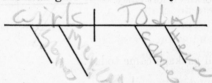

10. The gorgeous red sun was setting slowly.

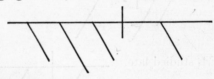

EXERCISE 17. Diagram the following sentences.

1. We will play tomorrow.
2. The other girls disagreed bitterly.
3. Beyond lies Manchuria.
4. There are no large cities here.
5. Where are your English books?
6. Come here immediately.
7. Has my father arrived?
8. She dances very gracefully and skates beautifully.
9. Study harder.
10. An old skipper and his grandson live and work here.

REVIEW EXERCISE A. Before continuing your study of the parts of a sentence, you should review what you have learned thus far. Be sure that you understand thoroughly everything you have covered because you will be building constantly upon what you have just learned. Can you give in your own words a definition of each of the following? After giving your definition, make up an example to illustrate it.

1. A sentence
2. A complete subject
3. A complete predicate
4. A subject (simple)
5. A verb (simple predicate)
6. A prepositional phrase
7. A verb phrase
8. A compound subject
9. A compound verb
10. An understood subject
11. A declarative sentence
12. An imperative sentence
13. An interrogative sentence
14. An exclamatory sentence

REVIEW EXERCISE B. Number in a column on your paper from 1 to 15. Select from each of the following sentences the verb and the subject and write them after the proper number on your paper. As you do this, be especially careful to include all parts of a *verb phrase*. This is a mastery test and will show how well you have learned to identify the verb and its subject.

1. Please give me your opinion of him.
2. Where has your brother been?
3. What did Mother say?
4. Tell him your story and note his reaction.
5. What were Jean and she doing?
6. Will one of you boys bring your dictionary to class?
7. There could have been several other reasons for his attitude.

8. Do you and Ralph see each other often?
9. All of these vegetables have spoiled.
10. Our journey will probably take us to Europe.
11. A handsome young fellow in an officer's uniform was approaching from the opposite corner.
12. There will be a lot of good things to eat.
13. None of my relatives live in the East.
14. Where did Phil leave my books?
15. Where will you and the other boys eat and sleep?

WORDS WHICH COMPLETE THE MEANING OF THE VERB

Every sentence has a base. This base may be compared to the foundation of a building or to the backbone of an animal. It is that part of the sentence upon which are built or from which are suspended all the other parts of the sentence. Sometimes the base itself is composed of only two parts. These are the subject and the verb.

EXAMPLES The *kettle* of boiling water *exploded*.
Base: *kettle exploded*
The *mystery* of the haunted house *was explained*.
Base: *mystery was explained*

Most sentences, however, have a base which is composed of three parts: the subject, the verb, and the *complement* of the verb.

2j. **The *complement* of the verb is a word or group of words which completes the meaning of the verb.**

The following example will show you how the complement does this.

EXAMPLE The firemen extinguished the blaze.

	Subject	Verb	Complement
BASE	firemen	extinguished	blaze

You can see that the complement *blaze* is a necessary part of this sentence base. The subject *firemen* and the verb *extinguished* by themselves would not be enough to make a complete thought. Study the following sentences and their bases. The bases are italicized. Name the part of speech of each complement. For instance, in the first sentence, the complement *captain* is a noun. In the second sentence, the complement *tall* is an adjective.

1. *Harold is* our *captain*.
2. Their *captain is* very *tall*.
3. *Jimmy defeated* his *brother*.
4. *Everyone* in the car *was* probably *afraid*.
5. Both *Matt* and *Paul knocked* the *ball* over the fence.
6. His little *house looked* quite *attractive*.
7. Our club *secretary read* the *minutes*.
8. The new *planes make* a terrifying *roar*.
9. This small donkey *engine can pull* a long *string* of cars.
10. *Jane* always *seems* quite *happy*.

EXERCISE 18. Using your imagination, construct sentences from the following sentence bases. Do not be satisfied with adding only one or two words. Make *interesting* sentences.

SUBJECT	VERB	COMPLEMENT
1. team	defeated	opponents
2. sky	was	blue
3. officer	caught	boys

4. visitors	departed	
5. teacher	is	friend
6. father	is	foreman
7. storm	was	violent
8. building	seemed	tall
9. dog	is	mine
10. bells	rang	

EXERCISE 19. Number in a column on your paper from 1 to 10. Select from each of the following sentences the sentence base. Write the base after the proper number on your paper.

1. His victory surprised all of us.
2. Everyone in school was proud of him.
3. For his achievement he received a gold medal.
4. The spectators cheered him.
5. The townspeople held a banquet in his honor.
6. The school bought twenty-five new typewriters.
7. The commercial students were very glad.
8. The old typewriters had been good machines in their day.
9. The new typewriters were noiseless.
10. I shall take typing next year.

THE SUBJECT COMPLEMENT

You may have noticed as you were selecting the bases of the sentences above that the complements are of several kinds. Some of them refer to the subject: for example, in the base *typewriters were noiseless*, *noiseless* refers to the subject *typewriters*. Also, in the sentence base *typewriters were machines*, *machines* refers to the subject, explaining what *typewriters were*.

2k. Complements which describe or explain the simple subject are called *subject complements*.

There are two kinds of subject complements. If the subject complement is a noun or a pronoun, it is called a *predicate nominative*. If the subject complement is an adjective, it is called a *predicate adjective*.

Predicate nominatives (nouns and pronouns) and adjectives are used after state-of-being verbs only. (See page 9.) The common state-of-being verbs are *be*,[4] *become, feel, smell, taste, look, grow, seem, appear, remain, sound, stay*.

EXERCISE 20. Number on your paper from 1 to 10. Select the subject complement from each of the following sentences and write it after the corresponding number on your paper. *Your work will be easier if you first find the verb and its subject.* After each complement write what kind of complement it is: predicate nominative or predicate adjective.

1. The large, awkward-looking machines in the fields were reapers.
2. Your trip may be dangerous.
3. When rescued, the explorers were ill.
4. The uniformed attendants were foreign soldiers.
5. The plane from South America was a beauty.
6. That is he.
7. Our days in prison seemed endless.
8. His account of the accident was a good story.
9. Beside him I felt very small.
10. The new teacher certainly looks young.

[4] For the other forms of *be*, see page 10.

DIAGRAMMING THE PREDICATE NOMINATIVE AND THE PREDICATE ADJECTIVE

A subject complement (predicate nominative or predicate adjective) should be placed on the same horizontal line with the simple subject and the predicate verb. It comes after the verb, and a line *slanting toward the subject* and drawn upward from the horizontal line separates it from the verb. The line slants toward the subject to show that the subject complement is closely related to the subject. The following examples show how to diagram a subject complement.

PREDICATE NOMINATIVE: Our storekeeper is a fat man.

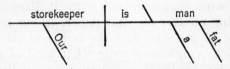

PREDICATE ADJECTIVE: He always seems very good-natured.

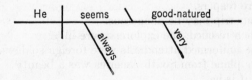

COMPOUND COMPLEMENT: He is an inventor and a
manufacturer.

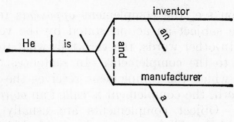

You look well and strong.

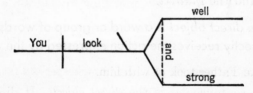

EXERCISE 21.   Diagram the following sentences.

1. The new president is a capable man.
2. Does that apple taste good?
3. That might have been they.
4. The thief probably was he.
5. The last few miles were very tiring.
6. Yesterday's homework seemed too difficult.
7. Are you the manager?
8. Jack will undoubtedly be our next pitcher.
9. The new mayor is a banker.
10. Mr. Jones was once my neighbor.

THE OBJECT COMPLEMENT

There is a kind of complement, however, which
does not refer to the subject. Instead, *it receives the
action of the verb.* Notice the word *opponents* in the
sentence on the next page.

EXAMPLE The first *team defeated* their *opponents* easily.

BASE *team defeated* *opponents*

Here, you see, the complement *opponents* receives from the subject an action stated by the verb *defeated*. In other words, the verb tells what the subject did to the complement. In sentences of this kind, in which the complement receives the action of the verb, the complement is called an *object complement*. Object complements are usually called simply *objects*. There are two kinds of objects, the *direct* and the *indirect*.

21. The *direct object* is a word or group of words that directly receives the action expressed by the verb.

EXAMPLE Father took *us* with him.

In this sentence, *us* is the *direct object*. It directly receives the action expressed by the verb *took*. Objects are used after *action* verbs only. Note that verbs like *think, believe, imagine*, which express mental action, are action verbs just as truly as verbs like *hit, fight, play, write*, which express physical action.

EXERCISE 22. Make a list of the direct objects in the following sentences. Be able to tell the verb whose action the object receives.

1. General Montgomery attacked the enemy's supply lines.
2. He used bombing and strafing planes.
3. On the desert the enemy could not hide supplies.
4. Montgomery drove the foe back.
5. His planes pounded them unmercifully.
6. The aviators destroyed many tanks.

7. They struck the enemy again and again.
8. The desert sun blinded the fliers.
9. The attack left miles of ruin.
10. The British infantry finished the job.

Caution: Just as the subject of a verb is never part of a phrase, so the object of a verb is never part of a phrase.

2m. An *indirect object* is a noun or pronoun in the predicate that precedes (comes before) the direct object. It usually tells *to whom* or *for whom* the action of the verb is done.

Study the following sentences:

The postman left a letter for me.
The postman left me a letter.

You recognized *letter* as a direct object in both sentences. It receives directly the action of the verb. In the second sentence you have another word which seems to receive, indirectly at least, the action of the verb. That word is *me*. *Me*, which comes before the direct object, tells *for whom* the letter was left. It is an *indirect object*.

What is the *indirect object* in this sentence?

I sent Harold a letter.

Letter is the direct object; *Harold* is the indirect object. It is Harold *to whom* the letter was sent.

If the words *to* and *for* are used, the word following them is part of a prepositional phrase and not an indirect object. Compare the following pairs of sentences.

I read a story *to her.* [no indirect object]
I read *her* a story. [*Her* is the indirect object.]
Mother made a new dress *for me.* [no indirect object]

Mother made *me* a new dress. [*Me* is the indirect object.]

EXERCISE 23. Make two columns on your paper. Label one column *direct objects*. Label the other column *indirect objects*. List in the proper column all the direct and indirect objects in the following sentences. You will not find an indirect object in every sentence.

1. We planned a long hike through the pine forest.
2. Our head counselor gave us permission.
3. He lent me his canteen.
4. The forest held no fears for such seasoned campers.
5. Usually they give campers a guide for this sort of trip.
6. I gave George the compass.
7. He gladly gave me the maps.
8. I showed the boys a short cut through the swamp.
9. The older boys told the younger boys stories about being lost.
10. We followed the fire lanes through the woods.

COMPOUND COMPLEMENTS

Like subjects and predicates, complements may be compound. Study the following examples of compound complements.

COMPOUND PREDICATE NOMINATIVE (NOUN):
  The winners were *Helen* and *Dot*.

COMPOUND PREDICATE NOMINATIVE (PRONOUN):
  The best players are *you* and *she*.

COMPOUND PREDICATE ADJECTIVE:
  He is *intelligent* and *industrious*.

COMPOUND DIRECT OBJECT:
  Father sent my *brother* and *me* to camp.

COMPOUND INDIRECT OBJECT:
　The coach gave *Jim* and *me* varsity letters.

EXERCISE 24.　Write 2 sentences containing a compound subject, 2 containing a compound verb, 2 containing a compound predicate nominative, 2 containing a compound predicate adjective, 2 containing a compound direct object.

DIAGRAMMING THE DIRECT AND INDIRECT OBJECT

The *direct object* is diagrammed in almost the same way as the predicate nominative.　The only difference is that the line separating the object from the verb is *vertical* (not slanting), as in the example below.

Tim kicked the ball.　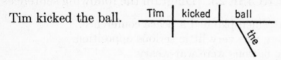

The *indirect object* is diagrammed on a horizontal line beneath the verb of which the word is the indirect object.

EXAMPLE Esther's friends gave her a party.

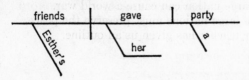

COMPOUND DIRECT OBJECT: We heard jokes and stories.

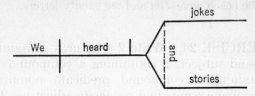

COMPOUND INDIRECT OBJECT: The speaker told Fred
and me several stories.

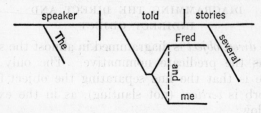

EXERCISE 25. Diagram the following sentences:

1. Statesmen planned a peace conference.
2. There was very little serious opposition.
3. The nations were war-weary.
4. The conference Big Three were the United States,
   Russia, and Great Britain.
5. The smaller nations gave the Big Three much con-
   cern.
6. Agreement is important.
7. Small nations can not alone cause a world war.
8. A large nation can cause a world war.
9. The large nations must preserve the peace.
10. Our teacher has given us an outline.

3. THE SENTENCE

PHRASES AND CLAUSES

For complete understanding of correct sentence structure you need to know phrases and clauses — how the various kinds are formed and what they do in a sentence. Since phrases and clauses are advanced items in grammar, you will probably want to study this chapter carefully, even though you may have found Chapters 1 and 2 to be mere review that you could cover rapidly.

THE PHRASE

You know that a group of words used as a verb is a *verb phrase*. *Have been sleeping, is sleeping, will be sleeping* are verb phrases. Groups of words may also be used as other parts of speech — as adjectives, adverbs, and nouns.

3a. **A group of words used as a single part of speech and not containing a verb and its subject is called a *phrase*.**

PREPOSITIONAL PHRASES

3b. **A group of words beginning with a preposition and ending with a noun or pronoun is a *prepositional phrase*.[1]**

EXAMPLES *by* + the old mill stream

to + him

[1] Do not confuse the infinitive form of a verb (*to see, to run*) with a prepositional phrase beginning with the preposition *to — to me, to the store.*

3c. The noun or pronoun which concludes the prepositional phrase is the *object of the preposition* which begins the phrase.

In the summer Bob went to a camp *for boys.*
[*Summer* is the object of the preposition *in; boys* is the object of the preposition *for.*]

During the entire afternoon I waited *for him.* [*Afternoon* is the object of the preposition *during; him* is the object of the preposition *for.*]

THE PREPOSITIONAL PHRASE USED AS AN ADJECTIVE [2]

If you will study the italicized phrases in this sentence, you will see that each modifies a noun:

EXAMPLE A lady *in the front row* was wearing a hat *with a big red feather.*

The phrase *in the front row* tells *which* lady, and since it thus modifies the noun *lady,* it is used as an adjective, for only adjectives modify nouns. The phrase *with a big red feather* describes the noun *hat.* It modifies a noun; it is an *adjective phrase.*

3d. A phrase that modifies a noun or a pronoun is an *adjective phrase.*

If you thoughtfully examine the pairs of sentences below, you will see just how a phrase is used as an adjective.

1. The *morning* delivery was late.
   The delivery *in the morning* was late.
2. The *wood* pile grew taller as the men worked.
   The pile *of wood* grew taller as the men worked.

[2] For work on the correct use of adjective phrases see "Misplaced Phrase Modifiers" on page 191.

3. The *Boston* papers opposed his election.
   The papers *in Boston* opposed his election.
4. Our *school* teams have been very successful.
   The teams *at our school* have been very successful.
5. *Chocolate* bars and *candy* boxes were on display.
   Bars *of chocolate* and boxes *of candy* were on display.

DIAGRAMMING ADJECTIVE PHRASES

Adjective phrases are diagrammed in much the same way as adjectives. The preposition which begins the phrase is placed on a slanting line leading down from the word the phrase modifies. The noun or pronoun which ends the phrase is placed on a horizontal line drawn from the slanting line.

EXAMPLE Planes with jet motors travel rapidly.

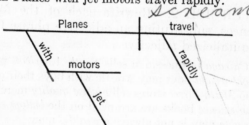

With jet motors is an adjective phrase modifying the noun *planes*.

EXERCISE 1. Each of the following sentences contains two adjective phrases. List these phrases in order on your paper. After each phrase write the noun it modifies.

EXAMPLE The man at the gate gave me a bundle of tickets.

Phrase	Word Modified
at the gate	man
of tickets	bundle

1. My friend in England sent me a book of short stories.
2. The men at work envied those on vacation.
3. This book by Charles Dickens gives a picture of nine-teenth-century England.
4. We had a piece of cake with chocolate frosting.
5. People from the South have an accent of their own.
6. The reason for our excitement was Bill's announcement of the victory.
7. The game at Yankee Stadium was a battle between pitchers.
8. The merchants in town honored the champions of the league.
9. The storms during our trip brought winds of great violence.
10. The teachers of science need laboratories with good equipment.

EXERCISE 2. Rewrite each of the following sentences, substituting an adjective phrase for each of the italicized adjectives.

1. A *Chicago* businessman sells *South American* products.
2. *Light-weight* boys may wrestle with boys their own size.
3. The *Main Street* stores sell *highest quality* merchandise.
4. The *science* books are arranged on the *bottom* shelf.
5. An *able* man is not always a *wealthy* man.
6. Most *college* boys were taken into the *United States* Army.

THE PREPOSITIONAL PHRASE USED AS AN ADVERB [3]

3e. A phrase that modifies a verb, an adjective, or an adverb is an *adverb phrase*.

Compare the sentences in each of the groups below.

[3] For work on the proper use of adverb phrases, see "Misplaced Phrase Modifiers" on page 191.

1. Our homeroom team won the game *easily*.
   Our homeroom team won the game *with ease*.
2. The spectators celebrated the victory *enthusiastically*.
   The spectators celebrated the victory *with enthusiasm*.
3. All day long we traveled *west*.
   All day long we traveled *in a westerly direction*.
4. He *mistakenly* gave me the wrong address.
   By mistake he gave me the wrong address.
5. *Earlier* we had eaten a big breakfast.
   At an earlier hour we had eaten a big breakfast.

All the adverb phrases in those sentences modify verbs. Name the modified verb in each sentence.

As you know, adverbs may also modify adjectives and other adverbs. Hence adverb phrases may likewise be used as modifiers of adjectives and adverbs.

EXAMPLES The new coat was too *large across the shoulders*. [Adverb phrase modifying adjective *large*.]

Later in the day the rain stopped. [Adverb phrase modifying adverb *later*.]

Adverb phrases modify other words in the same ways that adverbs modify other words. An adverb phrase may tell *how*, *when*, *where*, *why*, or *to what extent*.

DIAGRAMMING ADVERB PHRASES

Adverb phrases are diagrammed in the same way as adjective phrases.

EXAMPLE In high spirits we left the house.

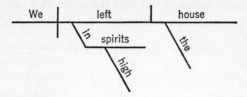

In high spirits is an adverb phrase modifying the verb *left*.

EXERCISE 3. Each of the following sentences contains two adverb phrases. List these phrases in order on your paper. After each phrase write the word the phrase modifies.

EXAMPLE He arrived at ten o'clock and left after lunch.

Phrase	Word Modified
at ten o'clock	arrived
after lunch	left

1. We went by ourselves but returned with the boys.
2. Gerald and I stood on the corner and talked for an hour.
3. Mr. Sikes walked into the room and put the assignment on the blackboard.
4. John arrived at dawn and left before nightfall.
5. In Detroit I stayed with my uncle.
6. The ball sailed toward the house and crashed through an attic window.
7. We waited for several hours and then returned to the camp.
8. Mother looked at us in amazement.
9. We met at the crossroads early in the morning.
10. Jan is good at diving and swims like a fish.

EXERCISE 4. Diagram the sentences in Exercises 1 and 3.

EXERCISE 5. Write 5 sentences containing an adjective phrase and 5 sentences containing an adverb phrase. Underline each phrase and draw an arrow pointing to the word the phrase modifies.

THE VERBALS: PARTICIPIAL, GERUND, AND INFINITIVE PHRASES [4]

In Chapter 1 you learned that there are eight parts of speech. There are some words, however, which cannot be classified in any one of these eight classes because these words are really two parts of speech in one. These words are called *verbals* because they are formed from verbs and act very much like verbs. They may, however, be used as other parts of speech. There are three kinds of verbals: the *participle*, the *gerund*, and the *infinitive*.

THE PARTICIPLE

A *participle* is a word formed from a verb and used as an adjective. From the verb *swim* you can form the participle *swimming*, as in the sentence:

The *swimming* beaver dove out of sight.

In this sentence the word *swimming* is partly a verb because it carries the action of the verb *swim*. Furthermore, it is partly an adjective because it modifies the noun *beaver*. It is a participle. Study the use of the word *standing* in the following sentence:

Standing in the back of the auditorium, we could not hear the speaker.

[4] For work on the proper use of verbals, see "Dangling Modifiers" on page 186.

In this sentence *standing* is a participle because it gives the action of the verb *stand*; yet, like an adjective, it modifies the pronoun *we*.

3f. A word which acts as both a verb and an adjective is called a *participle*. Participles which end in *–ing* are called *present participles*.

Caution: Not all words ending in *–ing* are participles. When used as a verb, a word ending in *–ing* is part of a verb phrase. Study the difference in use between the words ending in *–ing* in the following sentences.

1. *Walking* home from school, Jack *was whistling*. [*Walking* is a participle; *whistling* is a part of the verb phrase *was whistling*.]
2. Jean, *looking* out the window, *was watching* the children *playing* in the street. [*Looking* is a participle; *was watching* is a verb phrase; *playing* is a participle.]

EXERCISE 6. From the following sentences select the present participles and list them in a column. After each participle write the noun or pronoun which it modifies.

1. Hurrying from one shop to another, the foreman was soon exhausted.
2. Helen, working rapidly, finished the dishes in a few minutes.
3. Pete is the boy carrying the flag.
4. Believing he was right, the speaker would not listen to any arguments.
5. Jim, seeing the danger, called us back.
6. The books lying on the table are mine.
7. Expecting visitors, we turned on the porch light.
8. We saw a number of fish lying under the bank.
9. Carrying furniture upstairs, Father strained his back.
10. I saw Jim driving the car.

Participles which end in *-d*, *-ed*, *-t*, *-en*, or *-n* show action in the past and are called *past participles*. Study the italicized words in the following sentences.

1. She was an *excited* little girl.

Since *excited* in this sentence carries the action of the verb *excite* and at the same time modifies the noun *girl*, it is both verb and adjective — therefore a *participle*.

2. The dog, *left* alone in the house, kept all intruders away.

You can see that *left* carries the action of the verb *leave*, but it is an adjective too because it modifies the noun *dog*. Hence *left*, being both verb and adjective, is a *participle*.

3. *Blown* from her course, the vessel reached port two days late.

Blown, which is formed from the verb *blow*, modifies the noun *vessel* as an adjective would. It is a *participle*. Participles like *excited*, *left*, and *blown* are *past participles*.

EXERCISE 7. Select from the following sentences all the participles, both present and past. List them on your paper and after each one write the word which the participle modifies.

1. Our teacher, annoyed by our conduct, kept us after school.
2. The boxes shipped from abroad came by air.
3. Awakened by the noise, Harold sprang to his feet, trembling with fear.
4. Seeing the problem clearly, I was able to solve it.
5. The days spent at the seashore improved my health.
6. Looking for the treasure buried by the old Spanish explorers, we uncovered many ancient relics.

7. Surprised by the sudden appearance of George wearing a new white suit, we rushed to meet him.
8. She came bringing gifts for us and left loaded with presents from us.
9. Sensing a disturbance in the back of the room, the professor called for order.
10. Angered by his attitude, the clerk refused to listen.

THE PARTICIPIAL PHRASE

3g. When a participle introduces a group of related words, all of which act together as an adjective, this word group is called a *participial phrase*.

The participial phrase in each of the following sentences is italicized.   An arrow points to the noun or pronoun which the phrase modifies. Note that Sentences 1–5 contain present participles (ending in *–ing*) and Sentences 6–10 contain past participles (ending in *–ed, –d, –t, –en, –n*).

1. *Getting up from her desk,* Jane approached the teacher.

2. I found the child *crying for his mother.*

3. *Jumping with perfect form,* he cleared the bar at six feet.

4. *Working in his office all day,* Father gets very little exercise.

5. It was a shock to see you *coming around the corner.*

6. We were sorry for the dog, *chained to a stake all the time.*

7. *Admired by everyone,* he became conceited.

8. *Swept off his feet by the charge,* our quarterback was thrown for a loss.

9. *Taken completely by surprise,* the enemy was forced to surrender.

10. The sloop, *torn from its moorings,* ran aground.

EXERCISE 8. You have learned to identify adjective, adverb, and participial phrases. Select the adverb, adjective, and participial phrases from the following sentences and copy them on your paper. After each phrase write the word it modifies and tell what kind of phrase it is.

When identifying participles, do not be misled by verb phrases containing a word ending in *–ing* or *–ed: were talking, have been working, has jumped,* etc. (See *Caution* under **3f,** page 66.)

1. My cousins from Chicago are spending the summer with us.
2. Disturbed by the commotion, we could not sleep.
3. In the afternoon we played tennis with Jimmy and him.
4. The girls living in the next house helped us with our work.
5. Attracted by the promise of easy money, he accepted the job.

THE GERUND

3h. The *gerund* is a word formed from a verb and used as a noun.

Study the italicized words in the following sentences. They are *gerunds.* Prove that each word is part verb and part noun. For instance, *eating* in the first sentence is formed from the verb *eat,* yet it names an action. It is the name of something; therefore it is used as a noun. Further proof that *eating* is used as a noun is its use as subject of the sentence.

1. *Eating* is a great pleasure.
2. *Skiing* is my favorite winter sport.
3. We enjoyed *cooking* our dinner over a campfire.
4. The clever *playing* of the catcher saved the game.
5. Quick *thinking* is necessary in *playing* basketball.

You can see that each of the italicized words is used as a noun. In some sentences it is used as the subject; in others it is used as the object of the verb. How is *playing* used in the fifth sentence? Unlike participles, gerunds always end in *-ing*.

EXERCISE 9. From the following verbs make gerunds and use each one in a sentence which will show clearly that your gerund is used as a noun. It may be one of the following in the sentence: subject of verb, object of verb, predicate nominative, object of a preposition.

1. sleep
2. run
3. swim
4. walk
5. hear
6. talk
7. look
8. be
9. wait
10. serve

THE GERUND PHRASE

3i. A gerund phrase is a phrase containing a gerund.

Study these examples of gerund phrases.

1. *Getting up early* is very painful.
2. *Eating breakfast hurriedly* will give you indigestion.
3. Fran's trouble is *always being late*.

4. I dislike *studying late at night*.
5. *Writing an interesting composition* is hard for me.

Go back over the five examples above and tell how each gerund phrase is used in the sentence. Is it the subject, the predicate nominative, or the direct object?

EXERCISE 10. Write five sentences, each containing one or more gerund phrases.

THE INFINITIVE

3j. An *infinitive* is a verbal consisting of *to* followed by the verb. An infinitive is generally used as a noun, but may also be used as an adjective or an adverb.

To go, to see, to work are examples of infinitives. Study the infinitives in the following sentences and note how each is used.

1. *To skate* on thin ice is dangerous. (Noun, subject of *is*)
2. We like *to study* in the library. (Noun, object of *like*)
3. They had plenty of water *to drink*. (Adjective, modifies *water*)
4. He played *to win*. (Adverb, modifies *played*)
5. *To see* is *to believe*. (Nouns, subject of *is* and predicate nominative after *is*)

EXERCISE 11. List on your paper the infinitives in the following sentences. After each infinitive tell how it is used — as subject, object, predicate nominative.

1. To work rapidly in hot weather is impossible.
2. She promised to do her best.

3. I don't want to be late.
4. His ambition was to swim the channel.
5. To eat is a necessity as well as a pleasure.
6. She expects to see you.
7. To work by yourself is efficient.
8. To leave in the midst of such a storm would be to ask for trouble.
9. I love to listen to records.
10. She attempted to prevent my going.

THE INFINITIVE PHRASE

3k. A phrase which contains an infinitive is an *infinitive phrase*.

Study the make-up of the infinitive phrases in the sentences below.

1. My plan was *to leave early*.
2. The principal duty of the fire squad is *to prevent fires*.
3. Do you expect *to beat the champion?*
4. *To be a professional ballplayer* was Andy's ambition.
5. Jack has gone *to see his brother*.

EXERCISE 12.   Write 2 sentences containing an example of each of the following. There will be **10** sentences in all.

1. an adjective phrase   3. a gerund phrase
2. an adverb phrase   4. an infinitive phrase
            5. a participial phrase

THE CLAUSE [5]

3l. A group of words that contains a verb and its subject and is used as a part of a sentence is called a *clause*.

[5] For work on the proper use of clauses see "Misplaced Clause Modifiers" on page 193.

DISTINGUISHING BETWEEN PHRASES
AND CLAUSES

Study the following examples of phrases and clauses.

1. a man *with a black hat* — phrase
   a man **who wore** a black hat — clause
   [The verb in this clause is *wore;* the subject of the verb is *who.*]

2. an airport *with long runways* — phrase
   an airport **which has** long runways — clause
   [The verb in this clause is *has;* the subject of the verb is *which.*]

3. *Climbing the ladder* he lost his balance. — phrase
   While **he was climbing** the ladder, he lost his balance. — clause
   [The verb in this clause is *was climbing;* the subject is *he.*]

4. *Greatly disappointed,* Jack returned home. — phrase
   Because **he was** greatly **disappointed,** Jack returned home. — clause
   [The verb in this clause is *was disappointed;* the subject is *he.*]

5. *In the morning* we learned what had actually happened. — phrase
   When **morning came,** we learned what had actually happened. — clause
   [The verb in this clause is *came;* the subject is *morning.*]

The difference between a clause and a phrase is that a clause has a verb and a subject, whereas a phrase does not.

DISTINGUISHING BETWEEN MAIN[6] AND SUBORDINATE CLAUSES

3m. A *main clause* is a clause that expresses a complete thought and can stand by itself as a sentence.

Standing by itself, a main clause would be called a sentence, but when written as a part of a sentence it is called a clause. For example, the two sentences below become main clauses when they are combined into one long sentence.

SENTENCES

1. The train is pulled as far as Harrisburg by an electric locomotive. [complete thought]

2. From Harrisburg on, it is pulled by a steam locomotive. [complete thought]

MAIN CLAUSES (parts of a sentence)

3. The train is pulled as far as Harrisburg by an electric locomotive, *but* from Harrisburg on, it is pulled by a steam locomotive.

The two main clauses in this sentence are joined into one sentence by the conjunction *but*.

3n. A *subordinate clause* is a clause which does not express a complete thought and cannot stand alone.

[6] *Main* clauses are sometimes called *independent* clauses. *Subordinate* clauses are sometimes called *dependent* clauses.

EXAMPLES When the shop door opened . . . . .

. . . . . who was the shopkeeper

. . . . . that someone was in the shop

These clauses depend upon a main clause to make their meaning complete. Note how they become meaningful when linked to a main clause (complete thought).

When the shop door opened, *a bell rang*.
Mr. Simon, who was the shopkeeper, *heard the bell*.
He knew that someone was in the shop.

EXERCISE 13. The following list contains sentences, subordinate clauses, and some word groups which are not clauses — do not have a verb and subject. Number on your paper from 1 to 15. Identify each group of words and tell what it is (*sentence, subordinate clause, not a clause*) after the corresponding number on your paper. Be able to support your opinion.

1. To whom he was talking.
2. The conversation lasted ten minutes.
3. Since he had very little to say.
4. Although she bought us tickets for the game.
5. On the day of the big game.
6. The stadium stands on a small hill.
7. Which is an ideal location.
8. Standing outside the stadium.
9. During the intermission between halves.
10. While the referee and umpires discussed the penalty.
11. The crowd roared its biased opinion.
12. As soon as a decision had been reached.
13. One of the best games of the season.

14. If they hadn't been so overconfident.
15. The result might have been different.

RELATIVE PRONOUNS IN
SUBORDINATE CLAUSES

Read the following sentences, noting especially the words in boldface type. These words are the subjects of the clauses in which they appear. Do you know what part of speech these words are?

1. I can't remember the name of the girl **who** *spoke to me.*
2. This is the book **that** *contains the best recipes.*
3. It is this coat **which** *fits you best.*
4. Wait for Jim, **who** *is coming later.*

The subjects of these clauses are, as you have discovered, all pronouns. They *relate* to another word somewhere in the sentence.

In Sentence 1 *who* relates to *girl.*
In Sentence 2 *that* relates to *book.*
In Sentence 3 *which* relates to *coat.*
What word does *who* relate to in Sentence 4?

3o. A pronoun which introduces a subordinate clause and *relates* to another word or idea is called a *relative pronoun.*

The relative pronouns are *who, whom, which,* and *that. Relative* pronouns are frequently used as subjects of subordinate clauses. They may also be used as objects and as predicate nominatives, as you will learn in the following explanation.

COMPLEMENTS AND MODIFIERS IN
SUBORDINATE CLAUSES

The verb in a subordinate clause may have the same kinds of complements as the verb in a sentence.

It may have an indirect or a direct object, a predicate nominative or a predicate adjective. Naturally, it may also be modified by an adverb.

There is the man *whom* I saw. [*Whom* is the direct object of *saw*.]

I couldn't tell *who* it was. [*Who* is a predicate nominative.]

Although she bought *us tickets* for the game..... [*Us* is the indirect object of *bought*; *tickets* is the direct object of *bought*.]

.....which is an ideal *location*. [*Location* is a predicate nominative.]

If they hadn't been so *overconfident*..... [*Overconfident* is a predicate adjective.]

While he was working *for me*..... [*For me* is an adverb phrase modifying *was working*.]

EXERCISE 14. Copy on your paper the italicized subordinate clauses in the following sentences. In each clause name the kinds of words listed below by writing the proper abbreviation over that kind of word if you find it in the clause.

ABBREVIATIONS

s.	subject	i.o.	indirect object
v.	verb	p.n.	predicate nominative
d.o.	direct object	p.a.	predicate adjective

If the verb is composed of more than one word, label each word.

EXAMPLE *When* **she** **has finally given** **us** **her permission,**
I will thank her.

1. I'd like to know *who did this*.
2. I know *who the captain was*, but I don't know *which team won the game*.
3. He is the player *whom you were watching*.
4. Is this the suit *that you wore to church?*
5. We saw the man *who was eight feet tall*.
6. *When you see Joe*, please give him my message.
7. He left *before I could give him the message*.
8. *Although he had waited for me*, I missed him.
9. Do you know *what he gave us?*
10. *If you can possibly spare a dollar*, give it to him.

EXERCISE 15. Write 10 sentences containing subordinate clauses. Underline the clauses and, using the abbreviations in Exercise 14, name each part of the clause.

THE ADJECTIVE CLAUSE

3p. An *adjective clause* is a subordinate clause which — like an adjective — modifies a noun or pronoun.

EXAMPLE Bill has a horse *that jumps beautifully*.

That jumps beautifully is a subordinate clause. *That* is its subject, and *jumps* is its verb. The clause modifies the noun *horse*. Therefore it is an *adjective clause*.

EXAMPLE It is she *whom I mean*.

Whom I mean is a subordinate clause. Its subject is *I;* its verb is *mean;* its direct object is *whom*. The clause modifies the pronoun *she*. It is an *adjective clause*.

DIAGRAMMING THE ADJECTIVE CLAUSE

Since a subordinate clause has a verb and a subject and includes complements and modifiers, it is diagrammed very much like a sentence. An adjective clause beginning with a relative pronoun is joined to the noun it modifies by a slanting dotted line. The line runs from the modified word to the relative pronoun.

The knife *that Father carries on his watch chain* has a pearl handle.

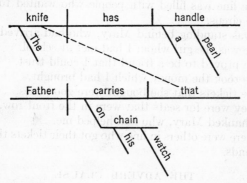

EXERCISE 16. Copy the italicized clauses in the following sentences on your paper. Label the subject, the verb, and the complements, if any. After each clause write the word it modifies.

1. Jane invited several girls *whom she had met recently*.
2. This is the one *about whom I was telling you*.
3. The gift *which you selected* pleased me most.
4. It was she *who told me the story*.
5. That was the time *when he made a grave mistake*.

From your study of those sentences you may have noticed that adjective clauses usually begin with the relative pronouns *who*, *whom*, *that*, and *which*. However, Sentence 5 shows that an adjective clause may begin with some other word.

EXERCISE 17. Each of the following sentences contains an adjective clause. Write the adjective clauses on your paper. Label the verb and the subject. After each clause write the word which the clause modifies.

1. The line which formed at the ticket window was very long.
2. The line was filled with people who wanted to go to the circus.
3. I was standing behind Mary, who had arrived early.
4. She was the girl whom I had met at school.
5. She proved to be a friend that I could trust.
6. She took the money which I had brought.
7. The tickets that she bought were good ones.
8. They were for seats that were in the front row.
9. I thanked Mary, who had helped me.
10. There were others in line who got their tickets through friends.

THE ADVERB CLAUSE

3q. **An *adverb clause* is a subordinate clause which — like an adverb — modifies a verb or an adjective or an adverb. Adverb clauses tell *how, when, where, why,* or *to what extent.***

Study the following sentences:

ADVERB CLAUSE MODIFYING A VERB

1. He played *as though his life depended on winning the game.* [In this sentence, *as though his life depended on winning the game* is a clause modifying the verb *played.* It tells *how* he played.]
2. *When he reached home,* he found the door locked. [In this sentence, *when he reached home* is a clause modifying *found.* It tells *when* he found the door locked.]
3. I will go *wherever you send me.* [In this sentence,

wherever you send me is a clause modifying the verb *go*. It tells *where* I will go.]

4. *Because there is so much to do,* we must hurry. [In this sentence, *Because there is so much to do* is a clause modifying the verb *must hurry*. It tells *why* we must hurry.]

ADVERB CLAUSE MODIFYING AN ADJECTIVE

5. Fred is as tall *as you are.* [In this sentence, *as you are* is a clause modifying the adjective *tall*. It tells *how tall* Fred is.]

ADVERB CLAUSE MODIFYING AN ADVERB

6. George plays better *than I do.* [In this sentence, *than I do* is a clause modifying the adverb *better*. It tells *how much* better George plays.]

THE SUBORDINATING CONJUNCTION

Adverb clauses are introduced by conjunctions. Conjunctions of this kind are *subordinating conjunctions*. *To subordinate* means to reduce something to a position of less importance, to a *sub order*. A subordinate clause is less important than the main clause in a sentence. The conjunction which introduces it is, therefore, known as a *subordinating conjunction*.

It may help you to learn a list of subordinating conjunctions. The following are the commonest ones. Usually, but not always, these words are used to introduce adverb clauses.

COMMON SUBORDINATING CONJUNCTIONS [7]

after	before	when
although	if	whenever
as	since	where
because	until	while

[7] *After, before, since,* and *until* may, as you know, also be used as prepositions.

DIAGRAMMING THE ADVERB CLAUSE

An *adverb clause* is joined to the rest of the sentence by a subordinating conjunction. This conjunction is written on a slanting dotted line which links the verb of the clause to the word the clause modifies.

When the telephone rang, three of us jumped up.

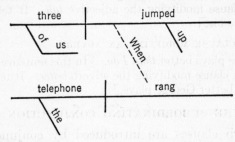

EXERCISE 18. From each of the following sentences copy onto your paper the adverb clause. Label the subject and the verb of the clause. After each clause write the word it modifies and state whether the clause tells *how, when, where,* or *why.*

1. Frank works as though he enjoys working.
2. I will use the wheelbarrow while you shovel sand.
3. We will build the walk whenever you want it.
4. We must get some water before we can mix cement.
5. Andy will help us after he has unloaded the cement.
6. Put the cement where you can reach it easily.
7. The old walk crumbled because the cement was poor.
8. As soon as the walk is finished, I will go swimming.
9. When you see Dad, tell him the truth.
10. He talks as though he is an authority.

EXERCISE 19. List on your paper the subordinate clauses in the following sentences. After each clause write the word it modifies and state whether the clause is an adjective clause or an adverb clause.

1. The party which the sophomore class gave was the best of the year.
2. When the decorations were planned, everyone wanted simple decorations.
3. There were green and gold streamers that hung from the ceiling.
4. Although the orchestra was small, it was very good.
5. John, who was the treasurer, reported a profit.
6. Since most of our dances had lost money, the sophomores were praised for their achievement.
7. The dance that lost the most money was the Senior Prom.
8. It lost money because the seniors would not admit underclassmen.
9. Because they had a big crowd the sophomores made money.
10. After the party was over, some of us went to Joe's.

EXERCISE 20. Diagram the sentences in Exercise 19.

EXERCISE 21. Write 10 sentences, using in each a different one of the subordinating conjunctions in the list on page 81. Underline the word which the adverb clause modifies in each sentence.

THE NOUN CLAUSE

3r. A clause which is used as a noun is a *noun clause.*

Compare the two sentences in each pair below. Notice that in the second sentence in each pair *a subordinate clause takes the place of a noun in the first sentence.*

Tell whether the clause in each of the following sentences is used as the subject, object, or a predicate nominative.

1. Nobody knew the *answer*.
   Nobody knew *what the answer was*.
2. The *defeat* made very little difference to the spectators.
   That the team was defeated made very little difference to the spectators.
3. Our *whereabouts* was a mystery.
   Where we were was a mystery.
4. The winner will be the best *player*.
   The winner will be *whoever plays best*.
5. I could not understand her *question*.
   I could not understand *what she asked*.

THE SUBORDINATE CLAUSE NOT INTRODUCED BY A JOINING WORD

Sometimes, especially in everyday speaking, we use a subordinate clause without a word to join it to the rest of the sentence. Compare the subordinate clauses in the paired sentences below.

1. I know **that** he will be on time.
   I know *he will be on time*. [The joining word *that* has been omitted.]
2. He is the man **whom** I saw.
   He is the man *I saw*. [The joining word *whom* has been omitted.]

EXERCISE 22. There are 10 noun clauses in the following sentences. Copy them on your paper. Label the subject and the verb. After each clause tell whether it is the subject of the sentence, the object, or a predicate noun.

1. I do not remember who told me this.
2. The storekeeper knows what you want.
3. Whoever wants a high mark must work hard.
4. I know where she is.
5. The captain will be whoever is appointed.
6. He asked me what I was doing.
7. I will do whatever you wish.
8. What he did surprised us all.
9. They wanted what they could not have.
10. Whoever wants library privileges must sign this card.

DIAGRAMMING A NOUN CLAUSE

A clause used as subject or object or predicate nominative is supported by an upright line resting on the subject or object or predicate nominative line.

1. NOUN CLAUSE AS SUBJECT: *What he said* surprised us.

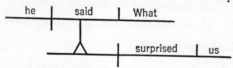

2. NOUN CLAUSE AS OBJECT: We knew *what he wanted*.

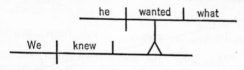

EXERCISE 23. Diagram the sentences in Exercise 22.

EXERCISE 24. In the following sentences there are adjective, adverb, and noun clauses. Copy each clause on your paper. Label the verb and subject, and name the kind of clause. Your teacher may prefer to have you diagram the sentences.

1. Father objected when he heard our plans.
2. He asked who was going with us.
3. That he took this attitude surprised me.
4. He told me that it would be late.
5. What we disliked was taking a chaperone.
6. It was Margaret who finally solved the problem.
7. She invited her older sister, whom everyone likes.
8. When he heard who was going with us, Father told us that we could go.
9. As soon as everyone was ready, we told Margaret where we were going.
10. Everyone said that it was the best outing of the summer.

SENTENCES CLASSIFIED ACCORDING TO FORM OR STRUCTURE

3s. Classified according to structure, there are four kinds of sentences — simple, compound, complex, compound-complex.

(1) A *simple sentence* is a sentence with one main clause and no subordinate clauses.

Simple sentences are not necessarily short.

EXAMPLE Philip, a young friend from Marblehead, [Subject] Massachusetts, and a born sailor, can handle a [Verb] sailing yacht with all the skill of an experienced mariner.

(2) A *compound sentence* is composed of two or more main clauses but no subordinate clauses.

EXAMPLES Franklin is an excellent yachtsman; *never-* [s. v.] *theless*, he was no match for Philip. [two [s. v.] main clauses]

His yacht was neither new nor handsome, *but*
it was trim, *and* it won every race. [three
main clauses]

Conjunctions most commonly used to join the clauses of a compound sentence are *and, but, nor, or*. When so used, these conjunctions are usually preceded by a comma.[8]

Other words used to join the clauses of a compound sentence are *consequently, therefore, nevertheless, however, moreover, otherwise,* etc. When so used, they are preceded by a semicolon.[9]

Each main clause in a compound sentence is diagrammed like a separate sentence. A dotted line joins them together. This line is drawn between the verbs of the clauses.

EXAMPLE Franklin is an excellent yachtsman; nevertheless, he is no match for Philip.

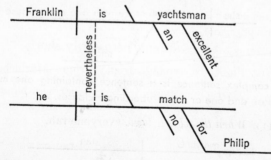

NOTE: Do not confuse the compound predicate of a simple sentence with the two subjects and two predicates of a compound sentence.

[8] For punctuation of compound sentences see pages 412-13.
[9] These joining words are called *conjunctive adverbs*.

SIMPLE SENTENCE WITH A COMPOUND PREDICATE

She left the room hurriedly *and* returned at once.

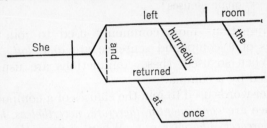

COMPOUND SENTENCE WITH TWO MAIN CLAUSES

She left the room hurriedly, *and* she returned at once.

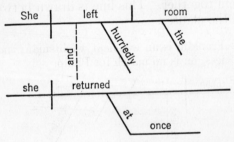

(3) A *complex sentence* is a sentence containing one main clause and one or more subordinate clauses.

EXAMPLE *When the whistle blew,* everyone ran.

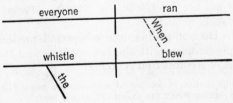

Since you have already learned how to diagram subordinate clauses (adjective, adverb, and noun clauses), you have learned to diagram a complex sentence. If you wish to refresh your memory, turn back to pages 79, 82, and 85.

(4) A *compound-complex sentence* contains two or more main clauses and one or more subordinate clauses.

EXAMPLE The book that I read was written by Kenneth Roberts, and it is a best seller. [two main clauses and one subordinate clause]

EXERCISE 25. Write 2 simple sentences, 2 compound sentences, and 2 complex sentences.

EXERCISE 26. What kind of sentence is each of the following? Be prepared to prove your answer.

1. After the plans have been completed, we will produce this complicated apparatus.
2. We appreciate the inconvenience which the delay caused, and we regret it very much.
3. Telephones must be placed where the need is greatest.
4. If you will limit your call to five minutes, we shall appreciate it.
5. Leave when you are ready.
6. I could hear his voice very clearly.
7. He was in San Francisco, and I was in New York.
8. She eagerly picked up the receiver and listened.
9. We take the telephone for granted, but we should appreciate it more fully.
10. The service which it gives us is remarkable.

EXERCISE 27. Diagram the sentences in Exercise 26.

4. WRITING COMPLETE SENTENCES

This chapter is for those of you whose compositions frequently contain incomplete sentences. When parts of sentences are written as though they were complete sentences, they are called *sentence fragments*. Many times sentence fragments get into your writing because you are careless in your punctuation, but they may also appear because you do not know very clearly what a sentence is or what the common sentence fragments are. This chapter will help you to avoid writing fragments as sentences.

In your study of the grammar of the sentence in Chapter 2 you learned that in order to be a sentence, a group of words must express a complete thought. You learned, furthermore, that a sentence contains a verb and its subject. If these terms are not now completely clear to you, return to page 27 and refresh your knowledge of them.

In analyzing your own sentences, you should ask yourself two questions. (1) Does this group of words express a *complete* thought? (2) Does it contain a verb and its subject? As you know, a subordinate clause [1] contains a verb and its subject, yet it is not a sentence because it does not state a complete thought. It depends upon the rest of the sentence for its meaning. By itself it is only a *fragment* of a sentence.

[1] See page 74.

EXERCISE 1. On your paper write *S* for each complete sentence, *F* for each sentence fragment (not a complete thought).

1. When the soldiers came back from Europe.
2. The missing dog having been found.
3. Waiting several hours for the bus.
4. While the ladies prepared the food.
5. The fire of the camp could be seen miles away.
6. Eagerly leaning out the window and looking down the street.
7. Please stop teasing the girls.
8. The penalty for cheating is very severe.
9. On the afternoon of the second day of school.
10. Low over the frightened crowd swung the airship.
11. Although she followed the directions exactly.
12. Didn't the cake turn out well?
13. Deserted by his friends.
14. Who mowed the lawn?
15. Who was an excellent workman.
16. The hero of the story which you were reading.
17. Not one of our players was able to hit the ball regularly.
18. Mr. Harris, the owner of the store.
19. Wait a minute, George!
20. If you want to go swimming tomorrow.

COMMON TYPES OF SENTENCE FRAGMENTS

4a. The subordinate clause must not be written as a sentence.

Although a subordinate clause does have a verb and a subject, it depends upon the main clause of the sentence for its complete meaning. In number 20 above, *If you want to go swimming tomorrow*, the verb in the clause is *want* and the subject is *you*, but not until we add a main clause, a complete thought, to the subordinate clause, do we have a complete sentence.

RIGHT   If you want to go swimming tomorrow, *I will give you a lift to the beach.*

WRONG   The principal advised us to take typing. Which will be useful in all our courses.

RIGHT   The principal advised us to take typing, which will be useful in all our courses.

WRONG   We left the party early. After we had reached home. We discovered we had lost the door key.

RIGHT   We left the party early. After we had reached home, we discovered we had lost the door key.

EXERCISE 2.   Add a main clause either at the beginning or at the end of each of the following subordinate clauses to make 10 complete sentences. An adverb clause at the beginning of a sentence is followed by a comma.

1. As we were rounding a bend in the river
2. While I was sitting in the barber shop
3. If you see my sister
4. Which I have never read
5. Until he had finished reading the book
6. After the victory had been announced
7. Who helped us with our work
8. Before you decide what to do
9. When the storm began
10. Which left us completely exhausted

EXERCISE 3.   In the paragraph below there are several sentence fragments. They are all subordinate clauses which should be attached to a main clause. Copy the paragraph, changing the punctuation so that there will be no subordinate clauses standing by themselves. In your copying, omit the numbers.

1. Helen and I are baseball fans. 2. Of course, we can't equal Jimmy Sullivan. 3. Who knows the batting average of nearly every player in the league. 4. We keep up on the standing of the teams, and we do know a lot about the Brooklyn Dodgers. 5. Which is our favorite team. 6. Whenever we can get our dads to take us. 7. We go into the city to a game. 8. This isn't very often. 9. Because our dads are busy men without many free afternoons. 10. We have suggested that they take us to a night game. 11. Which we would enjoy especially. 12. Because we could stay out so late. 13. Although we can't see many games. 14. We can listen to them on the radio. 15. Helen and I are looking forward to the television days. 16. When we can see a whole game at home. 17. Which is much more comfortable than a ball park.

4b. Participial phrases and gerund phrases must not be written as sentences.

You will recall from your study of pages 66–69 that the present participle and the gerund are verbals ending in –*ing*. *Words ending in* –**ing** *cannot be used as verbs unless they have with them a helping verb. By themselves they can never be used as the verb in a sentence.* With a helping verb like *am, are, has been, will be*, etc., they become complete verbs.

WRONG The girls *making* fudge [A phrase; no verb]

RIGHT The girls *were making* fudge. [A sentence; a helping verb *were* has been added.]

WRONG A thunderstorm *threatening* in the east. [A phrase; no verb]

RIGHT A thunderstorm *was threatening* in the east. [A sentence; a helping verb *was* has been added.]

The following *helping verbs* may be used with words ending in *–ing*.

am	were	can (may) be
are	will (shall) be	could (would, should) be
is	has been	will (shall) have been
was	had been	might have been

A participial phrase containing a past participle must not be written as a sentence.

WRONG We finally found him. *Bound* and *gagged* and in great pain.

RIGHT We finally found him, *bound* and *gagged* and in great pain.

A participial phrase appears as an error in writing usually because of incorrect punctuation which leaves the phrase standing alone, unattached to a sentence.

WRONG John was nearly drowned. Swimming in the forbidden pit on Farmer Bowle's property.

RIGHT John was nearly drowned, swimming in the forbidden pit on Farmer Bowle's property.

WRONG In going to the opposite shore. The commander lost his way.

RIGHT In going to the opposite shore, the commander lost his way.

WRONG Ben walked slowly along the street. Having only a few pennies in his pockets. He could not buy anything to eat.

RIGHT Ben walked slowly along the street. Having only a few pennies in his pockets, he could not buy anything to eat.

WRONG Left alone in the deserted house. Marilyn was terrified.

RIGHT Left alone in the deserted house, Marilyn was terrified.

WRONG   The final speaker was Mr. Lambert.   He argued
a long time.   Determined to change the minds of
his audience.

RIGHT   The final speaker was Mr. Lambert.   He argued
a long time, determined to change the minds of
his audience.

In the sentences above marked *Right,* the participial phrase is not left standing by itself but is attached to a main clause.   The phrase has become
part of a sentence; this is the only way it should be
written.

EXERCISE 4.   Using the phrases listed below,
write 10 complete sentences.

1. Springing upon the platform and waving his arms
   wildly
2. Upon reaching home after the celebration
3. Abandoned by his comrades
4. Hiding behind a tree just to the right of the front
   porch
5. Playing center on the varsity
6. Pleased by the excellent performance of the school
   actors
7. Creeping forward between two projecting boulders
8. Riding all day across the prairie
9. After waiting patiently for several hours
10. Praised by everyone

EXERCISE 5.   Some of the following groups of
words are sentences.   Others are subordinate clauses,
participial phrases, or improperly written constructions like those you have just studied.   On your
paper place an *S* after the number corresponding
to each complete sentence; correct the others by
making them parts of complete sentences and write
your sentences after the proper numbers.

1. Believing that he had lost the match, Jimmy stopped trying.
2. We were thrilled at our first view of the harbor. Which is one of the finest in the world.
3. If he had not given up so soon.
4. The coach scolded Jimmy for his lack of fight. Telling him he'd never make a champion that way.
5. Delighted by the news that he had won a fortune.
6. I couldn't understand where all the ships came from. Which were lying at anchor there.
7. Because his opponent was more tired than he.
8. Suffering from the heat and tired from our long walk. We decided to go directly to bed.
9. He handled his money carelessly. Giving it away in large amounts to people. Who didn't know how to handle it.
10. We enjoyed watching the antics of some sailors. Who apparently had just come ashore. After a long voyage.
11. You have learned a valuable lesson from your experience.
12. Whichever one you want.
13. Most thrilling was the Statue of Liberty. Standing strong and reassuring in the harbor.
14. Fran, hurrying down the street on her way to school.
15. We gazed a long time at the sights. As though we had never seen a harbor before.

4c. An appositive must not be written as a sentence. An *appositive* is a word or group of words which follows a noun or pronoun and means the same thing.

EXAMPLES Mike, *the janitor*, is the best natured man in our building. [*The janitor* is an appositive. It is "in apposition with" *Mike*.]

My good friend, *the pastor of St. Luke's Church,* has consented to speak to us. [*The pastor of St. Luke's Church* is in apposition with *friend.*]

Sometimes a hasty writer will treat an appositive as a complete sentence and leave it standing alone, although it has neither verb nor subject and does not express a complete thought.

WRONG We were talking about Mr. Altman. The newly appointed member of the board of directors.

RIGHT We were talking about Mr. Altman, *the newly appointed member of the board of directors.* [apposition with *Mr. Altman*]

Since an appositive is usually set off from the sentence by commas, the way to correct the error in the sentence above is to use a comma instead of a period after *Altman.*

WRONG Today the President had a long conference with an old friend of his. Our new ambassador to England.

RIGHT Today the President had a long conference with an old friend of his, our new ambassador to England.

WRONG I received my most valuable information from Mr. Scott. An experienced explorer who knows the arctic regions thoroughly.

RIGHT I received my most valuable information from Mr. Scott, an experienced explorer who knows the arctic regions thoroughly.

4d. Avoid other sentence fragments.

You have been studying how to improve your writing by not letting subordinate clauses, participial phrases, and appositives stand by themselves, unattached to a main clause. There are other kinds of fragments which you should know so that you will not let them stand alone either. These other fragments do have names, but it will not be necessary for you to learn them. Study the following examples of rather common fragments. Notice that each *wrong* item is corrected by attaching the fragment to a main clause. Then do the summary exercises which follow.

WRONG Sally was delighted with everything she saw on the farm. Especially the baby chickens and the new colt.

RIGHT Sally was delighted with everything she saw on the farm, especially the baby chickens and the new colt.

WRONG I begged Ray to let me go with him. To see a major league ball game.

RIGHT I begged Ray to let me go with him to see a major league ball game.

WRONG A freshman has many things to learn. Such as the plan of the high school, the student customs, and the best way to study.

RIGHT A freshman has many things to learn, such as the plan of the high school, the student customs, and the best way to study.

WRONG He made a great many friends. Became the most popular boy in his class and was elected class president.

RIGHT He made a great many friends, became the most popular boy in his class, and was elected class president.

EXERCISE 6. Each of the following contains a sentence fragment. Rewrite each item so that there will not be a sentence fragment in it.

1. We can profit from the mistakes of others. Taking care not to make the same mistakes ourselves.
2. I enjoy literature more than grammar. Because I like to read better than to write.
3. Walter worried about his math. Having failed it the first term. He found the second term even harder.
4. We felt sorry for Joyce. Kept after school for not doing her homework. She had to miss the game.
5. I promised that I would do my best. To get George the kind of portable radio set he wanted.
6. Our class wrote letters of congratulation to Senator Warren. The first graduate of our school to become a national figure.
7. We listened to everything Captain Cooper had to say. About life in the Air Corps. Which we thought the most exciting branch of the service.
8. My parents reserve the living room radio for themselves. Insisting that Jane and I listen to our programs on our own sets.
9. Sam picked up his books and raincoat with a flourish. As he left the room. He stumbled on the threshold Lost his balance and went down in a heap.
10. The foreman sent us out on the highway. To shovel crushed stone onto the new road.
11. Our ball team needs new uniforms this year. Which are too expensive for us to buy. Unless we can raise some more money.
12. We made a list of odd jobs we could do. To raise money for our uniforms. And to buy new equipment.

THE RUN–ON SENTENCE

It is not enough just to be able to avoid writing *parts* of sentences (subordinate clauses, participial phrases, appositives, and other fragments) as though they were whole sentences. It is equally important always to recognize where one sentence ends and the next one begins.

4e. A sentence should be followed by an end mark (period, question mark, exclamation point).

Sentences should not be separated by commas. To use a comma between sentences is an error in thought as well as in punctuation. In the following exercises are examples of poor writing in which sentences are not separated from each other properly. *Such constructions, because they consist of several complete sentences all run on together as though they were one sentence, are called* **run-on sentences.** *Avoid them.*

EXERCISE 7. Read the following aloud. Your ear will tell you where the complete thoughts begin and end. Write the last word in each complete sentence on your paper. Place the proper mark of punctuation after it. Then write the first word of the next sentence, beginning it with a capital letter.

EXAMPLE 1. We sailed out of the harbor just before dusk, a stiff breeze was blowing, lowering clouds forecast a storm coming from the north.

        1. dusk. A
        blowing. Lowering

1. I found it hard to believe his stories they were all too full of miraculous happenings, they didn't sound like true accounts of what had actually happened I doubt whether he believed them himself.

2. Having been excused early we hurried to the locker room and changed to our baseball suits, when the coach called us we were ready to go the big bus drew up in the drive and just as we had done a dozen other times we

piled in and took our usual seats this trip was different, however, every boy knew how different it was we would return either as champions of the state or as just another second-rate ball team.

3. It was the hottest day we could remember, coming down the street, we were sure we could see heat waves rising from the sidewalk, we felt as though we'd never get home we ambled up the street in a daze, hoping we'd last just one more block, we knew if we could make it there would be wonderful bottles of ice-cold cokes awaiting us.

4. Working on a lake steamer all summer was monotonous, it was also better than any other job I could have obtained, I loved the water and the ships and the rough and ready men with whom I worked, the food was good the work was not too strenuous, if it hadn't been for the sameness of the routine day after day, I should probably never have left.

EXERCISE 8. Copy the following paragraphs on your paper. Add punctuation and capital letters necessary to divide them into complete sentences.

1. When our evening chores were done, we'd gather in the lot behind the barn, lie down on our backs, and watch the night hawks they would be circling, sailing, and diving above us it was a matter of pride to see which of us could spot a diver first, the low whirr of the birds coming out of their dives was a music we loved to hear.

2. Spring was descending on Mr. Bush the neighbor to our left to anyone else it might mean birds in the trees, green things, blossoming catkins all over the place to Mr. Bush it meant only one thing, the grim business of planting his garden day after day we would see him digging like mad, turning over soil, raking, fertilizing then came the all-important planting, the moment toward which all his efforts had been bent. he dropped each seed in,

carefully muttering to himself meanwhile as though he were ordering each bit to grow and grow well for him it was wonderful to see him he concentrated so hard on what he was doing that he didn't hear even the ringing of the telephone, and he paid no attention whatever to his wife's strident call to dinner he was happy making mere seeds come to life.

3. Maybelle was a cute girl she used to have the nicest clothes when she walked, she always swished a little making taffeta-like sounds all the boys, the ones on our block anyway, whistled when she came by Maybelle pretended she didn't hear them, never pausing in her jaunts down the street she knew that she made them all want to date her her blue eyes were very blue her long yellow hair blew carelessly in the breeze, and her pretty legs seemed to twinkle as she sauntered by Maybelle was a cute girl the boys said she thought so too I never liked Maybelle.

EXERCISE 9. Copy the following selection on your paper, inserting punctuation so that there will be no sentence fragments and no run-on sentences. Every sentence must have a verb and its subject and must express a complete thought.

I'll never forget my first morning in camp much too early Pete and I were awakened by the bugler, who was standing right outside our cabin everything in camp was cold and damp because of the rain, which had been falling all night we had to decide whether to take a dip or not Pete said we should take a dip unless we wanted to be called sissies the lake looked icy, and as we climbed into our damp swimming trunks, we almost changed our minds we ran down to the dock and dived in without taking time to think about the cold water when we got used to the water, we enjoyed swimming in the light rain breakfast tasted especially good following our swim soon we were ready for inspection the first day at camp had started off pretty well after all.

EXERCISE 10. Copy the following selection on your paper, inserting punctuation so that there will be no sentence fragments and no run-on sentences. Every sentence must have a verb and its subject and must express a complete thought.

The airport was an exciting place we stood on a high platform near the observation tower, which was a glass-inclosed room in the distance the wide runways formed a huge white cross their pavements glistened in the sun, which was directly overhead great planes with the sun flashing from their sides turned and taxied on the large concrete apron above the roar of motors I shouted to George, and he shouted to me he was pointing to the blue water beyond the field, a part of Flushing Bay then he began to pound me on my back where I was sunburned I finally saw what he was pointing at the Pan American Clipper was coming in sweeping down to the bright blue water in a graceful glide, she was like a great white gull effortlessly she slid across the waves leaving a broad wake of white, blue, and green water behind her we turned to leave the airport thinking that it could offer nothing to surpass this final picture.

5. MAKING WORDS AGREE

AGREEMENT OF SUBJECT AND VERB

5a. A verb agrees with its subject in number.

In order to speak and write correctly you must be able to make the words you use *agree* with one another grammatically. If you will study the following sentences you will see at once how words *agree*.

RIGHT   Three *girls* from our class *were* going to the theater.

RIGHT   One *girl* from our class *was* going to buy the tickets.

RIGHT   *All* the tickets *were* lost.

RIGHT   *One* of the tickets *was* found.

RIGHT   The *pupils* in our class *have* been looking for the other tickets.

RIGHT   Our *teacher has* been hunting too.

In these sentences you can see how, in order to be correct, the verbs agree with their subjects. When the subject refers to *several* things, as in the first sentence in each pair, the verb takes a certain form to agree with that subject. When the subject refers to *one* thing, as in the second sentence in each pair, the verb changes to agree with the changed subject.

SINGULAR AND PLURAL NUMBER

5b. When a word refers to one thing, it is singular in number. When a word refers to more than one thing, it is plural in number.

In the sentences on page 104, which words are singular? Which are plural? [1] As you see, verbs change their number to agree with the number of their subjects.

EXERCISE 1. List the following words on your paper. After each plural word write *plural;* after each singular word write *singular*.

1. children	6. either	11. women
2. many	7. anyone	12. neither
3. one	8. all	13. several
4. each	9. no one	14. somebody
5. both	10. few	15. anybody

Have your list checked to be sure it is correct before going on to the next exercise.

EXERCISE 2. Decide which one of the words in parentheses should be used to agree with the subject given.

1. children (ask, asks)	8. books (appeal, appeals)
2. many (has, have)	9. no one (appear, appears)
3. one (seem, seems)	10. few (go, goes)
4. each (believe, believes)	11. women (is, are)
5. both (play, plays)	12. neither (look, looks)
6. either (was, were)	13. several (use, uses)
7. anyone (leave, leaves)	14. somebody (work, works)

15. anybody (lose, loses)

NOTE: *Is, was,* and *has* are singular. *Are, were,* and *have* are plural, except when used with the singular pronouns *I* and *you*.

EXAMPLES If I *were* boss, you would *have* to work harder.
Are you sure that I *have* no letter?

[1] See pages 466–68 for rules governing formation of plural of nouns.

Most verbs ending in a single *s* (*looks, meets, dresses*) are singular. Most verbs not ending in *s* are plural except when used with singular *I* and *you*.

SINGULAR	PLURAL
He appeals	They appeal
He believes	They believe
He learns	They learn
He leaves	They leave
He looks	They look
He makes	They make
He suits	They suit
He seems	They seem
He works	They work
He wants	They want
He goes	They go
He tries	They try

5c. The number of the subject is not changed by a prepositional phrase following the subject.[2]

One construction which may prove difficult for you is that in which a prepositional phrase comes between the subject and its verb.

RIGHT   *One is* late.

RIGHT   *One* **of the teachers** *is* late.

RIGHT   *Both are* courteous.

RIGHT   *Both* **of the men in the office** *are* courteous.

The subject is never in a prepositional phrase. The prepositional phrase cannot change the number of the subject, and so it cannot affect the number of the verb which agrees with the subject. Diagrams of these sentences will make this point clear.

---

[2] The pronouns *some, any, none, all,* when used as subjects, are exceptions to this rule. See **5e**.

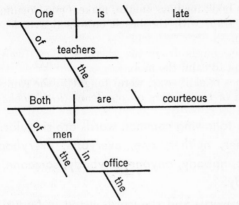

In doing the exercises which follow, do not be led astray by prepositional phrases coming between the subject and the verb.

EXERCISE 3.   In each of the following sentences you have a choice of verbs.   Write the subject of each verb on your paper.   After each subject write the correct one of the two verbs given in parentheses. You are now applying a grammar principle to usage. Remembering that verb and subject must agree in number, select the one of the two verbs which agrees in number with the subject.

1. The girls in the office (work, works) long hours.
2. A tree with wide-spreading branches (were, was) brushing the house.
3. The sound of the branches (was, were) weird and frightening.
4. The players on the first team (were, was) the most capable.
5. The buildings along the waterfront (seem, seems) to be unoccupied.

6. This book for boys (make, makes) good reading.
7. The train with the beach crowds (leave, leaves) at noon.
8. Some guards from the sheriff's office (were, was) trying to calm the mob.
9. Games of skill (was, were) taught to the campers.
10. Both of the players on our team (look, looks) good.

5d. The following common words are singular: *each, either, neither, one, everyone, everybody, no one, nobody, anyone, anybody, someone, somebody.*

These words and the words listed in **5e** are called *indefinite pronouns* because they do not refer to any definite thing or person. They refer only generally, *indefinitely*, to some thing or some person. Many persons, however, are confused by the plural noun in the phrase following the subject. Thinking this word to be the subject, they make the verb plural to agree with it, thus throwing the verb out of agreement with its true subject, the indefinite pronoun.

WRONG One of the apples are ripe. [Verb is incorrectly made to agree with *apples*, which is not its subject.]
RIGHT *One* of the apples *is* ripe. [Verb agrees with its subject, which is *one*.]

Study the use of the indefinite pronouns in the following pairs of sentences.

RIGHT *Each is* present.
RIGHT *Each* of the members *is* present.
RIGHT *Either* (*Neither*) *seems* good.
RIGHT *Either* (*Neither*) of the plans *seems* good.
RIGHT *One has* been answered.
RIGHT *One* of our questions *has* been answered.

RIGHT   *Everyone looks* happy.

RIGHT   *Every one* of the youngsters *looks* happy.

RIGHT   *Everybody takes* the same course.

RIGHT   *Everybody* in those classes *takes* the same course.

5e. **The following common words are plural: *several,*** ***few, both, many.* *Some, any, none,* and *all* may** **be either plural or singular.**

When the words *some, any, none,* and *all* are followed by a phrase, the phrase often helps you to decide whether the words are plural or singular. The phrase makes clear whether or not the writer is thinking of *several* things or *one* thing.

RIGHT   *Some* of the pencils *are* sharp. (plural)

RIGHT   *Some* of the food *has* spoiled. (singular)

RIGHT   *Have any* of the girls been here? (plural)

RIGHT   *Has any* of the order been shipped? (singular)

RIGHT   *None* of his reasons *were* sound. (plural)

RIGHT   *None* of his money *was* taken. (singular)

RIGHT   *All* of the tires *were* new. (plural)

RIGHT   *All* of the gasoline *was* spilled. (singular)

EXERCISE 4: *Oral Drill.* Repeat each of the following sentences *aloud* five times, stressing the italicized words.

1. *One* of these *is* mine.
2. *Every one* of them *looks* good.
3. *Neither* of the books *has* a clean cover.
4. *Some* of them *are* willing.
5. Not *one* of these stories *appeals* to me.
6. *One* of us *is* sure to win.
7. *Neither* of the teams *was* defeated.
8. *Either* of your proposals *is* acceptable.

9. *Several* of us girls *were* looking for you.
10. *Every boy* on the team *respects* the coach.

EXERCISE 5. Number from 1 to 10 on your paper. Select from the pair of verbs in each sentence the correct one to agree with the subject. Write this verb after the proper number on your paper.

1. (Is, Are) every one of these pens yours?
2. Neither of the ladies (were, was) afraid to work.
3. Every one of our trees (was, were) uprooted by the storm.
4. Each of the bushes (need, needs) trimming.
5. Both of your brothers (is, are) leaving school.
6. Several of the players (seem, seems) nervous.
7. Not one of these boys (has, have) finished the homework.
8. Everybody in the European countries (knows, know) what war is like.
9. One of your arguments (is, are) easily refuted.
10. A few of the boys in my class (were, was) on the honor roll.

EXERCISE 6. Number in a column on your paper from 1 to 20. Read each of the following sentences *aloud*. If the sentence is correct — the verb and the subject are in agreement — write a plus (+) after the proper number on your paper. If the sentence is incorrect, write a zero (0) after the proper number.

1. Every one of us have tried out for the tennis team.
2. One of the boats looks like a sloop.
3. Either of the older boys are able to do the job.
4. Some of the pages in this book are torn.
5. Every one of you have to report to the principal.
6. Each of those girls work conscientiously.

7. Neither of your arguments is convincing.
8. Both of the escaped prisoners was captured.
9. One of us has to be on time.
10. Several of our Presidents have come from Ohio.
11. All of the children look healthy.
12. Neither of my friends know how to dance.
13. Are one of the boxes large enough?
14. Either of your offers seems fair.
15. Each of the contests is sure to be close.
16. Every one of these dogs are thoroughly trained.
17. Some of the students was rather noisy.
18. Many of my answers were wrong.
19. Not one of us were going to tell on you.
20. If any one of you boys and girls knows the answer, raise your hand.

5f. *Don't* and *doesn't* must agree with their subjects. With the subjects *I* and *you,* use *don't* (do not). With other subjects use *doesn't* (does not) when the subject is singular, and *don't* (do not) when the subject is plural.

RIGHT   *I don't* know how.
RIGHT   *You don't* know my brother.
RIGHT   *It (he) doesn't* work.
RIGHT   *They don't* want to go.

The commonest errors in the use of *don't* and *doesn't* are made when *don't* is incorrectly used after *it, he,* or *she.* You can remove these common errors from your speech and writing if you will remember always to use *doesn't* after *it, he,* or *she.*

WRONG It don't seem possible.
RIGHT   It *doesn't* seem possible.

WRONG He don't know the answer.
RIGHT   He *doesn't* know the answer.

EXERCISE 7. Write in a column on your paper the correct form (*don't* or *doesn't*) for the following sentences.

1. This —— worry me.
2. It —— look right.
3. He —— appear until the second act.
4. They —— want any money.
5. We —— have enough time.
6. That —— sound right.
7. She —— know any better.
8. He —— feel well.
9. It —— matter.
10. You —— look very tall.
11. Fred —— study very hard.
12. My sister —— like college.
13. Some of the boys —— like the captain.
14. It —— appeal to me.
15. This work —— please the boss.

EXERCISE 8. Choose the correct one of the two verbs given in parentheses in the sentences below and list them in a column on your paper.

1. Mr. Bright, one of my teachers, (believe, believes) in more homework.
2. The ship which is crowded with sightseers (sail, sails) at ten o'clock.
3. The other ship, which carries freight and passengers, (leaves, leave) earlier.
4. It (don't, doesn't) matter how you go so long as you get there.
5. Harold says he (doesn't, don't) want to go.
6. Christmas, of all the holidays in the year, (appeals, appeal) most to us.
7. Some of us in the class (learn, learns) faster than others.

8. (Wasn't, Weren't) you surprised?
9. He (don't, doesn't) like to be kept waiting.
10. They (wasn't, weren't) at all helpful.

THE COMPOUND SUBJECT

5g. Most compound subjects joined by *and* are plural and take a plural verb.

RIGHT   Lewis *and* he **were** arguing.
RIGHT   The automobile *and* the train **are** not yet out-moded.
RIGHT   The beginning *and* the end of your story **are** good.

Some compound subjects joined by *and* are singular and take a singular verb.

RIGHT   *Bread and water* **is** a poor diet.
RIGHT   *Running and diving* into the pool **is** prohibited.
RIGHT   The *stress and strain* of flood waters on the bridge **was** carefully prepared for.

In compound subjects in which the *idea* is singular, the verb must be singular. In the sentences above, *bread and butter, running and diving, stress and strain* are thought of as units — as one food, one action, one force. When so thought of, they are naturally singular.

5h. Singular subjects joined by *or* or *nor* are singular and take a singular verb.

RIGHT   *Either* Fred *or* Jerry **is** coming.
RIGHT   *Neither* my brother *nor* my sister **was** at home.
RIGHT   **Has** *either* George *or* his mother called yet?
RIGHT   *Neither* Helen *nor* Jane **works** as fast as you.
RIGHT   *Neither* the president *nor* his secretary **speaks** very highly of the candidates.

(1) The word *either* may be omitted, but the number of the subject is not changed so long as its parts are joined by *or*.

RIGHT   Mary *or* her sister **was** trying to make a telephone call.

(2) Do not confuse this *either . . . or, neither . . . nor* construction with the other correlative conjunctions *both . . . and,* which take a plural verb.

RIGHT   *Both* the cat *and* the dog **are** very friendly.
RIGHT   *Neither* the cat *nor* the dog **is** very friendly.

5i. When two subjects, one of which is singular and the other is plural, are joined by or, nor, the verb agrees with the nearer word.

RIGHT   Either the President or his cabinet *members* **are** to be held responsible.

It is best to avoid such constructions entirely.

BETTER   The responsibility will be placed upon either the President or his cabinet members.

EXERCISE 9. From the parentheses in the following sentences choose the correct verb. Write the verbs in a column on your paper.

1. Neither James nor his brother (care, cares) for sports.
2. Both Jack and she (are, is) graduating this year.
3. Neither the teacher nor his pupils (were, was) right.
4. Either the principal or the class adviser (are, is) going with us.
5. Neither their team nor ours (have, has) a chance in the tournament.
6. Either the captains or the umpire (call, calls) time out.
7. Doris and he (was, were) dancing together.
8. Either the school or the village (pay, pays) the expenses.

9. Neither Marion nor Janet (seem, seems) to approve.
10. Both George and Joan (look, looks) like you.

EXERCISE 10: *Oral Drill.* Repeat each of the following sentences *aloud* five times, stressing the italicized words.

1. *Each* of us *has* finished.
2. *Neither* Beth *nor* Ned *is* at home.
3. A *few* of his ideas *are* excellent.
4. *Either* Julia *or* she *has* your pen.
5. *One* of my fingers *was* broken.
6. *Every one* of these seats *is* too small.
7. *Both* Don and Dave *are* absent.
8. *Each* of these magazines *looks* interesting.
9. *Not one* of your friends *has* been here.
10. *Several* of them *were* here yesterday.

OTHER PROBLEMS IN AGREEMENT

5j. **When the subject and the predicate nominative are of different numbers, the verb agrees with the subject, *not* with the predicate nominative.**

	Subject		Predicate Nominative
RIGHT	The ship's cargo	*was*	bananas.
RIGHT	Bananas	*were*	the ship's cargo.
BETTER	The ship carried a cargo of bananas.		

5k. **When the subject comes after the verb as in sentences beginning with *here is, there is,* and *where is,* be especially careful to determine the subject and make sure that it and the verb agree.**

WRONG There is too many in this car.
RIGHT There *are* too many in this car.

In our daily conversation we increase the likelihood of error by hurrying over *there is, there are* and making contractions of them.

WRONG Here's the pencils you ordered.
RIGHT   Here *are* the pencils you ordered.
WRONG Where's Harry and Joe?
RIGHT   Where *are* Harry and Joe?

51. *Together with, in addition to, including, as well as,* and similar constructions following the subject do not affect the number of the subject.

RIGHT   Mr. Leary, together with his two sons, *has* left for California.

The tendency of a careless writer might be to consider the subject of this sentence as plural, but strictly, the subject is *Mr. Leary,* and it requires a singular verb. Perhaps the logic of this will be clearer to you if you rearrange the sentence so that it reads:

Mr. Leary *has* left for California with his two sons.

RIGHT   The trapeze performer, as well as the spectators, *was* frightened.
RIGHT   This error, in addition to those made by the other players, *was* responsible for our losing the game.

EXERCISE 11: *Oral Drill.* Repeat each of the following sentences *aloud* five times, stressing the italicized words.

1. Where *are* those *papers?*
2. *Francis,* with several others, *has gone* to the movies.
3. *Both* Keith and Larry *are* with him.
4. There *are* your *notebooks.*

5. *Ruth* as well as Dot *is* taking chemistry.
6. *Either* Grace *or* Grant *has* a slide rule.
7. *One* of the officers *has* resigned.
8. The *superintendent*, together with the principals, *is* attending a convention.
9. *Neither* of them *feels* like playing.
10. Here *are* the *skates*.

EXERCISE 12. Number in a column on your paper from 1 to 20. Read each sentence aloud. If the verb agrees with the subject put a plus (+) on your paper after the proper number. If the verb does not agree with the subject, write a zero (0).

1. Here's your skates.
2. One of these stories is about the Revolutionary War.
3. Neither this book nor the other interest me.
4. Where's the gloves I left here?
5. Both you and he are taller than I.
6. Either Fred or Joe has been injured.
7. Macaroni and cheese are a popular dish in our family.
8. There are several answers to your question.
9. Every one of his themes are interesting.
10. There's several cars in the driveway.
11. Mr. Wheaton, with his two sisters, are going to Denver.
12. Have either of the dogs returned?
13. Your uncle and aunt, together with your cousins, are spending the summer on a ranch.
14. Both Frank and she have been abroad.
15. Do every one of your friends go to your school?
16. Neither of the policemen uses strong-arm methods.
17. Edward, as well as Ernest and Eugenie, were at home.
18. Here's your test papers.
19. Neither of the girls like to cook.
20. Each of us wants a vacation.

5m. Collective nouns may be either singular or plural,

You may be puzzled at times by words which name a *group* of persons or objects. Such words are known as *collective nouns.* They are puzzling because *they may be used with a plural verb when the speaker is thinking of the individual parts of the group; they may be used with a singular verb when the speaker is thinking of the group as a unit.* Study the following pairs of sentences.

1. The jury *was* locked behind closed doors. [*Jury* is thought of as a unit.]
   The jury *were* arguing among themselves. [*Jury* is thought of as individuals.]

2. The class *was* a very large one.
   The class *were* not all present.

3. The family *has* arrived.
   The family *have* given their consent.

Following is a list of common collective nouns:

crowd	herd	flock	squadron
committee	troop	group	army
jury	fleet	swarm	team
class	audience	club	faculty

EXERCISE 13. Select 5 collective nouns and write 5 pairs of sentences like those given above, showing clearly how the words you choose may be either singular or plural.

5n. Words stating amount (time, money, measurement, weight, volume, fractions) are usually singular.

RIGHT   *Two weeks* **is** the usual vacation.
RIGHT   *Five dollars* **was** more than I had expected.

RIGHT   *Four tons* is what I ordered.
RIGHT   *Three quarters* of our time **has** passed.

5o. The title of a book, even when plural in form, takes a singular verb.

RIGHT   *Short Stories for Boys* **is** worth reading.

REVIEW EXERCISE A. In some of the following sentences the verbs agree with their subjects; in others, the verbs do not agree. Number in a column on your paper from 1 to 25. If the verb and subject agree in a sentence write *A*, for agreement, after the proper number. If the verb does not agree with its subject, write the correct form of the verb after the proper number.

1. The committee was unable to agree among themselves.
2. Neither of the men leaves until five o'clock.
3. Several of the boys in the office are absent today.
4. Bacon and eggs is a tasty dish.
5. Either Joan or Betty are using my sled.
6. She don't mind very well.
7. Each one of them has a bike.
8. There are one set of books left on the shelf.
9. Do every one of you agree to take the test later?
10. Several of the boys seem to have colds.
11. She, together with her friends, seems to have come late.
12. Neither of us care to go.
13. He, as well as his brothers, seem to have gone out.
14. There is too many automobiles in this parking space.
15. Not one of them was invited.
16. *Popular Sports Stories* have been read by every member of the class.
17. Where's the books I gave you?
18. Some of the horses were running away.

19. Both of the students have good reports.
20. Few of Mother's friends like to play bridge.
21. One of our teachers seem like a good sport.
22. There is in this room two books which must be found now.
23. Basketry and riding is two things we do at camp.
24. Each of us has a long way to go.
25. Everyone in these rooms are excused for the day.

AGREEMENT OF PRONOUN AND ANTECEDENT

5p. A pronoun agrees with its antecedent in number and gender.

So far in your study of *agreement* you have learned how to make subject and verb agree. The next type of agreement is the agreement of a pronoun with its antecedent. A careful study of the following sentences will show you what is meant by the term *antecedent* and how the pronoun which refers to the antecedent agrees with it in number and gender.[3]

1. *One* of the players broke *his* racket.
2. *Each* of the girls did *her* best.
3. *Everyone* brought *his* own lunch.
4. *Neither* of the ladies recognized *her* child.

In each of these sentences the first pronoun (*one, each, everyone, neither*) is the *antecedent* of the second pronoun, which refers to it. *Antecedent* means *going before* (Latin *ante*, before + *cedere*, going). Notice that the first pronoun is singular in every case and that the second pronoun which refers to it is also

---

[3] Gender means sex: feminine, masculine, neuter. When the antecedent may be either masculine or feminine, use the masculine form of the pronoun. Example: Each of the boys and girls was eager to do *his* part.

singular. If the antecedent is plural, the pronoun which agrees with it is also plural.

RIGHT   Several *members* of the team failed to play *their* best.

If you will keep in mind all that you have learned about agreement of subject and verb, you will have no difficulty in making pronouns and antecedents agree. Keep in mind, for instance, that the indefinite pronouns — *each, either, neither, one, everyone, everybody, no one, nobody, anyone, anybody, someone, somebody* — are singular. They are referred to by singular pronouns: *he, she, him, her, his, hers, it,* and *its.* Keep in mind that a prepositional phrase following a subject does not alter the number of the subject.

RIGHT   *One* (of the artists) destroyed *his* own masterpiece.

(1) Two antecedents joined by *and* should be referred to by a plural pronoun.

RIGHT   Sid *and* Bill did *their* best.

(2) Two or more singular antecedents joined by *or* or *nor* should be referred to by a singular pronoun.

RIGHT   *Neither* Sid *nor* Bill did *his* best.

EXERCISE 14.   Number in a column on your paper from 1 to 12. For each blank in the following sentences select a pronoun which will agree with its antecedent and write it after the proper number on your paper.

1. Not one of the captives would give —— own name.
2. Either Steve or George can bring —— father's car.
3. One of my friends forgot —— hat.

4. No one in the group seemed sure of —— own destination.
5. Each girl in the troop had to make —— own bed.
6. Several members of the club were told to make —— protests to the president.
7. One of the children asked directions of us, but we told —— we were lost too.
8. Philip and his brother helped —— uncle harvest his wheat.
9. Every soldier is responsible for —— own equipment.
10. Both of the applicants brought —— credentials with them.
11. Neither did —— best.
12. Neither Molly nor she could do —— homework.

(3) When the idea of the sentence (the meaning of the antecedent) is clearly plural, the plural pronoun is acceptable, even though grammatically the singular may be preferable.

For example, in the following sentences, the idea of the speaker is so definitely plural that to use a singular pronoun would be unnatural. Usage here differs somewhat from grammar.

RIGHT　1. Did *everybody* have a good time at Jack's party? Yes, *they* seemed to.

RIGHT　2. If *everyone* comes, it will be impossible to seat *them*.

REVIEW EXERCISE B. In some of the following sentences subject and verb, and pronoun and antecedent agree; in others they do not. Number on your paper from 1 to 20. If a sentence is correct, place a + after the corresponding number; if it is incorrect, place a 0.

1. Neither of the roads were paved.
2. One of the girls brought her little sister to class.
3. Tim, with several other boys, have gone swimming.
4. Neither Ted nor Tom had finished their work.
5. Both Eileen and she make their own dresses.
6. Where's your brother and sister?
7. A few of the boys offered their services.
8. Either Thelma or Judy will bring her records.
9. Each of the campers cooked their own supper.
10. Neither of the boys wanted to do their homework.
11. Every one of the schools is closed.
12. Either of them could get an A, if he would work.
13. Here's the books I promised you.
14. Would anyone treat their dog so cruelly?
15. Some of the musicians own their own instruments.
16. Each boy had their own locker.
17. If anyone has not done their homework, they should see me.
18. No one could believe his eyes.
19. Where's the money your father gave you?
20. Both Byron and Lloyd string their own rackets.

EXERCISE 15: *Oral Drill.* Repeat each of the following sentences *aloud* 5 times, stressing the italicized words.

1. *Both* of the bats *were* cracked.
2. *Neither* of them *was* usable.
3. *One* of the workmen lent me *his* knife.
4. *Each* sailor did *his* own laundry.
5. Where *are* your *books?*
6. If *one* of the boys calls, ask *him* to wait.
7. *Neither Dad nor Mother* would give *his* consent.
8. *Each* of the students asked what *his* grade was.
9. *One* of them did not sign *his* name.
10. If *anyone* asks you, tell *him* your name.

AGREEMENT OF ADJECTIVE AND NOUN

5q. The adjectives *this, these, that, those* agree in number with the word they modify.

When the common pronouns *this* (plural, *these*) and *that* (plural, *those*) are used as adjectives they agree in number with the noun they modify. For example, in the sentence *Those papers are valuable* the adjective *those* must also be plural to agree with *papers*.

There are very few cases in which any English-speaking person would make an error in using the plural form of these adjectives. In fact, the only common error of this kind is illustrated in the following constructions.

WRONG   I like these kind of books. [incorrect because *these* is plural and *kind* is singular]
RIGHT   I like *these kinds*.
RIGHT   I like *this kind*.

Other words frequently used as *kind* is used in these sentences are *sort, sorts* and *type, types*.

EXERCISE 16. For the blanks in the following sentences choose the correct form of a suitable word: *this, these, those, kind, sort, type*. When your sentences have been corrected, repeat each *aloud* 5 times.

1. Mother prefers these —— of ice cream.
2. I don't care for those —— of people.
3. Which —— do you want, these or those?
4. I always buy —— kind.
5. If you use —— type of paper, you will get better results.
6. We sell these —— only.

7. —— sort of argument is foolish.
8. These —— can be found in any store.
9. —— kinds are more efficient.
10. I envy —— kind of student.

REVIEW EXERCISE C. Number on your paper from 1 to 20. In each sentence select the correct one of two forms given in parentheses and write it after the corresponding number on your paper.

1. If you help one of the girls, (she, they) will help you.
2. Neither of these knives (look, looks) sharp.
3. I never read these (kind, kinds) of magazines.
4. Each of the candidates (seems, seem) well qualified.
5. Mr. Wilson, as well as his wife and children, (enjoys, enjoy) the mountains.
6. Either Pete or his brothers (is, are) responsible.
7. Both trains and buses (were, was) delayed.
8. Do you like (this, these) type of uniform?
9. A few of our men (were, was) wounded.
10. (Here's, Here are) the groceries you ordered.
11. If anyone wishes to see the doctor, (he, they) will have to wait.
12. Neither of the objectors could make (himself, themselves) heard.
13. Mr. Longworth doesn't approve of (these, this) kind of monkeyshines.
14. Several of the students (was, were) tardy.
15. Neither of the boats could make (its, their) way against the tide.
16. Where (are, is) the girls?
17. If someone will help me, I'll pay (him, them) well.
18. I asked the clerk for a pound of (those, that) kind.
19. Everyone in our house (do, does) (his, their) share of the work.
20. Either of these students could do better, if (he, they) would work harder.

6. USING THE CORRECT CASE OF PRONOUNS

In the English language nouns and pronouns may be in one of three cases: *nominative, objective,* and *possessive.* Nouns and indefinite pronouns have the same form in the nominative and objective cases; they change form only in the possessive case when they require either an apostrophe and *s* or just an apostrophe.

Nominative [subject]	Objective [object of verb]	Possessive

The *captain* saw another *captain* reading the *captain's* orders.

Anybody there may ask *anybody* else. Has *anybody's* reply been received?

On the other hand, personal pronouns change their forms to denote the various cases. Since this changing results in so many different pronoun forms and each form has a definite use, there are many personal-pronoun problems in usage. To solve these problems, to use pronouns correctly, you must master the various case forms and know when to use them.

CASE FORMS OF PRONOUNS [1]

Examine the following table presenting the various case forms of pronouns in the singular and plural numbers.

[1] Personal pronouns are those pronouns which change form in the different persons. There are three persons, first, second, and third. The meaning of *person* is as follows:

PERSONAL PRONOUNS

Singular

	NOMINATIVE CASE	OBJECTIVE CASE
FIRST PERSON	I	me
SECOND PERSON	you	you
THIRD PERSON	he, she, it	him, her, it

Plural

	NOMINATIVE CASE	OBJECTIVE CASE
FIRST PERSON	we	us
SECOND PERSON	you	you
THIRD PERSON	they	them

RELATIVE AND INTERROGATIVE PRONOUNS

NOMINATIVE CASE	OBJECTIVE CASE
who	whom
whoever	whomever

EXERCISE 1. Referring to the table above, list on your paper in a column the pronouns which change their forms according to their case. Which pronouns keep the same form in both cases?

By doing the exercise just above, you have learned that the pronouns *you* and *it* do not undergo any changes. Therefore, these pronouns do not present any usage problem. Omitting them from considera-

---

1st person is the person speaking: (*I, We*) come.

2nd person is the person spoken to: *You* are coming.

3rd person is the person spoken about: *He* (*She, It, They*) will come.

Who and *whom* (*whoever* and *whomever*) are not personal pronouns. They may be relative pronouns (see page 76); when used to ask a question they are interrogative pronouns.

tion, you will have the following list of pronouns whose nominative case form is different from their objective case form. Memorize these lists.

NOMINATIVE CASE	OBJECTIVE CASE
I	me
he	him
she	her
we	us
they	them
who	whom
whoever	whomever

EXERCISE 2. Your teacher will read to you a mixed-up list of pronouns. You are to write the case of each pronoun. With practice you should be able to do this quickly, automatically.

EXERCISE 3. Write the following personal pronouns:

1. Third person plural objective case
2. First person plural nominative case
3. Third person plural nominative case
4. First person singular objective case
5. Third person singular objective case, feminine gender
6. First person singular nominative case
7. Third person singular nominative case, feminine gender
8. Third person singular objective case, masculine gender
9. First person plural objective case
10. Third person singular nominative case, masculine gender

When you have thoroughly memorized the nominative and objective pronouns, and not until then, you will be ready to study the correct use of pronouns as explained in the following pages.

THE NOMINATIVE CASE

6a. The subject of a verb is in the nominative case.

The pronouns used as subjects are the following: *I, you, he, she, it, we, you, they,* and *who.* A study of the following sentences will make this clear to you. Note that the case of the pronouns used as subjects is nominative.

RIGHT *He* and *I* — played in the backfield.
RIGHT My sister and *she* — went to the movies.
RIGHT *We* and *they* — have always been neighbors.
RIGHT *We* girls — have always been friends.

You should note that since the pronouns in those sentences are all subjects, they are in the nominative case. Failure to understand the reasons for these forms will lead to errors in usage such as

WRONG *Him* and *me* — played in the backfield.
WRONG My sister and *her* — went to the movies.

In these wrong sentences the objective form has been used for the subjects instead of the nominative form.

EXERCISE 4. Number your paper from 1 to 10. Choose correct pronouns for the blanks in the following sentences. Vary your pronouns. Omit *you* entirely.

1. Jimmy and —— make a good team.
2. Jack and —— played against them yesterday.
3. She and —— argued about the score.
4. My partner and —— practiced for several days.
5. The Browns suggested to us that —— and —— go on a picnic.
6. Tom and —— preferred to play golf.

7. —— and —— asked our dads to play with us.
8. —— boys accused them of being afraid of us.
9. Yesterday —— and —— played by ourselves.
10. Dad said that Mr. Brown and —— could have made better scores than ours.

EXERCISE 5: *Oral Drill*. Recite *aloud* 5 times each of the following sentences, stressing the italicized words. By *hearing* and *speaking* the correct form you will make your tongue and ear sensitive to it, and help yourself to speak correctly.

1. *He* and *I* are friends.
2. *You* and *I* will work together.
3. *Betty* and *I* expect to win.
4. *We* and *they* are cousins.
5. *We* boys (or girls) were late.

EXERCISE 6. Number in a column on your paper from 1 to 20. Read each of the following sentences *aloud*. Decide whether the italicized pronouns are in the correct case. If all of them in a sentence are correct, put a + after the proper number on your paper; if any one of them is not, put a 0 and write the correct form of the pronouns.

1. Bill and *I* believed that you and *she* would help.[2]
2. You and *I* will have to solve the problem.
3. Your friends and *him* are troublemakers.
4. *We* players respect the coach.
5. *Him* and *me* were going skating.
6. Helen and *her* preferred to ski.
7. The principal and *he* knew the whole story.

[2] Most errors in the use of pronouns are made when the subject (or object) is compound; i.e., it has two parts. *Bill and I* and *you and she* are compound subjects in this sentence. You can often arrive at the correct form by simply dropping the first word of the two in the compound subject: *I believe that she would help.* Your ear tells you the sentence is correct.

8. You and *I* ought to get together.
9. I wish you and *she* were more friendly.
10. You and *them* came from the same town.
11. Where do your aunt and *he* live?
12. *He* and *she* live on Tenth Street.
13. *Him* and *me* will graduate at the same time.
14. *Us* boys must stick together.
15. I think you and *she* are bound to win.
16. *Her* and *I* arrived an hour early.
17. My uncle and *they* were not able to come.
18. Sally and *I* will bring the sandwiches.
19. Bill and *me* decided to go to college together.
20. Hank and *he* enlisted in the Navy.

6b. A predicate nominative is in the nominative case.

Whenever you wish to use a pronoun as a predicate nominative, you will use one of the following: *I, you, he, she, it, we, you, they, who.*

A review of pages 50–53 where you previously encountered this predicate construction will remind you of these facts:

(1) A predicate nominative is a word which completes the meaning of the verb and means the same thing as the subject.

EXAMPLE That must be *they*.

(2) The verb *to be* and a verb followed by *to be* are the only verbs commonly followed by a predicate nominative pronoun.

EXAMPLES That is *she*.   I'd hate to be *she*.

EXERCISE 7.   Remembering that a predicate nominative is in the nominative case, supply the predicate pronouns specified for the following.

1. I thought it was ——. (third person singular masculine)
2. These are ——. (third person plural)
3. I thought it might be ——. (third person singular feminine)
4. It couldn't be ——. (third person plural)

NOTE: Observance of this rule among educated people varies greatly. In at least one instance, custom has changed the case of a predicate nominative. This instance is the expression "It's *me*." The objective pronoun *me* is correct.

In listening to conversations, you will also hear the objective case used after a form of *to be*. Expressions like *That's him, That was us, Had it been us* may be fairly classed as acceptable, everyday, *oral* English but should probably be avoided in *written* English. Your drills in this book contain only a few of these generally accepted constructions. They are included for the sake of drilling you on the rule which you should understand and be able to apply in case of need: *a predicate nominative is in the nominative case.*

REVIEW EXERCISE A. Number in a column on your paper from 1 to 20. Write after the proper number the pronouns which will correctly fill the spaces in the following sentences. You should be able to make a perfect score. Try to use *as many different pronouns* as you can. Omit *you* entirely. Be ready to explain the reason for your choice.

1. Sally and —— made the highest scores.
2. It might have been ——.
3. I didn't know that you and —— were sisters.
4. —— girls refused to agree to the plan.
5. When I asked them, both Jean and —— gave me the money.

6. I was sure that the family and —— wouldn't let you down.
7. Did you think it was ——?
8. The party leaders and —— were unable to get together.
9. Jill and —— tried to persuade them.
10. Are you sure that it was ——?
11. Jimmy and —— stayed at my house all afternoon.
12. Was that Mr. Bartlett or ——?
13. —— boys asked our parents.
14. Jed and —— are old friends.
15. The two captains are Albert and ——.
16. My uncle and —— came to call on us.
17. I thought it probably was ——.
18. I think that —— boys have a good chance to win.
19. —— and —— entered school the same year.
20. —— and —— are traveling in the same car.

OBJECTIVE CASE

6c. The object of a verb is in the objective case.

So far in your study of the correct use of pronouns, you have learned that *the nominative forms are used as subjects and as predicate nominatives.* Having learned the uses of the nominative pronouns, you are now ready to learn the uses of the objective pronouns. The objective pronouns, as you know, are:

me	us
you	you
him	them
her	whom
it	whomever

These pronouns are used as objects. There are two kinds of objects: objects of verbs, and objects of prepositions. You learned to identify the object of a verb in your study of complements on page 54. To refresh your knowledge of verbs and their objects, study these examples. The object is in boldface type.

(1) The object of a verb receives the action of the verb.

EXAMPLES Fire *had* nearly *destroyed* the **barracks**.

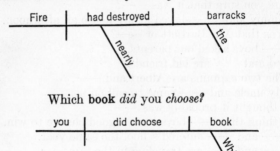

Which **book** *did* you *choose?*

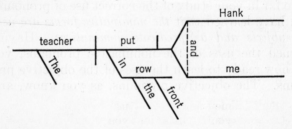

(2) An object may be compound.

EXAMPLE The teacher *put* **Hank** and **me** in the front row.

EXERCISE 8. In the following sentences, select the objects of the verbs.

1. We are expecting you at four o'clock.
2. They invited us.
3. Captain Brill booted the ball.
4. Did you defeat May or her?

5. Did you help Fred and him?
6. The family left me behind.
7. We shall expect you and your brother at one.
8. I believed him completely.
9. I tested Jerry and him.
10. Why have you been avoiding Roy and me?

Failure to use the objective pronouns as objects of the verb leads to rather serious errors in usage. Such errors can be avoided with a little thought, a little care, and a large amount of drill.

WRONG I have met Andy and he.
RIGHT I *have met* Andy and *him*.

WRONG They frightened Joe and I.
RIGHT They *frightened* Joe and *me*.

EXERCISE 9. Remembering that the pronoun objects are always in the objective case, supply the correct pronouns for the blanks in the following sentences. Avoid using the same pronoun throughout. Omit *you* entirely.

1. She met Mother and —— at the store.
2. I left Mother and —— together.
3. Have you seen either your father or ——?
4. Did you take Mary or ——?
5. She couldn't run fast enough to catch either Roy or ——.
6. Don't tell Jeff and —— what I told you.[3]
7. Did you ask Dr. Jones and —— for their opinion?
8. Mother refused to leave the baby and —— alone.
9. Please give —— and —— a better book.
10. They sent —— boys several letters.

[3] The indirect object, like the direct object, takes the objective case.
RIGHT: I asked Mother and *him*. [direct object]
RIGHT: I asked Mother and *him* a question. [indirect object]

EXERCISE 10: *Oral Drill.* Recite *aloud* 5 times each of the following sentences, stressing the italicized words. The purpose of this exercise is to tune your ear to the correct forms of the pronouns as objects of verbs.

1. He *asked* Harry and *me* for some help.
2. I *saw* Betty and *her* in the drugstore.
3. Dad *drove* Helen and *me* to the movies.
4. She *told* you and *him* the story.
5. We *saw* the other team and *them* on the field.
6. Mr. Harmon *brought* them and *us* in his car.
7. Please *call* George and *him.*
8. He *took* Fred and *me* with him.
9. Do you *mean* Jerry or *me?*
10. They *trusted us* boys completely.

REVIEW EXERCISE B. Remembering what you learned about the case of subjects and predicate nominatives as well as what you have just learned about the case of objects of the verb, fill the blanks in the following sentences. Use a variety of pronouns. Omit *you* entirely.

1. Please give Helen and —— extra time for our compositions.
2. You and —— had better ask for more time.
3. Did you and —— get an allowance of extra time?
4. Miss English refused Joyce and —— any special consideration.
5. It was Helen and ——.
6. Mrs. Lord and —— assigned Bill and —— some extra work.
7. Mr. Fletcher took Allen and —— to the game.
8. Jack and —— were the only soldiers the general could trust.
9. Were you chasing Alice or ——?

10. He sent my friend and —— on a dangerous mission.
11. Did he want you or ——?
12. The winner will be either Carl or ——.

REVIEW EXERCISE C.

Write 3 sentences containing pronouns used as subjects of verbs.

Write 3 sentences containing pronouns used as predicate nominatives.

Write 4 sentences containing pronouns used as objects of verbs.

After each sentence tell how the pronoun is used: subject, predicate nominative, or object of verb.

REVIEW EXERCISE D. Number in a column on your paper from 1 to 20. Select the correct one of the two pronouns in the parentheses and write it after the corresponding number on your paper. Be ready to explain your answers.

1. Our guide called Sandy and (I, me).
2. Sandy and (he, him) knew the woods and streams well.
3. (He, Him) and (I, me) were at the head of the line of canoes.
4. Fred and (they, them) were at the end of the line.
5. The guide gave (he, him) and (I, me) some good advice.
6. The guide and (we, us) boys told the hikers the trip was dangerous.
7. They refused to believe Sandy and (I, me), but they did believe him.
8. (They, Them) and (he, him) were on the best of terms.
9. It was (he, him) who collected the fees.
10. He knew it was (they, them) who paid the money.
11. The guide agreed to pay Sandy and (I, me) a small amount of money.

12. It must have been (they, them).
13. Her husband and (she, her) had never been in the north woods.
14. When their canoe capsized, (him, he) and (her, she) were thrown into the water.
15. Sandy and (I, me) swung our canoe toward them.
16. The guide and (us, we) realized our responsibility.
17. Mrs. Stanley, however, was not helpless. It was (she, her) who saved her husband.
18. When the guide and (we, us) reached them they were sitting calmly on a large boulder in midstream.
19. Neither her husband nor (she, her) was injured.
20. The rest of the party congratulated Mr. Stanley and (her, she) on their escape.

REVIEW EXERCISE E: *Oral Drill.* Recite *aloud* 5 times each of the following sentences, stressing the italicized words.

1. *He* and *I* are neighbors.
2. Do you mean Bill or *me?*
3. You resemble your mother and *her.*
4. Frank and *I* called you and *him.*
5. Sally and *we* are in the same class.
6. Ask Jean and *her.*
7. Is that *he?*
8. I saw both Bob and *him.*
9. I know Frank and *her.*
10. He caught Pat and *me.*

REVIEW EXERCISE F. Number in a column on your paper from 1 to 20. Read each of the following sentences *aloud.* If a sentence is grammatically correct put a + after the corresponding number on your paper. If it is incorrect put a 0. After each 0 write the correct pronoun forms.

1. One evening Barry Bond's brother and he were discovered to be missing from camp.
2. The guide sent Sandy and I after them.
3. It was they who had disappeared once before.
4. We asked Barry and he.
5. We boys began our search.
6. In the dark I couldn't see either Sandy or he.
7. I knew I'd never find Barry and him.
8. Mr. Stanley and they were urged to assist us.
9. Him and me scanned the woods south of camp.
10. The guide and them searched the woods to the north.
11. Who discovered Barry and him?
12. It was either you or them.
13. Sandy and me were the discoverers.
14. He and I found the boys rolled up in blankets.
15. Apparently Barry and he had decided to spend the night out.
16. They should have told either the guide or us about their plan.
17. When I heard voices in the woods, I knew it must be them.
18. They and we were the only human beings within 100 miles.
19. I brought Barry and he back to camp.
20. The guide and they gave them and me a fine welcome.

REVIEW EXERCISE G. Prepare a drill exercise of 10 sentences for use with your classmates. Be sure that every sentence presents a real problem in the correct use of pronouns. Errors in the use of pronouns are usually made when the subject or object is compound. You should use compound subjects and objects in your sentences. Do not put the answers on your paper. You may test someone with your exercise in class.

6d. The object of a preposition is in the objective case.

You will remember from your study of the parts of speech that a preposition is a word which shows the relationship between a noun or a pronoun and some other word in the sentence. There is a list of common prepositions on page 19. A preposition begins a prepositional phrase:

on the **train**   *for* my **father**

in the **house**   *of* the **story**

above the **trees**

The final or principal word in a prepositional phrase is the *object of the preposition* which begins the phrase. The boldface words in the phrases above are the objects. They are in the objective case. *When the object of a preposition is a pronoun, you must be careful to use the objective form.* The following pronouns are used as objects of prepositions: *me, you, him, her, it, us, you, them, whom, whomever.*

Examine the following sentences carefully to see how pronouns are used as objects of prepositions. The objects given are compound because it is the compound form that usually leads to errors in usage.

RIGHT   I am expecting letters *from* **Jane** and **her.**
RIGHT   The argument was *between* **John** and **me.**
RIGHT   These orders are intended *for* **you** and **them.**
RIGHT   He wrote *to* our **friends** and **us.**

EXERCISE 11. In the following sentences pick out the prepositions which take pronoun objects and list them on your paper. After each write the correct one of the two pronouns given in parentheses.

1. Send a letter to his father and (she, her).
2. He stood between Helen and (me, I).
3. I played against Stuart and (him, he).
4. Please keep behind Carl and (me, I).
5. The book was written by his brother and (him, he).
6. I ran into Alice and (them, they).
7. My aunt is coming after you and (we, us).
8. Did you see the picture of Paul and (me, I)?
9. I'll go with you and (her, she).
10. Are you looking at Pam or (me, I)?

EXERCISE 12. Select the correct one of the two pronouns in parentheses and write it on your paper.

1. This decision must be made by you and (I, me).
2. There is a mutual feeling of respect between the Republican candidate and (he, him).
3. Let's go to the movies with Dad and (she, her).
4. She told the secret to Martha and (I, me).
5. Packages were left for you and (them, they).
6. I was surprised to run into Fran and (her, she) in New York.
7. He was looking at Bob and (me, I).
8. The police were standing directly behind (them, they) and (we, us).
9. Why did you come without the family and (them, they)?
10. Did anyone ask about the Whites and (us, we)?

EXERCISE 13. Write sentences of your own, using each of the following prepositions with a compound object, one of whose parts is a pronoun.

EXAMPLE She was looking **for** *Barbara* and *me*.

1. for
2. at
3. with
4. near

5. to	8. toward
6. of	9. by
7. like	10. except

EXERCISE 14. *Oral Drill.* Read *aloud* 5 times each of the following sentences, stressing the italicized words.

1. The letters are *from* my brother and *her*.
2. They write *to* Alice and *me* regularly.
3. The mail is delivered *by* either Mr. Owen or *him*.
4. Mr. Owen had letters *for them* and *us*.
5. She refused to come *with* either Anne or *me*.
6. Who was sitting *between you* and *them?*
7. They played a trick *on* the boys and *us*.
8. I won't go *without you* and *her*.
9. Were you talking *about him* and *me?*
10. He looks *like* both *you* and *her*.

"WHO" AND "WHOM" AS INTERROGATIVE PRONOUNS

Like the use of the correct form of the pronoun as a predicate nominative (page 132), the use of *who* and *whom* in questions can no longer be reduced to a strict law. In modern *conversational* English usage the distinction between *who* and *whom* is gradually disappearing, and *whom* is going out of use. Among educated people, one sometimes hears **Who** *do you mean?* **Who** *do you know?* According to the rule you have learned about the case of the object of the verb, the speaker should say *whom* in these sentences. *In everyday conversation* you may use *who* for *whom* as an interrogative pronoun. *In written English* you should observe carefully the distinction between *who* and *whom*.

"WHO" AND "WHOM" AS RELATIVE PRONOUNS

When the pronouns *who* and *whom* introduce a subordinate clause, they are relative (not interrogative) pronouns. (See page 76.)

6e. The case of a relative pronoun is determined by its use in the clause which it introduces.

EXAMPLE It was James *who spoke to me.* [*Who* is in the nominative case because it is the subject of the verb *spoke* in the subordinate clause.]

EXAMPLE It was James *whom I saw.* [*Whom* is in the objective case because it is the object of the verb *saw*, the verb in the subordinate clause.]

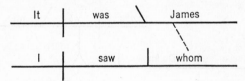

EXAMPLE I can remember *who was absent.* [*Who* is in the nominative case because it is the subject of the verb *was* in the subordinate clause. The object of the verb *can remember* is not *who* but the entire subordinate clause.]

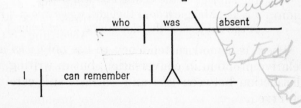

EXAMPLES He is the friend *of whom I spoke.*
He is the friend *whom I spoke of.* [*Whom* is in

the objective case because it is the object of
the preposition *of* in the subordinate clause.]

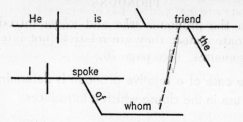

EXAMPLE Do you know *who it was?* [*Who* is in the nominative case because it is a predicate pronoun
after the verb *was.* This is clear when you
change the clause around so that the sentence
rather nonsensically reads, Do you know *it
was who?*]

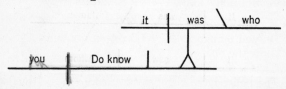

NOTE: Interrupting expressions like *I think* and *I believe*
do not affect the case of the relative pronoun.

RIGHT He is the one ***who,*** I believe, *will win.* [*Who* is
the subject of the clause *who will win.*]

RIGHT I asked Maggie ***who,*** I thought, *would know.* [*Who*
is the subject of the clause *who would know.*]

There is a modern tendency to use only *who* as a
relative pronoun in conversation, but in writing, the
distinction between *who* and *whom* is still carefully
observed.

What can we conclude about the proper use of
who and *whom?* In your daily conversations you

need not be too much concerned about the distinction, especially in questions.

In your writing, you should observe the distinction. The practice exercises which follow will contain *who* and *whom* problems, therefore, to help you in your written English. Since correct use of these pronouns is very difficult, you may wish to look back at the examples on this and the preceding page for help.

EXERCISE 15. Number in a column from 1 to 10. Write the correct form of *who* or *whom* for each of the following sentences. After each relative pronoun write how it is used in the clause which it introduces (subject, object of verb, object of preposition, predicate nominative).

EXAMPLE I don't know ―― is coming.

      who   subject of clause

1. Do you remember ―― borrowed my pen?
2. He is the one ―― I remember.
3. He is a plane pilot ―― has few equals.
4. The police have never discovered ―― the thief was.
5. There is a girl ―― I think will be a success.
6. What is the name of the girl ―― you introduced me to?
7. The actors ―― we saw were professionals.
8. I know ―― she went with.
9. We could not find out ―― the man was.
10. He is one of those boys ―― everyone likes.

EXERCISE 16. Supply the correct form of the relative pronoun (*who, whom, whoever, whomever*) to fill the blanks in the following sentences. List them on your paper.

1. I'll wait for ―― is late.
2. Everyone ―― I invited accepted my invitation.

3. The men —— the President appointed felt highly honored.
4. The President interviewed —— was sent to him.
5. The agency investigates anyone —— is suspected of treason.
6. Anyone —— he disapproves of is in great danger.
7. Jack is the only one —— I told the story to.
8. I am not sure —— he is.
9. That is the boy —— I saw.
10. Did anyone hear —— you were talking about?
11. The store gave a book to —— asked for it.
12. I have confidence in —— he selects.
13. We had no idea —— the speaker would be.
14. The man —— I was thinking of is tall and dark.
15. He refused to say —— he thought would win.

REVIEW EXERCISE H. Number on your paper from 1 to 20. After the proper number write how the pronoun in parentheses is used —

> subject
> predicate nominative
> object of verb
> object of preposition

On the basis of its use, select the correct pronoun and write it on your paper.

EXAMPLE 1. I know (who, whom) is coming.
> 1. subject, who

1. She offered to help Jack and (me, I).
2. It was either Henry or (him, he).
3. I haven't heard from either Sid or (she, her).
4. Tell your story to Jim and (me, I).
5. Do you know (who, whom) the winner was?
6. Betty and (she, her) are always arguing.
7. They finished the job without the teacher and (we, us).
8. (He, Him) and (I, me) are brothers.

9. Put Frank and (he, him) on the first team.
10. Was it Sally or (she, her) that told you?
11. I will interview (whoever, whomever) applies.
12. I know (who, whom) you mean.
13. Was the book written by Conrad or (he, him)?
14. We saw you and (he, him) on the corner.
15. You and (me, I) will take turns.
16. After the accident the police took Mr. Cole and (her, she) to the hospital.
17. Did you know (who, whom) Mr. Carlson appointed?
18. Do you think it could have been (they, them)?
19. I have worked for both Mr. Andrews and (him, he).
20. My sister and (me, I) do not always agree.

The three exercises which follow cover all you have so far learned about the correct use of pronouns. You should make a perfect score on them. If you fall below 90%, you had better review.

REVIEW EXERCISE I. Number on your paper from 1 to 20. Select the correct one of the two pronouns in parentheses in each sentence, and write it after the proper number on your paper.

1. Have you met Perry and (he, him)?
2. The coach wants you and (me, I).
3. Miss Smith sent for Marie and (her, she).
4. Bill and (I, me) did the homework together.
5. Was it you or (him, he) that did the first problem?
6. I am expecting you and (she, her).
7. (He, Him) and (me, I) took the late bus.
8. I don't know (whom, who) the pitcher was.
9. It was she (who, whom) I told you about.
10. The manager hired both Ellen and (me, I).
11. He will support (whoever, whomever) supports him.
12. Jerry and (they, them) are coming later.
13. I know (who, whom) you were talking to.
14. Please take Ann and (me, I) with you.

15. The fight was between Sanford and (he, him).
16. Mr. Thompson invited (us, we) boys into his office.
17. We'll take (whoever, whomever) comes first.
18. Tell Joan and (me, I) the whole story.
19. (We, Us) girls were sitting on the front porch.
20. He spoke to Sam and (me, I).

REVIEW EXERCISE J. Number on your paper from 1 to 20. For each correct sentence in which the pronouns are all in the proper case, place a + after the corresponding number on your paper; for each incorrect sentence, place a 0.

1. Will you and he be there?
2. Please ask Jane and her when they will arrive.
3. I remember who came with Pete.
4. The jury gazed intently upon the witness who the attorney was examining.
5. Hank reached the finish line just ahead of Allan and he.
6. The postmaster offered jobs to both Tim and I.
7. The doorman refused Larry and me permission to enter.
8. She hired Carl and him.
9. She expected him and me.
10. This he and I refused to do.
11. The librarian gave we boys some new books.
12. Ginger and me decided to share our earnings.
13. No one but Jessie and him could do the problem.
14. He and she received the highest marks.
15. Without you and she the party will be a flop.
16. Helen and me won the dance contest.
17. We met your family and them in Chicago.
18. Mother took Hazel and me home.
19. When she and I reached the beach we couldn't resist the water.
20. Us girls were severely punished.

REVIEW EXERCISE K. Number on your paper from 1 to 20. For each correct sentence in which the pronouns are all in the proper case, place a + after the corresponding number on your paper; for each incorrect sentence, place a 0.

1. Was it she whom we saw?
2. She and I went to the movies last night.
3. We saw Sally and her as we went into the lobby.
4. He and them didn't see us.
5. Was it him who won the award for Best All-Around Student?
6. No, it was she.
7. On our last picnic, Mr. Bush and them went with us.
8. He and they ate too many hot dogs.
9. Will you wait for Joe and I?
10. We waited for Mr. Bush and them.
11. Him and me didn't stay in very long.
12. As we were coming home, Mr. Lean and her saw us.
13. We told Mr. Lean and she we were sorry to be late.
14. They told Mr. Bush and I that it was all right.
15. When we got there, Mr. Bush and they were shivering.
16. Art and he said it had been worth while.
17. Elizabeth said Marty and she were going next time.
18. Whoever wants to go can call us next Saturday.
19. He is a man who you can trust.
20. I don't know who he said was coming.

THE PRONOUN IN AN INCOMPLETE CONSTRUCTION

The following are examples of incomplete constructions. In each one, part of the sentence is omitted and is written in brackets.

RIGHT 1. My brother is taller than I. [am tall]

RIGHT 2. The new boss paid him more than me. [than he paid me]

From these two examples of an incomplete construction you may notice that you should use the form of the pronoun which you would use if you completed the sentence. Thus, in Sentence 1, *I* is correct because it is the subject of the clause *I am tall*. In Sentence 2, *me* is correct because it is the object of the verb *paid* in the clause *he paid me*.

Now examine this pair of sentences:

RIGHT 1. I like Gerald better than *he*. [likes Gerald]
RIGHT 2. I like Gerald better than *him*. [than I like him]

As you can see, the case of the pronoun depends on how the sentence is completed. Both the sentences above are correct, but the sentences are quite different in meaning; they are completed in different ways.

6f. After *than* and *as* introducing an incomplete construction, use the form of the pronoun you would use if the construction were completed.

EXERCISE 17. Write out each of the following sentences, supplying the omitted part and using the correct form of the pronoun. After the sentence write the use of the pronoun in its clause — as subject, object of verb, object of preposition, etc.

1. No one worked harder than (I, me).
2. Did you do as well as (she, her)?
3. She did more for Mary than (me, I).
4. I told you more than (he, him).
5. The boys on our team are faster than (they, them).
6. My brothers boasted that they were stronger than (we, us).
7. She thought she could swim farther than (me, I).
8. Jane finished earlier than (I, me).

9. Did you study as long as (we, us)?
10. We ate more than (they, them).

REVIEW EXERCISE L. Number on your paper from 1 to 20. Select the correct one of the two pronouns given in parentheses and write it after the proper number on your paper.

1. Carol and (me, I) are twins.
2. I know (who, whom) you mean.
3. She played a better game than (I, me).
4. It might have been (they, them).
5. I came in several yards behind Ted and (he, him).
6. My father and (she, her) are listening to the radio.
7. Helen will tell you (who, whom) was absent.
8. Natalie will do the job as well as (she, her).
9. We are expecting Phil and (him, he) on the next train.
10. You and (I, me) ought to talk the matter over.
11. This car was sold to either Mr. Foster or (he, him).
12. I like both Janie and (she, her).
13. The play delighted the children and (we, us).
14. They left Fred and (me, I) alone.
15. The pictures were painted by Mr. Olsen and (she, her).
16. George took longer than (I, me).
17. Elise wants to stay with you and (us, we).
18. You told her more than (he, him).
19. He is a man (who, whom), I think, deserves a great deal of credit.
20. The band played a request number for Sally and (I, me).

REVIEW EXERCISE M. Fill in the blanks with the proper pronoun, making sure you use a variety of them throughout the exercise. Omit *you* entirely.

1. Phyllis and —— waited for Estelle and ——.
2. I don't remember —— he came with.

3. Perhaps you can tell —— and —— what happened.
4. He is a lot taller than ——.
5. With Geraldine and —— came the two dogs.
6. After closing the car door, Mother and —— went in opposite directions.
7. —— and Mother went shopping, and Elizabeth went with ——.
8. Kent and ——, together with Harry and ——, started a small orchestra.
9. —— and —— practiced faithfully for three weeks.
10. Then Kent and —— thought we were ready to perform.
11. Everybody came to Art and —— for advice.
12. Very freely, —— and —— gave it.
13. Why is Christmas shopping so hard on —— and ——?
14. Paul told Molly and —— not to be frightened.
15. I like desserts better than ——.
16. —— and —— ought to eat more of them.
17. The Fourth of July is fun for our dog and ——.
18. Grandfather met —— and —— for tea downtown.
19. Why do Grandmother and —— live so far away?
20. Was it Bill or —— who asked that question?

7. USING VERBS CORRECTLY

In grammar the word *tense* means *time*. It is applied to verbs because verbs indicate time. Study the verbs in the following sentences.

Now she *swims* across the river. [present tense]
She *swam* across the river yesterday. [past tense]
She *has swum* across the river often. [present perfect tense]

You can see that the verbs in these sentences express action happening at different times.

7a. **There are three basic forms of a verb. They are the *present*, the *past*, and the *past participle*.**

Study the following list of the six tense (time) forms of a verb. Giving all the forms of a verb in this way is called "conjugating" the verb.

Notice that the six tenses are formed from the three principal parts.

CONJUGATION OF *TO SWIM*

(Principal Parts: *swim, swam, swum*)

PRESENT TENSE

Singular	*Plural*
I swim	we swim
you swim	you swim
he swims	they swim

PAST TENSE

Singular	*Plural*
I swam	we swam
you swam	you swam
he swam	they swam

FUTURE TENSE

Singular	*Plural*
I shall swim	we shall swim
you will swim	you will swim
he will swim	they will swim

PRESENT PERFECT TENSE

Singular	*Plural*
I have swum	we have swum
you have swum	you have swum
he has swum	they have swum

PAST PERFECT TENSE

Singular	*Plural*
I had swum	we had swum
you had swum	you had swum
he had swum	they had swum

FUTURE PERFECT TENSE

Singular	*Plural*
I shall have swum	we shall have swum
you will have swum	you will have swum
he will have swum	they will have swum

(Present Participle: *swimming*)

REGULAR VERBS

A regular verb is one which forms its past and past participle forms by merely adding *–ed* or *–d* to the present form.

PRESENT	PAST	PAST PARTICIPLE
I walk	I walk*ed*	I have walk*ed*
I believe	I believe*d*	I have believe*d*

IRREGULAR VERBS

An irregular verb is one which does not form its past and past participle forms by adding *–ed* or *–d* to the present form. Irregular verbs form their past and past participle forms in various other ways: by changing the vowel, or by changing consonants, or by making no change at all.

PRESENT	PAST	PAST PARTICIPLE
I sw*i*m	I sw*a*m	I have sw*u*m
I s*ee*	I s*aw*	I have s*ee*n
I beat	I beat	I have beaten
I bid	I bid	I have bid

Since all tenses may be made from the three principal parts, it is important for you to know these principal parts of verbs you wish to use. The regular verbs are easy to use because the past and past participle forms of every regular verb are made in the same way, but each irregular verb forms its past and past participle forms in a different way, and this fact makes irregular verbs harder to use correctly.

On page 156 you will find a list of the principal parts of common irregular verbs. These verbs present a real problem in correct usage because failure to know their principal parts will lead you into noticeable errors.

WRONG I seen him yesterday. [The past participle has been used where the past should have been used.]

RIGHT I *saw* him yesterday.

WRONG I have went there many times. [The past has been used, but the past participle should have been used.]

RIGHT I *have gone* there many times.

The following irregular verbs are those which are most frequently misused. Most of your everyday errors in using verbs in conversational English can be prevented if you will learn the principal parts of these verbs. The drills which follow will give you practice in their correct use. When you memorize the principal parts, you will help yourself if you will always include *have* with the past participle. In repeating them to yourself, for instance, say: *go, went, have gone; see, saw, have seen, etc.*

The past participle of a verb which takes an object is also used in such expressions as the following in which the verb acts upon its subject rather than upon an object.[1]

EXAMPLES Our quarterback *was thrown* for a loss.

The report *had been written* by the secretary.

All the bells *were rung* at one time.

They *have been seen* downtown during school hours.

Two records *were broken* in Saturday's meet.

IRREGULAR VERBS FREQUENTLY MISUSED[2]

PRESENT	PAST	PAST PARTICIPLE
begin	began	(have) begun
break	broke	(have) broken
come	came	(have) come

[1] Verbs which act upon their subject are said to be in the *passive voice*. Verbs which act on an object are in the *active voice*. The whole matter of *voice* has been omitted from these pages as being difficult and of very little importance for young writers.

[2] The especially difficult verbs *lie, lay, sit, set, rise, raise* will be given special attention. See pages 159–69.

do	did	(have) done
drink	drank	(have) drunk
give	gave	(have) given
go	went	(have) gone
ride	rode	(have) ridden
ring	rang	(have) rung
run	ran	(have) run
see	saw	(have) seen
speak	spoke	(have) spoken
swim	swam	(have) swum
take	took	(have) taken
throw	threw	(have) thrown
write	wrote	(have) written

EXERCISE 1. Your teacher will dictate to you the present tense of these 16 irregular verbs. Write from memory the past and past participle forms for each verb. Place *have* before the past participle.

EXERCISE 2. Write sentences using correctly the past and past participle forms of the verbs you missed in the preceding exercise.

EXERCISE 3. Write in a column on your paper the correct form of the verb given at the beginning of each sentence. If necessary, refer to the list given above.

1. *do* Harold —— his best to win yesterday's match.
2. *come* He —— in late last night.
3. *begin* Yesterday everyone —— a new project.
4. *run* Although we —— after the thief, we did not catch him.
5. *see* I —— Bob at the game last week.
6. *write* I have —— the letter.
7. *ring* The bell had —— before we reached school.
8. *go* She has —— with him.

9. *give*   Andy —— us our instructions.
10. *drink*   He had —— the entire bottle.
11. *break*   They've —— out of their cage.
12. *speak*   He had —— to no one.
13. *swim*   Then the big fish —— toward us.
14. *throw*   Some valuable papers had been —— out.
15. *take*   She has —— more than her share.
16. *ride*   The sheriff had —— to the scene of the crime.
17. *do*   Although we —— all we could to prevent a collision, the cars collided.
18. *run*   You should have —— faster.
19. *come*   She —— on the late train yesterday.
20. *give*   He's —— us something to think about.

EXERCISE 4.   Choose the correct one of the two verbs in parentheses. Write the words in a column on your paper. When your paper has been corrected, read each sentence *aloud* several times, using the correct word.

1. After I told her, she (begun, began) to cry.
2. Have you (wrote, written) your theme?
3. You should have (thrown, throwed) the ball to me.
4. The doctors (did, done) all they could.
5. He (drank, drunk) three cups of coffee at breakfast.
6. Who (came, come) home with you?
7. We (seen, saw) the feature picture twice.
8. Have you (rode, ridden) horseback before?
9. She's never (took, taken) any advice from me.
10. The vacant house had been (broken, broke) into.
11. Who (give, gave) you permission to leave?
12. The car (run, ran) well for ten years.
13. Have you (spoken, spoke) to him yet?
14. Who (swum, swam) the channel?
15. Has the bell (rang, rung)?
16. We've (broke, broken) the lock.
17. This horse has never been (ridden, rode).

18. Who (gave, give) us away?
19. The troops (begun, began) their march at dawn.
20. I (seen, saw) you at the concert.

EXERCISE 5. Number in a column on your paper from 1 to 20. Read each of the following sentences aloud. If the form of the irregular verb is correct, place a + after the corresponding number on your paper. If it is incorrect, place a 0.

1. Our bicycles had been ran over.
2. The teacher had spoken sharply to Jane.
3. Both of us run in the quarter-mile relay last week.
4. I seen him go that way!
5. The clock had been broke for years.
6. It seemed as though we swam for miles.
7. Bill had thrown one over home plate.
8. Have you wrote to your aunt yet?
9. They'd went downtown for a soda.
10. It was the longest letter I ever wrote.
11. Who has given the best answer?
12. We have came back earlier than we expected to.
13. Which of you have saw the picture at the Rivoli?
14. We swum in the ocean for the first time yesterday.
15. Who has spoke to you about the dance?
16. We done the best we could.
17. They have taken their places in line.
18. He done the marketing for her.
19. We come to see your brother last night.
20. Has he drunk all the cokes yet?

"LIE" AND "LAY"

The verb *lie* means *to recline, to rest or remain in a lying position*. Its principal parts are *lie, lay, (have) lain*. The present participle is *lying*.

The verb *lay* means *to put, to place* something. Its

principal parts are: *lay, laying, laid, (have) laid.* The present participle is *laying.*

Study the following.

PRESENT	PRESENT PARTICIPLE	PAST	PAST PARTICIPLE
lie (to recline)	lying	lay	(have) lain
lay (to put)	laying	laid	(have) laid

The various forms of these two verbs are often confused. Careful thought and drill will help you to distinguish them and to use them correctly.

It may help you to know that *lie* [*lying, lay, (have) lain*] never has an object, whereas *lay* [*laying, laid, (have) laid*] may have an object.

RIGHT   All morning I lay on the davenport. (no object)

RIGHT   I laid the *child* on the davenport. (*child* is object of *laid*)

RIGHT   I found my glasses lying on the grass. (no object)

RIGHT   We watched the men laying *concrete.* (*concrete* is the object of *laying*)

EXERCISE 6. Study the *lie, lay* forms above until you can write them from memory exactly as given. Be sure you know which verb means *to recline, rest, remain in a lying position* and which means *to put* something.

EXERCISE 7. Read over *aloud* several times each of the following sentences in which the verbs are used correctly. Be able to explain, in the light of the information just given, why the verb is correct. For example: *She laid her sewing on the table. Laid* is correct because the sentence means *she put her sewing on the table,* and the verb required is *lay,* the past tense of which is *laid.*

1. I *laid* your coat on the chair.
2. We *lay* on the hot sand until we were sunburned.
3. You *lie* here while I get help.
4. For months the machine *lay* untouched.
5. Please *lay* your bundles over there.
6. The men were *laying* a cement foundation.
7. They used the sand which was *lying* about.
8. I had just *lain* down.
9. I had *laid* down my book and rushed to the door.
10. You must *lie* here.

EXERCISE 8. Supply the correct form of the proper verb (*lie—lay*) in the following. List the forms in a column on your paper. Ask yourself whether the action in the sentence is that of resting or placing. Refer to the forms on page 156 if necessary.

1. Where was the dog ——?
2. Who —— this book here?
3. I was —— in bed.
4. He has —— many plans before the school board.
5. John was —— the pictures out to dry.
6. Our ship had —— at anchor all night.
7. Engineers —— a new road through the swamp last year.
8. I grew tired of just —— around the house.
9. We —— under the overturned canoe until the storm had passed.
10. We might have —— there an hour.

EXERCISE 9. Write 8 sentences using the following:

lie	lay (to place)
lying	laying
lay (reclined)	laid
lain	have laid

EXERCISE 10. Select from each sentence the correct one of the two words in parentheses and write the words in a column on your paper. Think carefully of the *meaning* of the verb.

1. The vessel (lay, laid) across a sand bar.
2. Fran (lay, laid) down about an hour ago.
3. I'll (lay, lie) here for a while.
4. He (lay, laid) it there.
5. (Lay, Lie) here until we call you.
6. Before noon the men had (laid, lain) a new road.
7. (Laying, Lying) there, we fell asleep.
8. The enemy had been (lying, laying) in wait all night.
9. Before the battle began, destroyers (lay, laid) a smoke screen.
10. After the launching, a new keel was (laid, lain).
11. Had he (laid, lain) there long?
12. Where were you (lying, laying)?
13. The eggs are carefully (lain, laid) in cardboard boxes.
14. (Lying, Laying) there in the rain, I caught a severe cold.
15. The lake (lies, lays) at the foot of a mountain.
16. He (laid, lay) the book open on the desk and began to read.
17. A vast forest (laid, lay) before us.
18. We found fossils which had (lain, laid) there for centuries.
19. He (lay, laid) the white paper over the red.
20. I found it (lying, laying) beside the walk.

EXERCISE 11. Number in a column on your paper from 1 to 20. Read each of the following sentences and determine whether it is correct or incorrect. If it is correct, place a + after the corresponding number on your paper; if it is incorrect, place a 0. Think of the *meaning* of the verb.

1. After laying on the beach for a while, we took a swim.
2. We saw four fishing boats lying in the small harbor.
3. A piece of candy lay on the table, completely melted.
4. Have you lain in the sun all this time?
5. We had lain our clothes on the river bank.
6. They must have been lying here for an hour.
7. He lay his watch on the balcony railing.
8. The workmen laid the keel last week.
9. I have been laying here waiting for you.
10. Pete and Bob are always laying around the sun porch.
11. I'd get fat if I laid around so much.
12. Our pet hen laid two eggs yesterday.
13. When Betty and Joan come home, they usually lay their books on the table.
14. The books are never left laying around on chairs.
15. Somehow, mine are always lying where they shouldn't be.
16. Laying down to read is a bad but comfortable habit.
17. The crew lay the foundation in one day.
18. The hounds were laying in wait for the fox.
19. The fox lay in his den, panting.
20. I know I lay them right here, yesterday afternoon.

"SIT" AND "SET"

The verb *sit* means *to rest in an upright, sitting position*. The principal parts of *sit* are *sit, sat, (have) sat*. The present participle is *sitting*.

The verb *set* means *to put, to place* something. The principal parts of *set* are *set, set, (have) set*. The present participle is *setting*.

Study the following:

PRESENT	PRESENT PARTICIPLE	PAST	PAST PARTICIPLE
sit (to rest)	sitting	sat	(have) sat
set (to put)	setting	set	(have) set

You will have little difficulty using these verbs correctly, if you will remember two facts about them.

(1) *Sit* is like *lie* and *set* is like *lay.* Can you tell in what respects the verbs in each pair are alike?

(2) *Set* does not change its form. Whenever the meaning is to *place* or to *put,* you use *set.*[3]

Memorize the principal parts of *sit* and *set* so that you can give them readily from memory.

EXERCISE 12. Read over *aloud* several times each of the following sentences in which *sit* and *set* are correctly used. Think of the *meaning* of each sentence as you read it.

1. I prefer to *sit* here.
2. *Set* the box down.
3. She had been *setting* out tomato plants.
4. Where have you been *sitting?*
5. Please *sit* down.
6. I *sat* there for an hour.
7. Rover *sat* up and began to bark.
8. He *set* the lamp in the corner.
9. He is content just to *sit* on the porch all day long.
10. You have *sat* there long enough.

EXERCISE 13. Write 8 sentences using all the principal parts of *sit* and *set.* Be able to explain why your sentences are correct.

EXERCISE 14. Select from each sentence the correct one of the two words in parentheses and write the words in a column on your paper.

---

[3] The expressions "the sun sets" and "the setting hen" are exceptions to this rule.

1. Which chair were you (sitting, setting) in?
2. Would you like to (set, sit) here?
3. This is a comfortable place to (sit, set).
4. We found him (setting, sitting) in the living room.
5. I have (sat, set) here too long.
6. The doctor (sat, set) his bag on the table.
7. Mother's flower pots were (sitting, setting) in the window.
8. We (set, sat) waiting for hours.
9. I couldn't have (set, sat) there a minute longer.
10. They were (sitting, setting) in the car, ready to leave.
11. I (set, sat) my suitcase down beside me.
12. You may (sit, set) in any seat you wish.
13. Do you expect me to (sit, set) here all day?
14. He (sat, set) unnoticed throughout the performance.
15. We (set, sat) and talked the evening away.
16. We found the farmer (sitting, setting) under a tree.
17. (Set, Sit) down and relax.
18. Have I (set, sat) here long enough?
19. I tried to (sit, set) perfectly still.
20. (Set, Sit) the packages on the table, please.

REVIEW EXERCISE A. Number in a column on your paper from 1 to 20. Read each of the following sentences and determine whether it is correct or incorrect. If it is correct, place a + after the corresponding number on your paper; if it is incorrect, place a 0.

1. She prefers to set in the rocking chair.
2. Where should the movers set the piano?
3. Lie as still as you can.
4. Sitting in the grandstand, we were uncomfortable.
5. I'll lay down right here.
6. Lay the pillows down first.
7. Please set them in a row.
8. Lay down and go to sleep.

9. Just set there until you are called.
10. Why are you sitting in the principal's office?
11. Who lay his briefcase on my desk?
12. How long have I laid here?
13. We were told to set down and wait our turn.
14. The coach advised us to lie down until we were rested.
15. I lay the mail on your desk an hour ago.
16. From where we were laying we could hear the radio.
17. Father laid out a badminton court on the lawn.
18. Set down a minute, please.
19. I had lain down for a brief nap.
20. We were forced to lay in an uncomfortable position.

"RISE" AND "RAISE"

The verb *rise* means *to go in an upward direction*. Its principal parts are *rise, rose, (have) risen*. The present participle is *rising*.

The verb *raise* means *to force something to move in an upward direction*. Its principal parts are *raise, raised, (have) raised*. The present participle is *raising*.

PRESENT	PRESENT PARTICIPLE	PAST	PAST PARTICIPLE
rise (go up)	rising	rose	(have) risen
raise (force upward)	raising	raised	(have) raised

Like *lie* and *sit*, *rise* never has an object. Like *lay* and *set*, *raise* may have an object.

EXERCISE 15. Fill the blanks in the following sentences with a correct form of *rise* or *raise*, whichever is required by the meaning.

1. The thermometer had —— rapidly since morning.
2. At the appointed hour, plane after plane —— from the field.

3. Everyone cheered as the balloon —— above the trees.
4. Men stood with tears in their eyes as the flag —— to the top of the pole.
5. By noon, the temperature had —— to 100 degrees.
6. As the river ——, men piled sandbags on the levee.
7. My grades have —— this term.
8. As the barometer ——, our spirits —— with it.
9. At last the clouds —— above the peaks.
10. Prices had —— alarmingly.

EXERCISE 16. Number in a column on your paper from 1 to 20. Select from each sentence the correct one of the two words in parentheses and write it after the corresponding number on your paper.

1. When stocks (rise, raise) the broker is happy.
2. (Rising, Raising) from my seat, I demanded an explanation from the chairman.
3. His importance has (raised, risen) steadily.
4. Tomorrow the sun will (rise, raise) at six o'clock.
5. The mercury was (raising, rising) steadily.
6. Clouds of dust were (raising, rising) skyward.
7. He (rose, raised) rapidly in his profession.
8. The little ships were (rising, raising) and falling on the surf.
9. Hands (rising, raising) from all over the class showed the students had many questions.
10. Spires of several churches could be seen (raising, rising) above the village.
11. The curtain had just (risen, raised) when we found our seats.
12. The plane (rose, raised) slowly.
13. Swollen streams (raised, rose) until they overflowed their banks.
14. He had (raised, risen) his arm in protest.
15. She (rose, raised) from her chair to greet us.

16. Crippled, the plane (raised, rose) sharply and then fell.
17. Storm clouds are (raising, rising) in the west.
18. The sudden appearance of a ghost made my hair (raise, rise) straight up.
19. Will prices (raise, rise) further?
20. We watched the gulls (rising, raising) from the water.

REVIEW EXERCISE B. Number in a column on your paper from 1 to 40. Read each of the following sentences and determine whether it is correct or incorrect. If it is correct, place a + after the corresponding number on your paper; if it is incorrect, place a 0.

1. We found her lost gloves lying in the top drawer.
2. Wouldn't you rather set here?
3. We laid on our sleds, ready for a push.
4. The bird sat on her nest.
5. The doctor advised him to lay still.
6. The men raise the flag to the top of the pole each morning.
7. Judy sets the table every night.
8. Why are you laying around here instead of working?
9. The river has raised six inches since last night!
10. We were just setting there, talking.
11. Quacky laid her first egg yesterday.
12. Shall we sit out this dance?
13. The sun raises at a later hour in winter.
14. Will you rise from your seats, please?
15. We laid out a tennis court on the old baseball diamond.
16. All of us had raised from our chairs.
17. The balloon raised out of sight.
18. It was too hot to lie in bed all night.
19. Please set in that chair, Mrs. Johnson.
20. We laid the light bulbs down carefully.
21. The ducks rose and waddled in a solemn line to the pond.

22. Don't just set there; do something!
23. We got sunburned from laying still too long on the beach.
24. Sit down with us for a while.
25. The whole audience raised up in protest.
26. Buster set there blinking his eyes and wagging his tail gently.
27. We lay out all the clothes we needed for the trip.
28. The Thompsons raised wonderful tomatoes last year.
29. Their voices rose in a loud shout of approval.
30. Lucky, our dog, laid in wait for the unwary mouse.
31. He was laying there for almost an hour, perfectly still.
32. Finally he raised his head ever so slowly.
33. Being tired, Mary lay down.
34. We set there watching him.
35. We set the pudding there to cool, and the cat ate it.
36. He set there looking very guilty.
37. Then he laid down over in the corner and went to sleep.
38. Lay right down and go to sleep!
39. Market prices have raised 100% in the last year.
40. Lie down, Rover!

CONSISTENCY OF TENSE

7b. Do not change needlessly from one tense to another.

WRONG   Henry *spoke* to me about the show and *says* he *has* a part in it for me. [inconsistent tenses]

RIGHT   Henry *spoke* to me about the show and *said* he *had* a part in it for me. [consistent tenses]

Young writers, especially when writing informal essays or narratives, sometimes begin their compositions in one tense and then lapse into another tense. Such lapses are due largely to carelessness, for students usually understand the error when it is pointed out to them. The exercises on the next few pages are intended to make you aware of this kind of error in written English. Let's look at a few isolated examples of sentences in which the writer has been inconsistent in his use of tenses.

WRONG The gun *went* off with a bang, and he *runs* away as fast as his legs *would carry* him. [tenses inconsistent]

RIGHT The gun *went* off with a bang, and he *ran* away as fast as his legs *would carry* him. [tenses consistent]

RIGHT The gun *goes* off with a bang, and he *runs* away as fast as his legs *can carry* him. [tenses consistent]

WRONG He *saw* the cause of the trouble, and *decides* to report it. [tenses inconsistent]

RIGHT He *saw* the cause of the trouble and *decided* to report it. [tenses consistent]

WRONG He *sees* the cause of the trouble and *decided* to report it. [tenses inconsistent]

RIGHT He *sees* the cause of the trouble and *decides* to report it. [tenses consistent]

EXERCISE 17.   Such sentences as those above are, of course, extreme examples. The paragraph below will illustrate a normal case of inconsistency in the use of tenses. List on your paper the verbs which are in the wrong tense. After each write the verb in its proper tense. You must, of course, decide first of all whether the paragraph should be in the present or the past tense throughout.

1. At the age of four I was learning to row a boat. 2. One evening my sister and I are playing in the boat which was tied to the dock. 3. Ruth decides to untie the boat and go exploring. 4. A sudden wind comes up and whitecaps covered the lake. 5. Much to my surprise I found myself in the middle of the lake while my frantic parents stood at the dock anxiously looking for us. 6. I wanted to stand up in the tossing boat and wave to them, but Ruth screams at me to sit still. 7. Our faith in our parents' ability to solve any problem was again strengthened as Dad comes speeding toward us in the launch. 8. He towed us back to shore.

EXERCISE 18. Prepare to read aloud the following paragraph, changing the tenses of the verbs whenever necessary to make them consistent.

1. I closed my eyes, and before me was the main room of a little Cape Cod farmhouse. 2. Near the big open fireplace was a spinning wheel. 3. On the mantle were a cuckoo clock and gay dishes standing up against the wall. 4. A square mahogany table adorns the center of the room, and scattered about the floor were colorful hooked rugs. 5. A large grandfather's clock stands in one corner, and an ornate desk in another. 6. Next to the desk were a large, deep, high-backed chair and a triangular table with a basket of sewing on it. 7. The fire on the hearth crackles cheerfully and throws patterns on the comfortable, soft chairs gathered around it. 8. Flashes of light were cast from the cut-glass candle-holders flanking the silver

tea set on the gleaming highboy. 9. The grandfather's clock chimes eight, and the gray cat, softly purring on the hearthstone, gives the room a deep sense of tranquillity.

EXERCISE 19. In the following passage the tenses are mixed. Read the entire passage through carefully and decide in which tense it should be written. Then copy it carefully, changing those verbs which are in the wrong tense.

1. There was bound to be trouble at the crossroads when the stagecoach arrived. 2. The highwaymen had hidden themselves in the bushes at the edge of the road. 3. Although the sun is setting, it looks as though there would be light enough so that they could make the attack. 4. The branches are motionless, and the thick dust lay undisturbed on the wagon tracks. 5. The two thieves lie on the dry ground completely covered by the leaves and branches.

6. Faintly, from the north, comes the regular patter of horses' hoofs. 7. As the sound grew louder, it became a rhythmic thud. 8. The robbers heard it and, their revolvers drawn, they rise to a kneeling position, ready to spring into the open at the first sight of the horses' ears. 9. With a thundering roar the high coach lurches into view just a hundred yards away. 10. Amid the cries of the driver and the screaming of the axles, the blundering vehicle swung into the straightaway. 11. The whole swaying pile is enveloped in a cloud of dust as the brakes were applied. 12. Two dark figures, their faces masked, slip from the shadows beside the road and glide toward the corner. 13. A sharp cry pierced the groans of the coach; and as the red rays of the lowering sun glint on the hard steel of revolvers, the confused mass of horses, wheels, and dust careened to the side of the highway and halted perilously near a deep ditch.

8. USING MODIFIERS CORRECTLY

In your study of grammar you learned that a modifier is a word or group of words which modifies (makes more definite) the meaning of another word. You know that there are two parts of speech which are modifiers. One is the adjective, which modifies a noun or pronoun. The other is the adverb, which modifies a verb or an adjective or another adverb. The purpose of this chapter is to help you use modifiers correctly and effectively. If you feel that you need to review adjectives and adverbs, turn to pages 5 and 13 and study them again before beginning work on this chapter.

USING ADJECTIVES AND ADVERBS CORRECTLY

Can you answer the questions below concerning the italicized words in these two sentences?

1. The child was *happy*.
2. The child played *happily*.

What word does *happy* modify in Sentence 1?
What part of speech is it?
What word does *happily* modify in Sentence 2?
What part of speech is it?

If you were able to answer those questions correctly, you will understand clearly the matter of good usage which you are to study next. *Happy* is an adjective modifying the noun *child*, subject of the sentence. *Happy*, because it is a part of the predicate and modifies the subject, is a *predicate adjective*. *Happily* is an adverb modifying the verb *played*. It tells *how* the child played.

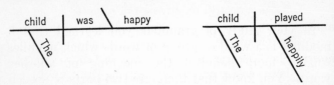

Most adjectives become adverbs by adding *-ly*.

ADJECTIVE	ADVERB
neat	neat*ly*
strange	strange*ly*
beautiful	beautiful*ly*

Caution: A few *adjectives* also end in *-ly* (*daily, sickly, lovely*), so that you cannot always be sure than an *-ly* word is an adverb.

In each sentence in the following exercise you are given a choice between two words, an adjective and an adverb. If the word modifies the subject of the sentence, choose the *adjective* to complete the sentence correctly. If the word modifies the verb, choose the *adverb*. In these sentences the adverbs end in *-ly*.

The following information may be of help to you in deciding between adjective and adverb.

(1) The state-of-being (or linking) verbs (see page 9) are usually followed by a predicate adjective. The following are most commonly used as state-of-being verbs: *be, become, seem, grow, appear, look, feel, smell, taste, remain, stay, sound.*

However, many of these verbs are not always state-of-being verbs; they may be action verbs, and as action verbs they may be followed and modified by an adverb.

RIGHT   The plants *grew tall.* [state-of-being verb followed by an adjective modifying the subject]

RIGHT   The plants *grew rapidly.* [action verb modified by an adverb]

RIGHT   She *appeared worried.* [state-of-being verb followed by an adjective modifying the subject]

RIGHT   She *appeared suddenly.* [action verb modified by an adverb]

RIGHT   He *looked heavy.* [state-of-being verb followed by an adjective modifying the subject]

RIGHT   He *looked sharply* in my direction. [action verb modified by an adverb]

(2) In many sentences requiring an adjective after the verb, the words *is, are, was, were* may be substituted for the verb without greatly changing the meaning.

EXAMPLE   She *felt* happy. [She *was* happy.]

EXERCISE 1.   Select the word in parentheses (adjective or adverb) which correctly fits the meaning of the sentence. Decide first whether the word modifies the subject or the verb. Write the word on your paper and after it write the word it modifies.

1. The berries tasted (bitter, bitterly).
2. She cried very (bitter, bitterly).
3. Displeased by our report, she looked (coldly, cold) at us.
4. The girls in swimming suits looked (coldly, cold).
5. She feels (bad, badly).
6. She played (bad, badly).
7. The new man seems (capable, capably) enough.

8. The new man works (capable, capably) enough.
9. The flowers smelled (sweetly, sweet).
10. The girl smiled (sweetly, sweet).

8a. When a modifier in the predicate modifies the subject it must be an adjective; when it modifies the verb it must be an adverb.

EXERCISE 2. Choose the correct one of the two words in parentheses. Write the words in a list on your paper. After each write the word it modifies.

1. The darkened vessel slipped (rapid, rapidly) out to sea.
2. We all thought she danced most (gracefully, graceful).
3. In her white gown she looked (beautifully, beautiful).
4. Everyone set to work very (enthusiastically, enthusiastic).
5. Helen said she felt (confidently, confident) about winning.
6. The coffee tasted rather (strong, strongly).
7. They appeared very (sudden, suddenly) at the entrance.
8. In spite of the danger the audience remained (quiet, quietly).
9. In reply to our question, the child looked (sad, sadly) up at us.
10. "Why do you look so (sad, sadly)?" we asked.

SPECIAL STUDY OF ADJECTIVES AND ADVERBS

Certain adjectives and adverbs very commonly misused deserve special study. These are *bad, badly; good, well;* and *slow, slowly.*

"BAD" AND "BADLY"

RIGHT   The situation *looks bad.* [After the state-of-being verb *looks*, the adjective *bad* modifies the subject *situation.*]

RIGHT I *played badly*. [The adverb *badly* modifies the verb *played*.]

WRONG He *looks* very *badly*.

RIGHT He *looks* very *bad*. [The adjective *bad* modifies the subject *he*.]

WRONG This *smells badly*.

RIGHT This *smells bad*. [*Smell* is a state-of-being verb here. *Bad* modifies the subject *this*.]

"WELL" AND "GOOD"

Well may be used as either an adjective or an adverb. As an adjective, *well* has three meanings.

1. To be in good health:

RIGHT He is *well*.   He feels *well*.

2. To appear well-dressed or well-groomed:

RIGHT It pays to look *well*.

3. To be satisfactory:

RIGHT It is *well*.   All is *well*.

As an adverb, *well* means to perform an action capably.

RIGHT He washed the car *well*.

Good is always an adjective. It should not be used to modify a verb.

WRONG The team played good.

RIGHT The team *played well*.

WRONG The actors did good.

RIGHT The actors *did well*.

"SLOW" AND "SLOWLY"

Slow is used as both an adjective and an adverb. *Slowly* is an adverb.

RIGHT   Go *slow*. [*Slow* is an adverb modifying the verb *go*.]

RIGHT   Go *slowly*. [*Slowly* is an adverb modifying the verb *go*.]

In most uses (other than *Go slow* and *Drive slow*) it is better practice to use *slowly* as an adverb instead of *slow*.

RIGHT   Move as *slowly* as you can.

RIGHT   He walked *slowly* up the stairs.

Caution: There are certain words like *loud, hard, deep, fast, tight, etc.,* which may be used as adverbs without changing their forms.

EXAMPLES   He spoke *loud* and *long*.

He played *hard*.

Dig *deep*.

They ran *fast*.

Hold on *tight*.

REVIEW EXERCISE A.   Number on your paper from 1 to 20. If the sentence is correct, place a + after the corresponding number; if it is incorrect, write the correct form of the modifier in question and after it write the word it modifies.

1. The children have behaved very good.
2. Pickles smell sour.
3. Your suit fits you well.
4. I thought she seemed happy.
5. This plum tastes badly.
6. He always does his work well.
7. Mary looked beautiful at the dance.
8. He said he felt strongly enough to make the journey.
9. I thought she left us rather sudden.
10. We agreed to proceed as slowly as possible.
11. I did the homework easy.

12. She prides herself on always looking well.
13. He does his work as careful as he can.
14. Drive slow!
15. When the chemistry class finished experimenting, the whole school smelled badly.
16. Jane speaks very slowly.
17. The key turned easy.
18. Did you think the team played good?
19. He took the bad news calmly enough.
20. The juice of some oranges tastes sweet.

REVIEW EXERCISE B. Number on your paper from 1 to 20. If the sentence is correct, place a + after the corresponding number; if it is incorrect, write the correct form of the modifier in question and after it write the word it modifies.

1. Harry felt pretty bad about losing his match.
2. You're looking well.
3. The results of the experiment were good.
4. He won the race easy.
5. We came as rapidly as we could.
6. Your suit fits good.
7. The announcement came suddenly.
8. They worked slow but sure.
9. Rain fell very heavily all day.
10. The room smelled badly.
11. His eyes look sad.
12. You did very well.
13. Does he feel strong enough to travel?
14. Please leave as quiet as possible.
15. The child slept peacefully.
16. This dress looks well on you.
17. If the meat smells badly, throw it out.
18. The little children behaved badly.
19. She felt rather bad all day.
20. The orchestra didn't play so good as the band.

COMPARISON OF ADJECTIVES AND ADVERBS

COMPARISON OF ADJECTIVES

Adjectives state qualities of nouns or pronouns.

> *tall* building
> *beautiful* day
> *good* dinner

8b. When you wish to *compare the degree* or *extent* to which one noun has a quality with the degree to which another noun has the same quality, you change the form of the adjective. This change is called *comparison*.

EXAMPLES The Empire State Building is *tall*.

The Empire State Building is *taller* than the Chrysler Building.

The Empire State Building is the *tallest* building in New York.

Today is *beautiful*.

Today is *more beautiful* than yesterday.

Today is the *most beautiful* day we have had.

The new restaurant served a *good* dinner.

The new restaurant served a *better* dinner than the old restaurant.

The new restaurant served the *best* dinner I have ever eaten.

There are three degrees of comparison: *positive, comparative, and superlative.*

POSITIVE	COMPARATIVE	SUPERLATIVE
tall	taller	tallest
beautiful	more beautiful	most beautiful
good	better	best

FORMATION OF THE COMPARATIVE AND SUPERLATIVE DEGREES

(1) Adjectives of one syllable form their comparative and superlative degrees by adding –er and –est.

POSITIVE	COMPARATIVE	SUPERLATIVE
strong	stronger	strongest
fine	finer	finest

(2) Some adjectives of two syllables form their comparative and superlative degrees by adding –er or –est; other adjectives of two syllables form their comparative and superlative degrees by means of more and most.

When you are in doubt as to which way an adjective is compared, consult an unabridged dictionary.

POSITIVE	COMPARATIVE	SUPERLATIVE
happy	happier	happiest
pretty	prettier	prettiest
rapid	more rapid	most rapid
helpful	more helpful	most helpful

(3) Adjectives of more than two syllables form their comparative and superlative degrees by means of more and most.

POSITIVE	COMPARATIVE	SUPERLATIVE
beautiful	more beautiful	most beautiful
industrious	more industrious	most industrious

(4) Comparison to indicate less or least of a quality is accomplished by using the words less and least before the adjective.

POSITIVE	COMPARATIVE	SUPERLATIVE
gray	less gray	least gray
satisfactory	less satisfactory	least satisfactory

IRREGULAR COMPARISON

Adjectives which do not follow the regular methods of forming their comparative and superlative degrees are said to be compared irregularly.

POSITIVE	COMPARATIVE	SUPERLATIVE
bad ⎫ evil ⎬ ill ⎭	worse	worst
good ⎫ well ⎭	better	best
little	less	least
many ⎫ much ⎭	more	most

EXERCISE 3. Write the comparative and superlative forms of the following adjectives. If you are in doubt about the two-syllable words, look them up in an unabridged dictionary.

1. big	6. successful	11. bad
2. strange	7. capable	12. honest
3. wealthy	8. short	13. little
4. eager	9. difficult	14. famous
5. lonely	10. certain	15. good

COMPARISON OF ADVERBS

(1) Adverbs of one syllable form their comparative and superlative degrees by adding –er and –est.

POSITIVE	COMPARATIVE	SUPERLATIVE
(run) fast	faster	fastest
(play) hard	harder	hardest

(2) Adverbs ending in *–ly* form their comparative and superlative degrees by means of *more* and *most*.

POSITIVE	COMPARATIVE	SUPERLATIVE
easily	more easily	most easily
carefully	more carefully	most carefully

USE OF COMPARATIVE AND SUPERLATIVE FORMS OF ADJECTIVES AND ADVERBS

Besides knowing how to form the comparative and superlative degrees of adjectives and adverbs, you should follow certain customs in using them which are commonly observed by educated people.

8c. Use the comparative degree when comparing two things, and the superlative degree when comparing more than two.

COMPARISON OF TWO THINGS

RIGHT We rode *more slowly* than the other party.

RIGHT Frank is *older* than his sister.

WRONG Of the two children, the girl is youngest.

RIGHT Of the *two* children, the girl is *younger*.

WRONG Which of the two spoke most clearly?

RIGHT Which of the *two* spoke *more clearly?*

COMPARISON OF MORE THAN TWO THINGS

RIGHT Dr. Jones was the *least excited* man in the crowd.

RIGHT He is the *most ambitious* student in school.

WRONG Which of the three books did you like better?

RIGHT Which of the *three* books did you like *best?*

WRONG Among the four available routes, we chose the shorter one.

RIGHT Among the *four* available routes, we chose the *shortest* one.

8d. Do not say "He is taller than any member of his class" because obviously he too is a member of his class and cannot be taller than himself. The sentence should read, "He is taller than any *other* member of his class."

WRONG George played better than any boy on his team.
RIGHT George played better than any *other* boy on his team.
WRONG New York is larger than any city in the Americas.
RIGHT New York is larger than any *other* city in the Americas.

8e. Avoid the *double comparison.*

A double comparison is one in which the degree is formed incorrectly by both adding *er* or *est* and using *more* or *most.*

WRONG She was more lovelier than a movie queen.
RIGHT She was *lovelier* than a movie queen.
WRONG I found the city the most loveliest place I had ever visited.
RIGHT I found the city the *loveliest* place I had ever visited.

EXERCISE 4. Number in a column on your paper from 1 to 20. If the sentence is correct, place a + after the corresponding number on your paper; if it is incorrect, place a 0.

1. Of the three brothers, Jim is the better looking.
2. I saw both *Othello* and *Hamlet,* and I thought *Othello* was the better play.
3. Your story is bad, but mine is badder.
4. In fact mine is worse than any story written in our class.

5. Jane is the most happiest girl I know.
6. Of the three pens I like this one best.
7. We were arguing as to which one of the two writers was best.
8. Of the many suggestions I received, yours was the most helpful.
9. The coach seemed hopefuller than the players.
10. He thinks he can run more faster than I.
11. Shakespeare is more famous than any other English author.
12. The policemen seemed more calm than the firemen.
13. I was sick, but he was sicker.
14. The President is better known than any figure in the world.
15. Do you think you're more strong than I?
16. He is regarded as the ablest member of the President's cabinet.
17. I have never heard anyone sing more beautifully.
18. Who's the honestest merchant in town?
19. I used to think the littlest men were the most conceited.
20. Al seemed to be the most angriest member of the mob.

EXERCISE 5. Fill the blanks with the correct comparative forms of the italicized words.

1. This book may be *bad*, but that one is ——.
2. You may be *good*, but she is ——.
3. He is *difficult*, but his brother is ——.
4. This is *pretty*, but that is ——.
5. He is *fat*, but his father is ——.
6. The river is *clear*, but the lake is ——.
7. I am *patient*, but you are ——.
8. I thought I was *efficient*, but you are ——.
9. Helen was *ill* on Monday, but she was —— on Tuesday.
10. Their argument was *good*, but ours was ——.

EXERCISE 6. Number on your paper from 1 to 20. If the comparison is correct, place a + after the corresponding number; if it is incorrect, place a 0.

1. We tried more harder than they.
2. Marvin did more than any other boy to help us.
3. Who is the wealthiest, Mr. Long or Mr. Short?
4. The results were worser than anyone expected.
5. He is the least successful of the four brothers.
6. Which of the two is the better?
7. Late at night the wind blew more stronger.
8. His manner is strange, but yours is stranger.
9. I feel worser every minute.
10. She is more pretty than her sister.
11. She's traveled more farther than I.
12. Are you more tall than your brother?
13. This mountain is taller than any other in the range.
14. Which is the most heaviest of the three boxes?
15. She is more capable than I.
16. We were tireder than they.
17. This is the simplest of the ten problems.
18. Of the two he is the less capable.
19. Today's homework was more easier than yesterday's.
20. The seniors work harder than any students in the school.

DANGLING MODIFIERS

8f. A modifying phrase or clause must clearly and sensibly modify a word in the sentence. A phrase or clause which does not clearly and sensibly modify a word in the sentence is a *dangling modifier*.

WRONG Looking out the window, every passer-by could be seen.

In this sentence the participial phrase *looking out the window* is a dangling modifier. It seems to modify *passer-by*, but such modification is neither clear nor sensible. The passer-by could not be looking out the window. The sentence should read

RIGHT *Looking out the window,* **we** could see every passer-by.

EXAMPLES OF DANGLING MODIFIERS

WRONG Waiting in the station, the newsstand attracted me.

RIGHT Waiting in the station, I was attracted by the newsstand.

WRONG Recommended by the president, the job was offered to me.

RIGHT Recommended by the president, I was offered the job.

WRONG After swimming all afternoon, our appetites were tremendous.

RIGHT After swimming all afternoon, we had tremendous appetites.

WRONG To get to the theater on time, a taxi had to be hired.

RIGHT To get to the theater on time, we had to hire a taxi.

WRONG While waiting in the principal's office, all my misdeeds came back to me.

RIGHT While waiting in the principal's office, I recalled all my misdeeds.

RIGHT While I was waiting in the principal's office, all my misdeeds came back to me.

EXERCISE 7. Study the following sentences containing dangling modifiers. As was done with the preceding examples, rewrite each sentence so that the modifier *clearly* and *sensibly* modifies a word in the sentence. You will have to supply words.

1. Sitting in the last row of the theater, the actors could not be heard.
2. Standing on the river bank, many beautiful fish could be seen.
3. To solve these problems, an answer book should be bought.
4. By working hard and fast, the lawn was soon mowed.
5. While in the army, his wife worked in a factory.
6. Coming across the lake, several mountain peaks can be seen.
7. On the way home from the dance, a thunderstorm drove us to shelter.
8. Convinced of my honesty, I persuaded her to lend me the money.
9. Reading rapidly, the book was soon finished.
10. When at home, the whole family waits on him.
11. Undecided about plans, the future looked uncertain.
12. When in school, your parents expect you to behave yourself.
13. Walking in the rain all day, our shoes were ruined.
14. Having looked forward to a holiday, the disappointment of the children was keen.
15. Entering the burning building, heat and smoke overcame the firemen.

EXERCISE 8. Eliminate the dangling modifiers in the following sentences by rewriting each sentence so that the modifier clearly and sensibly modifies a word in the sentence. You will have to supply words.

1. After failing to pass the examination, the teacher advised me to try again.

2. Speaking to the entire student body, plans for the celebration were explained by the president of the council.

3. While standing on the corner, an automobile horn startled me.

4. By taking the longer route, many historic sites can be visited.

5. To enjoy traveling, very little luggage should be carried.

6. To play a good game of tennis, new balls must be used.

7. When but a small child, my great-uncle left me his fortune.

8. After being fired, the boss gave me a tip on a new job.

9. To go aboard one of the large aircraft carriers, a permit must be obtained.

10. After being away so long, home seemed good to us.

11. Sailing on the Sound this afternoon, the sun was very hot.

12. When in town, our house is the first place he visits.

13. To understand this process, the third chapter must be mastered.

14. While listening to the radio, the weather report discouraged us in our plans for an outing.

15. Picnicking on the mountain, the red roofs of the college glistened in the distance.

MISPLACED MODIFIERS

In doing the exercises on the preceding pages, you noticed the absurd meaning of the sentences containing dangling modifiers. The modifiers either seemed to modify a word which they could not sensibly modify or they were left without any word to modify at all. Writing just as absurd as dangling modifiers will also result from misplaced modifiers.

8g. Modifying words, phrases, and clauses should be placed as near as possible to the word they modify.

MISPLACED SINGLE-WORD MODIFIERS

There are two common words (used as either adjective or adverb) which are often carelessly placed in relation to the word they modify. These words are *only* and *just*. In conversation these words are used carelessly, and yet no confusion results because the tone of the speaker indicates the meaning intended. In written English, which is more exact and lacks the tone of voice to convey meaning, a careful writer will use *only* and *just* with exactness.

(1) To make your meaning clear, place *only* and *just* near to the word they modify and usually before it.

EXERCISE 9.   Explain the difference in meaning between the sentences grouped together in pairs. Show that by modifying a different word in each sentence the modifier changes the meaning. What word is modified in each sentence?

1. We had *only suggested* having dinner together.
   We had suggested having *only dinner* together.
2. I have *just earned* a dollar.
   I have earned *just a dollar*.
3. We *only argued* for an hour.
   We argued for *only an hour*.
4. We had *only enrolled* the day before.
   We had enrolled *only the day before*.
5. I *just glanced* at the book this morning.
   I glanced at the book *just this morning*.

Notice that the meaning is changed by shifting the position of the modifier.

EXERCISE 10. Change the meaning of the following by shifting the position of the modifier in italics.

1. He came in second in *only* the first race.
2. He nodded to me *only* yesterday.
3. She *just* baked a cake.
4. The children *only* looked at their ice cream.
5. The speaker mentioned *only* you.
6. Did you *just* see John?
7. We *only* suggested a senior dance.
8. The wind *just* blew down the elm tree.
9. He *only* talked about what he was going to do.
10. She *only* cried a few minutes.

MISPLACED PHRASE MODIFIERS

(2) Modifying phrases should be placed as near as possible to the words they modify.

The sentences below will indicate the importance of observing this rule.

WRONG   Did you see a boy in the bus with a brown cap?

RIGHT   Did you see a boy *with a brown cap* in the bus?
[The phrase *with a brown cap* obviously modifies *boy*. It should be placed next to *boy*. Otherwise it appears to modify *bus* and gives the impression that it was a bus with a brown cap.]

WRONG   I expect co-operation in wrapping these packages from everyone.

RIGHT   I expect co-operation from everyone in wrapping these packages.

BETTER   In wrapping these packages, I expect co-operation from everyone.

WRONG   We borrowed an extension ladder from a neighbor 35 feet long.

RIGHT   We borrowed an extension ladder 35 feet long from a neighbor.

BETTER From a neighbor we borrowed an extension ladder 35 feet long.

WRONG   We came upon a magnificent view rounding the bend.

RIGHT   Rounding the bend, we came upon a magnificent view.

WRONG   John asked her to marry him sitting in the moonlight.

RIGHT   Sitting in the moonlight, John asked her to marry him.

EXERCISE 11. Read each of the following sentences. Pick out the misplaced phrase, decide what word the phrase should modify, and rewrite the sentence, placing the phrase near this word.

1. We saw a lady talking to a policeman in a green dress and a white coat.
2. He tried to shoot himself after writing a farewell note with a shotgun.
3. He spoke of the need of building new tennis courts in the strongest possible terms.
4. A plane flew over the school building with red wings.
5. Mrs. Stevens went to Florida after her husband had been sent to jail to live with relatives.
6. Parry was stung by a bee hoeing weeds in his garden.
7. I came upon an interesting old book shop wandering about the narrow streets.
8. The judge sentenced the prisoner to five years in prison with fire in his eyes.
9. The children were offered a piece of chocolate layer cake by a strange lady with white frosting.

10. I told the teacher that I had lost a book on the play-ground with a red cover.
11. We saw a great deal of farming country riding along in our car.
12. We were told to leave the school building by the principal.
13. A collision occurred in the middle of the block between a delivery car and a fire truck.
14. The telegram was delivered by a messenger boy in a yellow envelope.
15. I had been talking to a lady on the train with three children.
16. We decided to finish trimming the house after we'd had a swim in white paint.
17. A strange-looking dog was led onto the stage by one of the actors with shaggy hair and a stubby tail.
18. We watched plane after plane land and take off sitting in the control tower at the airport.
19. I saw them leave before the sun came up in a long red car.
20. He told us about killing the lion in the auditorium.

MISPLACED CLAUSE MODIFIERS

A thoughtless writer may misplace a subordinate clause in the same way that he may misplace a prepositional phrase. In using modifying clauses, you should follow the rule which applies to phrases.

(3) Place the clause as near as possible to the word it modifies.

These sentences will show you how a misplaced clause may make a sentence ridiculous.

WRONG   She had diamond rings in her ears which she had bought in Paris.

RIGHT   In her ears she had diamond rings which she had bought in Paris.

The modifying clause *which she had bought in Paris,* of course, modifies *rings,* not *ears.* In the second sentence the clause has been shifted so that it comes next to the word it modifies. The second sentence is, therefore, clear.

WRONG I borrowed a book from the library that contained nothing but detective stories.

RIGHT From the library I borrowed a book that contained nothing but detective stories.

WRONG We caught a dozen fish with the new bait which we fried for supper.

RIGHT With the new bait we caught a dozen fish which we fried for supper.

WRONG We took a swim in the lake after our day's work which left us cool and refreshed.

RIGHT In the lake we took a swim which left us cool and refreshed after our day's work.

EXERCISE 12. Read each of the following sentences. Take out the misplaced clause, decide what word the clause should modify, and rewrite the sentence, placing the clause near this word. If you find a misplaced phrase, correct it.

1. The new bicycle was standing on the porch which we had ordered from Chicago.
2. A large automobile drew up to the curb which was profusely draped with flags.
3. I liked the picture of you on the diving board that you sent me.
4. There are several men selling newspapers that are blind in New York.
5. We strapped the antique chair onto the old truck which was about a hundred years old.
6. He left the hotel in an automobile where he had spent the night.

7. My uncle bought a young terrier who is very fond of animals.
8. Dr. Longstreet cured our pet dog who is our family doctor.
9. An explosion in the refinery awoke everyone in town that had a hundred storage tanks.
10. The fireplace heated the entire cabin which was six feet long.

PHRASES AND CLAUSES WHICH MODIFY TWO WORDS

Sometimes a writer will place a modifying phrase or clause so that it seems to modify either of two different words. This is not clear writing, because the reader may read the sentence in either of two ways. Naturally, the writer has only one meaning in mind when he writes his sentence. To be sure of being understood, he must place modifiers so that they clearly modify only one word.

NOT CLEAR He asked me *on the way home* to call him.

Here the phrase *on the way home* may modify either *asked*, meaning that it was while we were on the way home that he asked me; or *to call*, meaning that he wanted me to call him while I was on my way home. Both of the following arrangements of the sentence are correct. Which one the author meant would probably be clear if we had the context from which the sentence was taken. A modifier placed so that it can modify either of two words may mislead the reader.

CLEAR *On the way home* he asked me to call him.

CLEAR He asked me to call him *on the way home*.

A modifying *clause* may be similarly misplaced so that the sentence does not make clear which of two words the clause modifies.

NOT CLEAR   I asked Mary *when she reached camp* to send me my mail.

The sentence might mean either:

CLEAR   *When she reached camp,* I asked Mary to send me my mail.

or

CLEAR   I asked Mary to send me my mail *when she reached camp.*

NOT CLEAR   We expected on Monday to make a trip to town.

CLEAR   On Monday we expected to make a trip to town.

CLEAR   We expected to make a trip to town on Monday.

NOT CLEAR   I asked Jerry when he finished mowing the lawn to repair the dog house.

CLEAR   When he finished mowing the lawn, I asked Jerry to repair the dog house.

CLEAR   I asked Jerry to repair the dog house when he finished mowing the lawn.

EXERCISE 13. Rewrite each of the following so that it is clear which word the clause modifies.

1. I thought when he came in I would speak to him.
2. We knew when the bell rang we would be late.
3. I advised Phil after he returned from abroad to go to college.
4. I told him, when we met in New Orleans, we would see the sights together.

5. Mrs. Abbot asked me before I returned to New York to call her.

REVIEW EXERCISE. The sentences in the following exercise contain dangling modifiers and misplaced modifiers. Rewrite the sentences so that the meaning is clear.

1. We saw a number of deer driving through the state park.
2. When cooking dinner, the roast was badly burned.
3. To make the trip in two days, all thought of a stop-over had to be abandoned.
4. I was hoping when school was out you would go home with me.
5. She went out with Harry dressed in her best clothes.
6. Amy said she would be back by the first of September in her last letter.
7. I saw a box in the post office that was addressed to you.
8. Having given away our position, the enemy attacked at once.
9. She pleaded for a new doll with tears in her eyes.
10. While working in Gover's store, the customers teased her.
11. There is a copy of the speech that I gave in my brief-case.
12. The archaeologists found a skeleton near their camp which, they thought, was a million years old.

9. SENTENCE VARIETY

"Variety," the saying goes, "is the spice of life." Variety is also the spice of writing. The dramatist varies his play by placing a comic scene between two serious scenes. The public speaker tells anecdotes and jokes in the course of an address. The novelist relieves the tension of his book with humor. In one respect writing is like living: both become dull when they lack variety.

To be sure, working for variety in the structure of your sentences before you have learned to write a sentence would be putting the cart before the horse. But if you have learned the principles taught so far in this book, you should be ready to master one of the finer points of good writing. This chapter will show you how to avoid monotonous writing — how to vary the structure of your sentences.

9a. Vary the beginnings of your sentences.

Beginning every sentence with the subject is a common cause of sentence dullness. Read the following paragraph in which every sentence begins in the same way — with the simple subject. Then read the next paragraph. You will see the difference between monotonous style and a style which has some variety.

NOT VARIED The trial had been scheduled for two o'clock. The audience was noisily settling itself in the courtroom for the coming show. The lawyers were quietly talking and shuffling piles of papers at the polished tables in the front of the room. The bell in the court-house tower struck two in resounding tones. Judge Walker, dignified in his long black gown, walked slowly to his bench. The clerk rasped out, "Everyone rise." The room seemed suddenly to lift for a moment; then it settled back into an ominous silence. The judge opened the case of the People vs. John Strong in a bored manner which seemed to imply that murder trials happened every day of his life.

VARIED The trial had been scheduled for two o'clock. In the courtroom the audience was noisily settling itself for the coming show. At the polished tables in the front of the room, the lawyers were quietly talking and shuffling piles of papers. When the bell in the court-house tower struck two in resounding tones, Judge Walker, dignified in his long black gown, walked slowly to his bench. "Everyone rise," rasped the clerk. Suddenly the room seemed to lift for a moment; then it settled back into an ominous silence. In a bored man-ner that implied that murder trials happened every day of his life, the judge opened the trial of the People vs. John Strong.

There are, as you may have noticed, several ways of beginning a sentence. Beginning with the sub-ject is the most natural way. The normal order of an English sentence is subject first, then predi-cate; furthermore, most of the sentences used in con-versation begin with the subject. But in order to avoid writing sentences which begin always in the same way, you can begin your sentence by placing a modifying word, a phrase, or a clause *first* in the sentence.

(1) You may begin a sentence with a single-word modifier — an adverb, an adjective, or a participle.

EXAMPLES *Suddenly* the room seemed to lift for a moment; then it settled back into an ominous silence. [adverb]

Cold and hungry, the survivors were brought into town. [adjectives]

Screaming, the frantic child beat her fists against the door. [present participle]

Disgusted, the teacher refused to continue the lesson. [past participle]

EXERCISE 1. The following sentences, all of which begin with the simple subject, contain a modifier which can be placed at the beginning of the sentence. Find this modifier and rewrite the sentence, placing the modifier first. The sentences in this and the following exercises are good sentences. You are asked to rewrite them so that you will learn a variety of ways of expressing the same idea.

EXAMPLE She opened the door cautiously.

Cautiously she opened the door.

1. The disappointed crowd filed dejectedly from the gym.
2. He stretched out lazily upon the thick rug.
3. Donald, strong and healthy, showed that his vacation had done him good.
4. The President, grinning, refused to answer the reporter's question.
5. Harold strode confidently toward the principal.
6. The boxer, bruised and beaten, stood swaying in the center of the ring.
7. My paper, illegible and messy, was returned for rewriting.
8. The mechanic expertly removed several pieces of rust from the carburetor.
9. The curtain finally rose.

10. The children, surprised, greeted the announcement enthusiastically.

EXERCISE 2. Write 5 sentences of your own beginning with single-word modifiers. Include at least one adjective, one adverb, and one participial modifier.

(2) You may begin a sentence with a phrase: a prepositional phrase or a participial phrase.

EXAMPLES *At the end of the game,* the crowds swarmed across the playing field. [prepositional phrase]

Having taken my position behind the wheel, I was ready for my first driving lesson. [participial phrase]

Angered by the repeated insults, Draper clenched his fists and stepped forward. [participial phrase]

EXERCISE 3. The following sentences, all of which begin with the subject, contain phrase modifiers which can be placed at the beginning of the sentence. Rephrase the sentences by placing the modifying phrases at the beginning.

1. We had fifty cents left after paying our expenses.
2. Everyone finally relaxed on the way home.
3. Joe and I, having seen the picture before, wanted to go to another theater.
4. John's long legs, stretched across the aisle, exerted an upsetting influence on his fellow students.
5. Our team, inspired by the words of the coach, came back in the second half to win.
6. The Bordens had built a beautiful playroom in their basement.
7. We went to the library in search of more information.

8. Tommy rushed into the house with tears streaming in white streaks through the grime on his face.
9. Mr. Hurley, accompanied by two detectives, returned to the scene of the robbery.
10. We tried, in spite of the bad weather, to celebrate the event in the usual way.

EXERCISE 4. Rewrite the following sentences so that each begins with either a word or a phrase modifier. In rearranging the sentences, you may wish to drop some of the words or add others; you may do so provided you keep the original meaning. Hints are given to help you with the first 5.

EXAMPLE We were discouraged and retraced our steps.
         Discouraged, we retraced our steps.

1. We left Perry at the station and went back to school. [Begin with *leaving*.]
2. Every horse looked like a winner at the starting line. [Begin with *at*.]
3. I found all the information I needed in the latest *World Almanac*. [Begin with *in*.]
4. He found himself alone in the big city and began to make inquiries. [Begin with *finding*.]
5. Mr. Kramer, generous and kindly, was soon cheated out of his money. [Begin with *generous*.]
6. Our school is equipped with an excellent pool and always turns out a strong swimming team.
7. The sound of riveters and pneumatic hammers, coming from the building next door, made it impossible for us to work.
8. The crew worked day and night for a week and completed the job earlier than expected.
9. Our science teacher helped us set up the apparatus but told us to do the experiment by ourselves.
10. They approached the entrance to the tunnel, scared to death.

11. We examined the array of instruments on the panel and wondered how anyone could fly a plane like this.
12. The witness told simply and sincerely all that he knew about the case.

(3) You may begin a sentence with a subordinate clause.

EXAMPLES Our absence was discovered after we had been gone half the day.
After we had been gone half the day, our absence was discovered.
We planned the party in December, and our idea was to have a dinner dance.
When we planned the party in December, our idea was to have a dinner dance.

EXERCISE 5. Rephrase each sentence so that it begins with a subordinate clause instead of the subject. Place a comma after an adverb clause coming first in the sentence.

1. Stuart came to Student Council meeting as though he had been invited. [As . . .]
2. Mr. Steinberg asked him what he wanted, and he said he wished to present a petition. [When . . .]
3. The other Council members finally arrived, and the meeting came to order. [After . . .]
4. President Al Mills was absent from school; hence Billy Thom, the vice-president, conducted the meeting. [Since . . .]
5. This was the first petition the Council had ever received, and no one knew exactly how to proceed. [As . . . *or* Since . . .]
6. Billy simply called on Stuart when the time came for new business.
7. Stuart read his petition and kept a perfectly straight face.

8. The Council members tried to preserve their dignity, but they finally broke down.

9. The signers of the petition asked for a free afternoon for every pupil once a week, and the Council sympathized with them.

10. Mr. Steinberg pointed out that this was not a matter for the Council and suggested that Stuart carry his petition to the Board of Education.

11. The idea, he thought, would be excellent if it applied to teachers too.

EXERCISE 6. Write 2 sentences beginning with single-word modifiers, 3 with a prepositional phrase, 2 with a participial phrase, and 3 with a subordinate clause.

EXERCISE 7. Change the following sentences in the manner suggested.

1. Mrs. Sweet was agreeable and charming that day, and she treated us with perfect courtesy. [Begin with single-word modifiers.]

2. Towser was feeling unusually vicious, and he nearly succeeded in removing the seat of the stranger's pants. [Begin with a participle.]

3. The workmen finished their job at four o'clock, but they stayed on the job until five. [Begin with a subordinate clause.]

4. I left school early, and I met the attendance officer on the front steps. [Begin with a participle.]

5. The mob surged expectantly down the street. [Begin with a single-word modifier.]

6. The clock said 12:15, and I knew I could never catch the bus. [Begin with a subordinate clause.]

7. Our team looked good at the beginning of the game. [Begin with a prepositional phrase.]

8. Lieutenant Hardman was promoted twice during the

year and was a major by December. [Begin with a past participle.]

9. The junior high school in this town is in the same building as the high school. [Begin with a prepositional phrase.]

10. Miss Smith was dissatisfied with our dancing and refused to give us a place on the program. [Begin with a past participle.]

11. Detective Harle came in at midnight and told us the case had been solved. [Begin with a subordinate clause.]

12. The campers left their packs at the foot of the mountain and made the ascent in record time. [Begin with a participle.]

13. The librarian told us the book was out of print, and we gave up all hope of getting it. [Begin with a subordinate clause.]

14. The fish markets are scenes of bustling activity every morning before dawn. [Begin with a prepositional phrase.]

15. She was quiet in manner and was not good at directing others in an emergency. [Begin with a single-word modifier.]

16. We stood on the top of the mountain and could see the entire valley. [Begin with a participle.]

17. The President finished his address, and every reporter in the room rushed for a telephone. [Begin with a subordinate clause.]

18. Additional election returns kept coming into party headquarters during the day. [Begin with a prepositional phrase.]

19. Tennyson was poet laureate of England from 1850 to 1892, but his best poetry was written before 1850. [Begin with a subordinate clause.]

20. We thought the doors and the windows were locked, and we didn't even try to get in. [Begin with a participle.]

9b. Vary the kinds of sentences.

On page 86 you learned that when classified according to their structure, there are four kinds of sentences: *simple, compound, complex,* and *compound-complex.* If you are not sure of the characteristics of each of these, you should turn back and refresh your memory before going further.

Just as it is possible to achieve variety in your writing by varying the beginning of your sentences, it is also possible to achieve variety by varying the kinds of sentences you use. Using simple or compound sentences all the time tends to make your style monotonous. For example, read the following paragraph composed entirely of simple and compound sentences.

1. Nick arrived in class one minute late and was promptly sent to the office for a late permit. 2. He returned a few minutes later and took his seat. 3. I gave him an inquiring look, and he muttered, "Two hours." 4. This meant no touch football for Nick this afternoon; it probably meant the same for me. 5. Nick and I were the backfield, and besides, Nick owned the only football. 6. The teacher droned on in the front of the room, and Nick, tired from his long walk to the office, settled down for a little nap. 7. Mr. Wakeman had noted this further evidence of weakness, and he strode with determination up the aisle. 8. He stood before the sleeping beauty. 9. He rapped lightly on the nodding head and awaited results. 10. There were none. 11. Everyone was watching and snickering — everyone but Nick. 12. He was dreaming of a schoolless world, without classes, teachers, or bells. 13. The bell did it! 14. Nick grabbed his books automatically and leaped with half-closed eyes straight into Mr. Wakeman's arms.

Now read the next paragraph which tells the same tale but contains 6 complex sentences (the subordinate clauses are italicized). You will see the superiority of this version over the first one.

1. Nick arrived in class one minute late and was promptly sent to the office for a late permit. 2. In a few minutes he returned and took his seat. 3. *When I gave him an inquiring look,* he muttered, "Two hours." 4. This meant no touch football for Nick this afternoon; it probably meant the same for me, *because Nick and I were the backfield and Nick owned the only football.* 5. *As the teacher droned on in the front of the room,* Nick, *who was tired from his long walk to the office,* settled down for a little nap. 6. *When Mr. Wakeman noted this further evidence of weakness,* he strode with determination up the aisle and stood before the sleeping beauty. 7. He rapped lightly on the nodding head and awaited results. 8. There were none. 9. By this time everyone was watching and snickering — everyone but Nick, *who was dreaming of a schoolless world without classes, teachers, or bells.* 10. The bell did it! 11. Automatically, Nick grabbed his books and leaped with half-closed eyes straight into Mr. Wakeman's arms.

Actually, all that had to be done to break the monotony of the first version was to change some of the less important ideas from main clauses to subordinate clauses. A subordinate clause in a sentence makes the sentence complex.

EXERCISE 8. The following paragraphs consist entirely of simple and compound sentences. Rewrite them, varying the style by changing or combining some of the sentences into complex sentences. Naturally you will not try to make all your sentences complex, for your purpose is to get variety.

1. The Frosh Flurry was the first big social event of my high school career. It turned out to be big all right, but not very social for me. I was chairman of the decorating committee, and I asked most of my friends to be committee members. Everyone likes to be a committeeman, but nobody wants to do any work. I called meeting after meeting, but only the same faithful three would show up. The rest always seemed to have dentist appointments. The dentists around here were certainly busy during the weeks before the Frosh Flurry.

2. We planned our decorations, made a list of necessary things, and completed our shopping on Friday. On Saturday morning I was at the gym right after breakfast. I waited alone. Mr. Jones, the janitor, looked puzzled. About 11 o'clock, the "faithful" trio waltzed in. I thought they'd probably all been to the dentist, and I didn't say anything.

3. Then followed the wildest day of my life. Nothing went right. Colored streamers were arranged in a great panoply on the gym floor. This was raised to the ceiling and fastened there by Jerry. He teetered on a spindly ladder, and I had visions of broken bones and hospital bills. A few hours later we thought the job was nearly done, and we were about to start cleaning up. Suddenly we felt streamers floating down upon us. They fell lightly over everything in the gym. The wire had pulled loose!

4. The lights wouldn't work right either. You can't have much light at a dance, but the chaperones disapproved of dancing in complete darkness. The boys showed themselves to be very poor electricians. They wanted a big *G* in lights over the orchestra, and it took them all afternoon to make it.

5. Jerry called for me at 9 o'clock in the evening. I was asleep. We managed to drag ourselves to school. Everyone was having a good time. The chairman of the decorating committee danced one dance and went home to bed!

EXERCISE 9. Write a one-page account of one of your own experiences working with a class committee or preparing for a special event — a school picnic, a family reunion, Christmas, an assembly program, etc. The purpose of your writing is to show that you can avoid a monotonous style by varying the form of your sentences. Before writing, review the three ways of beginning a sentence. Include some complex sentences in your composition.

EXERCISE 10. Rewrite the following paragraphs, varying the beginnings of the sentences and the kinds of sentences.

1. The play, in the opinion of several people, was not worth seeing. There were, they admitted, some exciting scenes, but they thought the action as a whole was slow. The leading lady had made her reputation in the movies. She could not act well enough on the stage. Neither the heroine nor the supporting cast understood the play, and the audience was completely confused. Carl Adams was the producer. He had had many Broadway successes. But even his master hand could not produce a hit this time. The play had been on the road for several weeks and had been mildly successful. The New York critics thought the settings excellent, but they said the play would last only a few weeks. It closed after a two weeks' run.

2. It was a September night. A family had gathered around their hearth. They had piled it high with the driftwood of mountain streams. This was the dry cones of pines and the splintered ruins of great trees. These trees had come crashing down the precipice. The fire roared up the chimney. It brightened the room with its broad blaze. The faces of the father and mother had a sober gladness; the children laughed; the eldest daughter

was the image of Happiness at seventeen; the aged grand-mother was the image of Happiness grown old. She sat knitting in the warmest place. They had found the herb, heartsease, in the bleakest spot of all New England. This family were situated in the Notch of the White Hills. The wind there was sharp throughout the year. It was pitilessly cold in the winter.... They dwelt in a cold spot. It was also a dangerous spot. A mountain towered above their heads. It was very steep. The stones would often rumble down its sides. This would startle them at night.[1]

9c. Vary the length of your sentences.

A composition consisting entirely of short sentences gives the effect of being chopped up. A series of short sentences may sometimes be used to describe exciting action because short sentences give the effect of speed. In general, however, avoid such style as that in which the following paragraph is written. There are too many sentences for such a short passage.

1. The Army Air Force had a quantity of obsolete air-plane engines. 2. They offered these to schools. 3. Our industrial arts department asked for one of the engines. 4. One day a large truck drew up to the school. 5. In no time at all, two massive boxes had been dumped on the drive. 6. The generous Army had sent *two* engines. 7. By working for hours the shop classes finally unpacked the motors. 8. The teachers beamed with pleasure. 9. Now they really had something to show their students. 10. With the help of nearly everyone they began to move the heavy motors toward the door. 11. Then the shock came! 12. Neither motor would go through. 13. It took several days of outdoor work to tear down the motors. 14. Then they were moved into the shop, part by part.

[1] Adapted from *The Ambitious Guest* by Nathaniel Hawthorne.

15. Finally they were reassembled there. 16. The boys had learned more about airplane engines than they had ever expected to know.

EXERCISE 11. Using any means you wish — compound verbs, appositives, modifying phrases, subordinate clauses, etc. — combine the sentences in the preceding paragraph into sentences of greater length. Do not make them too long. Vary them. Compare your finished paragraph with the one on page 241, in which the number of sentences has been reduced from 16 to 9.

EXERCISE 12. Combine the short sentences grouped below into one long sentence. Take special pains to make the long sentences read smoothly. Appositives, introductory expressions, subordinate clauses, compound subjects and verbs are suggested means.

1. Chet shivered. He stopped writing. He drew his coat closer about him. He decided to speak to the janitor about keeping the heat up.
2. The tree was large and shapely. It was a maple. It stood in the center of the wide lawn. It was the only tree there.
3. Art asked her to go to the movies with him. The date was to be Friday night. She didn't want to go. She accepted.
4. Elinor often watched the doctor rush out late at night. He was on an emergency call. His face was grave and white under the street lamp.
5. The girl across the street always wanted life to be like the movies. She tried to elope one night with an usher from the Royal. Her father stopped them.
6. Tom's opponent hit a beautiful shot down the middle

of the fairway. Tom stepped up to drive. All he could think of was another failure under pressure.

7. We had not done our homework. The teacher was angry. She assigned four exercises. This was twice as much as usual.

8. *David Copperfield* was written by Charles Dickens. It is a story of a boy's growing up. Much of it is autobiographical.

9. Red Barnes is president of the Student Council. In assembly today he introduced Myra Atkinson. She asked everyone to support the Red Cross.

10. Nathaniel Hawthorne was an American writer. He wrote short stories. His stories are beautifully written. They are not very exciting.

11. Helen took her first driving lesson yesterday. It lasted half an hour on a deserted highway. She was a nervous wreck after it.

12. Lucerne is a lakeside city. Around it stand the lofty Alps. Their massive shoulders are outlined against the blue sky. They are reflected in the glassy surface of the lake.

10. WRITING THE PARAGRAPH

WHY WE WRITE IN PARAGRAPHS

You know what a paragraph looks like. You could point one out on any page of writing. Paragraphs are parts of a composition that are set off by themselves by means of spacing and, generally, by indenting the first line.

You may have seen a long composition written as one paragraph. You know how discouraged you felt as you began to read and how confused you became as you read on. The confusion came because without paragraphs the various divisions of the composition did not stand out. There was no clear indication as to when the author was about to take up another part of his subject. You felt like a traveler who can find no road signs to guide him.

The break between paragraphs is like a road sign. It tells the reader that at this point there is to be a small change in the subject — perhaps a change to a new idea, perhaps a change in time or place, perhaps a change to another argument. In any case, paragraphing makes easier reading.

When you are reading a properly paragraphed story or essay, you know that each paragraph presents one topic. You can see this topic clearly because you know where the discussion of it begins and where it ends.

Strange as it may seem, one of the main weaknesses of young writers, as any English teacher will tell you, is neglecting to write their compositions in paragraphs at all. Perhaps you have found the familiar sign ¶ on your paper. The sign means, "Begin a new paragraph here." The teacher marking your paper had found that you were introducing a new topic without beginning a new paragraph.

Good planning of your compositions will make paragraphing easier. When you have organized a composition into a number of ideas or topics, you can devote a paragraph to each topic or part of a topic.

10a. A *paragraph* is a series of sentences developing one topic.

The topic is usually, but not necessarily, stated in a sentence somewhere in the paragraph.

10b. The sentence which states the topic of the paragraph is called the *topic sentence*.

The other sentences in the paragraph develop the idea expressed by the topic sentence.

HOW TO DEVELOP A TOPIC SENTENCE

A topic sentence may be developed in many ways, depending on the kind of thing you are writing. In general, you give in your paragraph *examples*, *details*, or *facts* which make the meaning of the topic sentence clear. In order to see how this is done, let's take a paragraph from Christopher Morley's famous essay *On Doors*. Take the one beginning with the topic sentence, "Also, there are many ways of opening doors." This sentence states the central thought of the paragraph which it introduces. You know at once that Mr. Morley is going to discuss the "many ways of opening doors." He does not disappoint you. Every one of the other sentences in the paragraph describes ways of opening doors. Now read the entire paragraph.

Also, there are many ways of opening doors. There is the cheery push of elbow with which the waiter shoves open the kitchen door when he bears in your tray of supper. There is the suspicious and tentative withdrawal of a door before the unhappy book agent or peddler. There is the genteel and carefully modulated recession with which footmen swing wide the oaken barriers of the great. There is the sympathetic and awful silence of the dentist's maid who opens the door into the operating room and, without speaking, implies that the doctor is ready for you. There is the brisk cataclysmic opening of a door when the nurse comes in, very early in the morning — "It's a boy." [1]

This method of developing the paragraph is a simple one. The writer merely gives you *examples* to support his central idea stated in the first sentence. The following paragraph is also developed by examples. Notice that every sentence is closely related to the idea in the topic sentence.

People vary a great deal in the conditions they require for efficient study. Silence and solitude are craved by some; noise and company by others. Many young people want fast and merry radio programs when they work. One person likes the same room, chair, and pencil day after day. The next one studies wherever he is: a phone booth, a trolley car. [2]

[1] From "On Doors" by Christopher Morley from *Mince Pie*, copyright 1919. Reprinted by permission of J. B. Lippincott Company.
[2] From "Do You Know How to Study" by George Lawton. Reprinted by permission of *Scholastic Magazines*.

EXERCISE 1. Choose one of the following skeletons of a paragraph and by completing the unfinished statements, build a good paragraph. Be sure that every sentence is a complete sentence. You are supporting the topic sentence by means of examples.

1

Anyone planning a trip from New York to San Francisco finds several ways of making the journey. If he is in a hurry, he will naturally choose to fly, and he will reach his destination the same day that he leaves New York. On the other hand, if he likes the leisureliness of an ocean voyage, he will .... The traveler who has plenty of time and is interested in seeing America will .... The next best thing to driving is .... Finally, in speed and comfort he may make the trip in three days by ....

2

There are certain standard types of student in every high school. There is the grind who .... Then there are those happy-go-lucky kids who .... The teachers' pets .... The politicians .... Of course, the rest of us ....

3

Every time I make my plans a long time in advance, I get sick just before the big day arrives. Last year I was looking forward to Christmas with special pleasure, but .... That big date with George when he came home from prep school had to be broken because .... This spring vacation Dad had offered to take me with him on a business trip, but .... Then I missed the biggest dance of the year because .... From now on I'm not going to ....

STICK TO THE TOPIC

Since a paragraph is a series of sentences developing one topic, every sentence in a paragraph must be closely related to the topic of the paragraph. Although usually part of a longer composition, a paragraph is also a complete unit in itself. Any sentence in a paragraph which does not relate to the topic of that paragraph spoils the unity and should be taken out.

The following paragraph contains a sentence which is unrelated to the topic of the paragraph. This sentence is italicized. Read the paragraph and note how this sentence spoils its unity.

The educational possibilities of radio broadcasting are almost unlimited. Lectures on important social and political subjects are available to everyone who will take the time to listen to them. Educational programs on matters of world interest may be presented with popular appeal through radio plays and radio forums. Everyone who can turn a dial can be better informed about world events than he ever could have been before the arrival of broadcasting. Furthermore, the news is interpreted several times a day by competent commentators. More and more people are learning to enjoy good music which is readily available at almost any hour of the day or night. *Dance music and comedy programs are the most popular radio broadcasts.* Finally, the schools are using radio broadcasts. They can buy recordings of good educational programs and play them in classes, and teachers can assign their students to listen to important broadcasts on literature, science, and national and international affairs.

EXERCISE 2. In each of the following paragraphs there is one sentence which is not closely related to the topic. Find this sentence and copy it on your paper.

1

Fourth Street is more a playground than a street. It is the place chosen by all the neighborhood children for skating, for bicycle and scooter races, games of keepaway and softball. The houses on Fourth Street are small and close together, and they are situated very near to the street. On a summer afternoon the crowd is so great that a motorist who happens to drive his car through the block must think he has missed the street entirely and ended up in a village playground. Cars are generally regarded as bold intruders, and the driver who tries to speed through endangers his own life as well as those of a dozen children. It was not surprising to find that last week someone had actually painted a baseball diamond in white on the pavement.

2

The most time-consuming job in painting a house is painting the trim and the little crosspieces of the windows. The man who thinks the job is half done when he has merely painted the walls is in for a surprise. Painting the windows will take twice as much time as painting the walls. A good brush and an extension ladder are essential for doing an efficient job. There are always many unexpected spots on the sill and sash which have to be scraped and sandpapered before any painting can be done. Finally there is the exacting task of painting the crosspieces without spreading paint all over the panes. Count the windows in your house and multiply by one hour, and you will have a fair idea of how long this part of the job will take you.

3

There are many things to learn about paddling a canoe. Since a canoe can be pushed from its course by a slight breeze, the paddler must sit in such a way that the bow will not be forced too high out of the water where it will catch too much wind. In calm weather, the canoeist should sit in the stern, but in windy weather he should kneel just aft of the middle, for in this position he can control his craft with less effort. He should paddle on the side opposite the direction of the wind because the wind then actually helps him to hold to a straight course. ⟨A canoe should never be loaded with stones for ballast because the stones will sink the canoe should it capsize.⟩ Steering is done by a twist of the paddle at the end of each stroke, the extent of the twist depending upon the force of the stroke and the strength of the wind against the bow.

4

Many a poor boy has risen to high position. Abraham Lincoln was born in a humble log cabin, spent part of his life as a rail splitter, and later became the emancipator of the slaves and President of the United States. Louis Pasteur was born of poor parents, but through great struggle became world-renowned for his pasteurization process. Giuseppe Verdi was born poor in a small Italian village, and as a youth played an organ for the community church. As a young man, he wrote the unforgettable opera *Aïda*. In the present day, Eddie Cantor is a man who was born in the New York slums, and today he is a favorite actor. ⟨Both Theodore Roosevelt and Franklin D. Roosevelt were sons of wealthy parents, but they had to overcome handicaps in their rise to the Presidency.⟩ Indeed, there are many people in this world who were born of poor parentage, but as men or women made for themselves high positions in life.

5

Walking is more than an everyday necessity — it can be used for all kinds of reasons. As a recreation it serves to pass your leisure time. When you are feeling lonely and depressed, a long walk in the crisp air does heaps of good toward cheering you up. Then again, if you're filled with the glorious feeling that everything is perfect, you enjoy a walk outdoors where everything in nature seems to be happy with you. ⟨Campers make many wonderful and surprising discoveries on their hikes.⟩ A nervous businessman, waiting to hear whether the stock market has gone down another point, puts his hands behind him and paces impatiently up and down the room. The sleep-walker is utterly unconscious of where or why he is walking, but still he walks. Riding in a car everywhere you go is faster but not so good for you as walking. Next time you're bored or happy or unhappy or worried, take a walk.

THE CLINCHER SENTENCE

It is a good plan, in descriptive and explanatory writing especially, to add a concluding sentence to a paragraph. This sentence sometimes repeats the idea expressed in the topic sentence. Its purpose is to sum up, to "clinch" the central thought. Teachers of composition call it the "clincher" sentence. Read the two paragraphs which are given below. Notice that the final sentence in each is a "clincher."

1

When Jackson was inaugurated, an old Federalist grunted, "the reign of King Mob seemed triumphant." But to a friend of democracy, "it was the people's day, the people's President, and the people would rule." And Jackson would have agreed fully with the last. Jackson's main purpose was to make a workable scheme of government out of Jefferson's ideals. A natural-born fighter and a man strong of tongue and temper, "Old Hickory" was determined to fight for the rights of the common people. As champion of the masses he was opposed to the greed and the power of the few; and the privileged classes soon discovered where Jackson stood. *When the common man looked to Jackson for leadership, he looked to the right man.*[3]

2

After the 1850's other kinds of magazines were published. Chief among these were the *Nation* and the illustrated *Harper's Weekly*. These did much to show up graft in the days after the War between the States. Later

[3] From *The American Way of Life*, by H. U. Faulkner, T. Kepner, and H. Bartlett. Reprinted by permission of Harper & Brothers.

Edward Bok brought out the *Ladies Home Journal*.
McClure's magazine and others, like the *Cosmopolitan*, appeared in rapid succession. These were for people who
found the older magazines too "high-brow." At about
the same time, humorous periodicals such as *Judge* were
started. *Magazines for the masses had become part of
American life.*[4]

EXERCISE 3. Write a paragraph on any topic
you wish. Make the first sentence a topic sentence
and the last sentence a "clincher" sentence.

EXERCISE 4. Choose one of the topic sentences
below and write a well-knit paragraph. Begin with
the topic sentence. Be sure that every sentence
deals with the subject introduced by the topic sentence. All the sentences lend themselves to development by examples.

1. Teachers may be classified in four types.
2. To me most of my sister's girl friends seem crazy.
3. There are many beautiful buildings in this city.
4. There are five days in every year that I always look
   forward to.
5. He can find more ingenious excuses for not doing his
   homework than anyone I know.

SUMMARY

(1) A composition should be divided into paragraphs. Correct
    paragraphing helps the reader.
(2) A paragraph is a series of sentences developing one topic.
(3) The topic of a paragraph is usually stated in a sentence
    which is called the *topic sentence*. This sentence is usually

[4] From *The American Way of Life*, by H. U. Faulkner, T. Kepner,
and H. Bartlett. Reprinted by permission of Harper & Brothers.

the first one in the paragraph, although it may come at some other point.

(4) Every sentence in a paragraph must be closely related to the topic.

(5) In general, a paragraph is developed by means of *examples, details,* or *facts* supporting the topic sentence.

THE DESCRIPTIVE PARAGRAPH

A descriptive paragraph is usually developed by means of a series of *descriptive details* which together make up the picture the writer is trying to describe.

In the paragraph below about the tropical night, the author gives details which "paint" the picture introduced in the topic sentence. To the story writer this is a common way of building a paragraph.

It was a beautiful night, dewy and still and fresh, with a full moon rising above the palm trees on the Taravao isthmus. The road wound this way and that around the shoulders of the hills, now skirting the sea, now crossing the mouths of broad valleys where the *hupe* — the night breeze from the interior — blew cool and refreshing. I had glimpses through the trees of lofty precipices festooned with the silvery smoke of waterfalls and, on the left hand, of the lagoon bordered by the barrier reef where great combers, rising to break on the coral, caught the moonlight in lines of white fire. From native houses along the road came snatches of song, a strange mixture of airs, part French, part Tahitian, to the accompaniment of guitars, accordions, and mouth organs. On verandas here and there women were busy with their ironing, sitting crosslegged on the floor with a lamp beside them, and far out on the lagoon the lights of the fishermen were already beginning to appear.[5]

[5] From "Sing a Song of Sixpence" by James Norman Hall. Reprinted by permission of *The Atlantic Monthly.*

THE ORDER OF DETAILS IN A DESCRIPTIVE PARAGRAPH

When you have planned what you are to include in a paragraph and have written a topic sentence, you must decide in what order you will give the various details. The natural order in a descriptive paragraph is the order in which the various parts of the picture appeared to you. You may, of course, for the sake of clearness, describe your scene from left to right, foreground to background, top to bottom. On the other hand, you may go from picture to picture in whatever order you think most effective, provided you keep the reader informed as to where you are going. The use of "connecting" words and phrases will help the reader to follow you. Observe the use of the italicized "connecting" words in the following paragraph.

Football practice presents a lively and colorful picture. As I hurry down the gravel path toward the practice field. I can smell the crisp autumn air with its faint tinge of burning leaves. I hear *in the distance* the harsh cries of the coaches mingled with the high-pitched voices of the younger boys. I approach the field, and the scene, as I stop to take it in, presents a pageant of color and movement against a background of green grass and the orange glow of the setting November sun. *On my left* are the lightweights, scampering about, their shrill voices shrieking louder and louder. Leaping into position, they prepare for the play. One stout little fellow seems momentarily lost and stands bolt upright hesitating before he finds his place. In a sudden blur of colors the play swings *toward the right* and ends abruptly in a splash of maroon and gray jerseys, a milling pile bristling with legs and kicking feet. I hear the insistent wail of the whistle and watch the referee dive hard down into the wriggling mass to find the ball.

USE OF CONNECTIVES IN A DESCRIPTIVE PARAGRAPH

The following words and phrases will prove useful in making clear to the reader the location of each thing you are describing:

here, beyond, on my left, on my right, near by, opposite to, adjacent to, on the opposite side, in the distance, above, below

EXERCISE 5. Below are the skeletons of two descriptive paragraphs. Write the paragraphs, filling in the descriptive details suggested. Use connectives to make the order of details clear. Your ability to select vivid words will determine the effectiveness of your paragraphs.

1

Most American high school classrooms are alike. A row of windows.............. The blackboards.....
.... A bulletin board............... The teacher's desk .... Pupils' desks and chairs .... The American flag...............
This plan and these furnishings are repeated thousands of times in schools throughout the United States.

2

The village pond on a January afternoon presents many entertaining sights. The little tots "just learning" ......
.... Their older brothers and sisters..........
..... At the far end, within a roped-off space, the hockey players.............. Of course, weaving in and out and around are the lovesick couples who ....

EXERCISE 6. Select one of the following topic sentences and, by supplying descriptive details, build a descriptive paragraph presenting in full the picture introduced by the topic sentence. Use connectives to make the picture clear. Choose the best words you know to make the picture vivid.

1. Out of doors, we found as colorful a landscape as a clear autumn day could provide.
2. She presented a picture of complete misery.
3. The crowded beach was a confusion of sound and color.
4. The decorating committee had transformed the gym.
5. The fury of the storm was unbelievable.
6. Marcie's first day at high school was one she would never forget.
7. The river, which had risen to flood height, had destroyed the whole village.
8. The lion house in the zoo presented a fascinating picture at feeding time.
9. It was fun to watch Uncle Ned set up the trains he'd given Bobby for Christmas.
10. "My first date was wonderful," Barbara said dreamily.

THE EXPLANATORY PARAGRAPH

Creating a paragraph by giving details of information in support of the topic sentence is a technique which may also be used when you are *explaining* something. In the following paragraph John Muir is explaining the construction and operation of a large thermometer which he built when he was a young man. Read it carefully. Note the topic sentence at the beginning and how it is developed by additional details of information.

1

One of my inventions was a large thermometer made of an iron rod, about three feet long and five-eighths of an inch in diameter, that had formed part of a wagon-box. The expan-

sion and contraction of this rod was multiplied by a series of levers made of strips of hoop-iron. The pressure of the rod against the levers was kept constant by a small counterweight, so that the slightest change in the length of the rod was instantly shown on a dial about three feet wide, multiplied about thirty-two thousand times. The zero point was gained by packing the rod in wet snow. The scale was so large that the big black hand on the white painted dial could be seen distinctly, and the temperature read, while we were ploughing in the field below the house. The extremes of heat and cold caused the hand to make several revolutions. The number of these revolutions was indicated on a small dial marked on the larger one. This thermometer was fastened on the side of the house, and was so sensitive that when anyone approached it within four or five feet the heat radiated from the observer's body caused the hand of the dial to move so fast that the motion was plainly visible, and when he stepped back, the hand moved slowly back to its normal position. It was regarded as a great wonder by the neighbors, and even by my own all-Bible father.[6]

There is often no difference at all in method between a paragraph developed by examples and a paragraph developed by explanatory pieces of information. The paragraph which follows is really explanatory; yet, as you will see, it is developed by examples.

2

A study of the penmanship of your friends will reveal some interesting things. Women are usually neater with the pen than are men — perhaps because their sense of beauty is often higher and their patience greater. The age of a person, his condition of health, his tidiness, carefulness, determination, nervousness, and various other traits of his character are all more or less clearly revealed by penmanship. No two persons write alike. The letters

[6] From *Story of My Boyhood and Youth* by John Muir. Reprinted by permission of Houghton Mifflin Company.

which are written with the greatest variety of form are *F, S, T, H, I, M, L* and *r, s, t, e, o, a, d, p,* and *n.* You will be interested in comparing the ways in which you and your friends form these particular letters.[7]

The following paragraph is developed by giving details of information.

3

The simplest and most practical type of bridge for spanning a wide river is the suspension bridge. A suspension bridge is constructed on the simple theory that if you can string cables across a space, you can hang a bridge on them. The bridge consists of steel cables of great strength passing over high towers and anchored in the ground at each end. The platform for the roadway is suspended from the dipping cables by means of vertical cables. In order to keep the bridge from swaying, stiffening girders are installed under the roadway. Because a suspension bridge is not likely to be so stable as some other kinds, it has not always been practical for railways, whose rails must be kept in strict alignment; but modern suspension bridges are so firm that they can carry as many as eight railway tracks. The length limit of the main span of a suspension bridge, according to engineering theory, is about 7,000 feet. The George Washington Bridge across the Hudson River in New York has a main span of 3,500 feet.

THE ORDER OF DETAILS IN AN EXPLANATORY PARAGRAPH

Details in an explanatory paragraph should be arranged so that the reader can follow the explanation clearly from beginning to end. In general, one of two arrangements is used.

1. From the *familiar to the unfamiliar* or from the *easy-to-understand to the hard-to-understand:* This method is especially important when you are han-

[7] From "Are You Handy with the Pen?" by Julia W. Wolfe. Reprinted by permission of *Scholastic Magazines.*

dling new and difficult subject matter or vocabulary — making a scientific explanation, for instance. This is generally the order used by the authors of paragraphs 2 and 3 just above.

2. *Chronological order:* This is time order and is especially useful in explaining a process or an operation consisting of a series of actions. It is the order used by Mr. Muir in his explanation of how his large thermometer worked. (See page 225.)

CONNECTIVES IN THE EXPLANATORY PARAGRAPH

Connective words or phrases are especially useful in writing the explanatory paragraph which follows a chronological order. The following words will be helpful in keeping the time order clear:

first, second, third, finally, next, at the same time, similarly, likewise, for this purpose, then, thereupon

Observe the italicized connective words in the following chronologically arranged paragraph.

In building a brick wall, the *first* thing the builder must do is prepare a bed which is perfectly horizontal. *At the same time* he must be sure that the bed is firm enough to hold a wall without sinking. *For this purpose* cement or cement blocks may be used. On this foundation the bricklayer *next* builds up the ends or corners several layers high. *After* he has got these absolutely true, he stretches a line between the corners at the exact height of his first layer of bricks, and *then* lays the entire row to fit this line. He lays only a few layers of brick at a time all around the building or the full length of his wall because bricks are liable to settle and so carry the work out of plumb. *Finally* when his day's work is finished, the bricklayer covers his wall to protect it from excessive weathering during the drying process.

EXERCISE 7. The following topic sentences are the kind that must be developed by additional explanatory details of information. Select one that you think you know enough about and write an explanatory paragraph. Use connectives to keep the explanation clear.

1. In making a dress you should follow several distinct steps.
2. Buying materials for a model railroad requires experience and judgment.
3. Since it is the forward movement of an airplane that creates a vacuum over the wings, an airplane has no buoyancy when its motors die.
4. Mother taught me some important things about making a cake.
5. The make-up editor of a newspaper has to know a great many things.
6. The typical camp day keeps everyone busy almost every minute.
7. There are many things to think about when you drive a golf ball.
8. Sailing a boat is not so simple as it looks.
9. Organizing a club turned out to be more complicated than we had thought.
10. In learning how to dive, one must keep many things in mind.

THE NARRATIVE PARAGRAPH

Much of the writing that you do is devoted to telling what happened. This is narrative or story writing, and you divide it into paragraphs to make it clear and interesting to the reader. A narrative paragraph, however, does not need to be so carefully constructed as paragraphs in other kinds of writing. It is not always possible to have a topic sentence in every paragraph when you are relating an experience or telling a story. You change paragraphs when the action of your story shifts to a different scene, when you bring in a new character, when you wish to insert a descriptive passage, or when you change to a different time.

Nevertheless, even in story writing, you can often use the topic sentence and additional details effectively. The following are narrative paragraphs of this kind. Notice how the authors have begun their paragraphs with a general statement — like a topic sentence — and then have gone on to explain by giving further details.

1

About this time I found out the use of a key. One morning I locked my mother up in the pantry, where she was obliged to remain three hours, as the servants were in a detached part of the house. She kept pounding on the door, while I sat outside on the porch steps and laughed with glee as I felt the jar of the pounding. This most naughty prank of mine convinced my parents that I must be taught as soon as possible. After my teacher, Miss Sullivan, came to me, I sought an early opportunity to lock her in her room. I went upstairs with something which my mother made me understand I was to give to Miss Sullivan; but no sooner had I given it to her than I slammed the door to, locked it, and hid the key under the wardrobe in the hall. I could not be induced to tell where the key was. My father was obliged to get a ladder and take Miss Sullivan out through the window — much to my delight. Months after I produced the key.[8]

2

But the trick that set the town talking was her bowing to anyone I spoke to. "Lennie Steffens' horse bows to

[8] From: *The Story of My Life* by Helen Keller, copyright 1902. Reprinted by permission of Doubleday & Company, Inc.

you," people said, and she did. I never told how it was done; by accident. Dogs used to run out at us and the colt enjoyed it; she kicked at them sometimes with both hind hoofs. I joined her in the game, and being able to look behind more conveniently than she could, I watched the dogs until they were in range, then gave the colt a signal to kick. "Kick, gal," I'd say, and tap her ribs with my heel. Anyway, she dropped her head and kicked — not much; there was no dog near, so she had responded to my unexpected signal by what looked like a bow. I caught the idea and kept her at it. Whenever I wanted to bow to a girl or anyone else, instead of saying "Good day," I muttered "Kick, gal," spurred her lightly, and — the whole centaur bowed and was covered with glory and conceit.[9]

A narrative paragraph is almost always written in chronological order because, by its very nature, a story moves in the time order in which its events happen. The following words are commonly used in narrative writing to make the order of events clear: *first, second, third, finally, next, hence, therefore, consequently, as a result, meanwhile, at length, immediately, soon, afterward, after a few days, in the meantime, later, now.*

Observe the italicized connectives in the following narrative paragraph.

3

Now we all had leisure to notice two things. *First*, the movement had not been of the whole jam, as we had at first supposed, but only of a block or section of it twenty rods or so in extent. *Thus* between the part that had moved and the greater bulk that had not stirred lay a hundred feet of open water in which floated a number of loose logs. *The second fact* was, that Dickey Darrell had

[9] Reprinted from *Autobiography of Lincoln Steffens*, by permission of Harcourt, Brace and Company. Copyright, 1931, by Harcourt, Brace and Company.

fallen into that open stretch of water and was in the act of swimming toward one of the floating logs. That much we were given just time to appreciate thoroughly. *Then* the other section of the jam rumbled and began to break. Roaring Dick was caught between two gigantic millstones moving to crush him out of sight.[10]

EXERCISE 8. Write a good narrative paragraph developing one of the following topic sentences or one of your own creation.

1. Herb held the advantage throughout the first four rounds.
2. The blaze was nearly under control when we discovered that sparks had set the barn afire.
3. It looked for a minute as though our heroic efforts to rescue the animals were going to fail.
4. Bewildered as I was by the confusion of the county fair, I grew frantic when I realized that I had become separated from my father.
5. Anger in every line of his face, Mr. Strong strode into the auditorium.
6. All of a sudden I felt my ski strap break.
7. Down the hill came the driverless Ford, careening from side to side.
8. There I was, on my first date, facing a barrage of questions from Elsie's father.
9. There came a horrible burning smell from the kitchen.
10. Suddenly Terry growled and headed for the door.

THE ARGUMENTATIVE PARAGRAPH

Writing which expresses the author's opinions and argues in favor of them is argumentative writing. Newspaper editorials and the talks of some radio

[10] From "The Riverman," in *Blazed Trail Stories*, by Stewart Edward White, copyright 1902. Reprinted by permission of Doubleday & Company, Inc.

commentators are often of this kind. You yourself occasionally use this type of writing in your class tests when you are asked to give an opinion and to support it with facts learned in the course. The purpose of argumentative writing is usually to convince the reader that the author is right. You must present your arguments clearly if you wish them to be convincing.

The argumentative paragraph usually begins with a statement of the opinion to be supported in the rest of the paragraph. This statement is the topic sentence. There are several ways of supporting opinion. Perhaps the way most commonly used is the listing of facts or examples (evidence) in support of the opinion. A writer may also prove his point by giving reasonable arguments arrived at through logical thinking. A combination of evidence and reasonable arguments is probably the most effective. At the end of the paragraph you may wish to add a summarizing sentence to clinch your point.

The paragraph which follows is an argumentative paragraph. Notice how the author begins by announcing his opinion, then gives facts and examples in support of his argument.

If Claiborn High School is to be the best kind of high school, it will have to have a strong injection of school spirit now. The need for school spirit has been shown by the fact that the recent campaign to sell General Organization tickets barely reached its goal even after being extended two weeks and after every kind of argument had been brought out and shined up. Of course, you should buy G. O. tickets because they will admit you to all school functions at a real saving. But it ought not to be necessary to base this sales campaign on dollars and cents considerations. You ought to buy a G. O. ticket for one reason and only one — because your school needs this money and it is asking you to give it. Students should have enough school spirit to want to support their school in whatever it undertakes. It's easy enough to support a winning football team or a school dance because those things are fun, but the quieter, less spectacular support of the whole school's General Organization is even more important even though it isn't fun. A dose of school spirit injected into the bloodstream of every student in C. H. S. is what Dr. Commonsense recommends, and we hope he'll inject it.

THE ORDER OF IDEAS IN AN ARGUMENTATIVE PARAGRAPH

The order in which your examples, details, and arguments should be arranged in an argumentative paragraph will be determined by their importance. Usually, you should begin with the least important and work through to the most important, saving your most powerful argument or your most convincing evidence until the last, when you may present it as a kind of climax. Observe the arrangement of ideas *in order of importance* in the following paragraph.

I have very little use for the man who takes pride in his ability to keep himself aloof from other people and hides his talents from the world. Such a man not only exhibits a distastefully self-centered character, but he is a piece of useless timber in the social structure. For example, this hermit shows himself unwilling to pay for what he gets. I do not mean that he doesn't pay his bills. He must do that to avoid the law. I mean that all the things in civilization which make it possible for him to enjoy his comforts he owes to the efforts of others; yet he himself contributes nothing to others. He does not interest himself in the problems of society — in the poor, the suffering, the struggling. He does not strive to make the world any better. He creates nothing. As a result, he is of little good in the world or to the world. Therefore, I neither approve of him nor respect him.

CONNECTIVES IN THE ARGUMENTATIVE PARAGRAPH

The following words will be helpful in carrying the thought smoothly from one idea to the next in an argumentative paragraph: *moreover, first, second, third, finally, furthermore, in addition, then too, equally important, on the contrary, at the same time, hence, therefore, accordingly, thus, in fact*. Observe the use of connectives in the following argumentative paragraph.

There are several reasons why homework should not be assigned over the week-end. *First,* five days out of seven devoted to school are enough for teen-agers, who really do have other things to do besides study. *For instance,* when are we going to work on the lawn for Dad, clean house or run errands for Mother, go shopping, get outdoors, see a show, or just read that book we have been waiting to get into? *Second,* week-end homework must be left until Sunday night unless you're one of those rare souls who, after five days of school, can settle down to the books on a Friday night in spite of the movies, games, and dates which Friday seems to inspire. *Then, too,* week-end homework is so often either not done at all or so poorly done that teachers have nervous breakdowns all day Monday trying to work with students who don't have the vaguest idea what the lesson is all about. *In fact,* it would be easier on everyone if the assignment had never been given at all. *Finally,* you come back to school on Monday fresher, more willing to start in again, if you have had a clean break from school for two days. A change is good for everyone, and anyone knows what all work and no play does to Jack.

EXERCISE 9. Each of the following topic sentences can be developed into an argumentative paragraph. Choose one which interests you and write a paragraph. Use connectives to make your point of view clear.

1. To become a famous athlete can be very bad for a boy.
2. Seeing a moving picture of a great book is not a substitute for reading the book.
3. Personality is more important than beauty.
4. Every boy should be required to participate in at least one sport.
5. The legal driving age should be eighteen.
6. Eighteen-year-olds should be allowed to vote.
7. All public transportation should be run by the Federal Government.
8. A small college is preferable to a large state university.
9. I am against co-education.
10. We need a new school building.

EXERCISE 10. From an old copy of a newspaper or magazine, cut out three paragraphs which you consider good examples of what a paragraph should be. Underline the topic sentence (it need not be the first sentence) and underline the summarizing sentence at the end if there is one. Paste the clippings on a piece of notebook paper. Under each tell what kind of paragraph it is — descriptive, explanatory, narrative, argumentative — and tell how it is developed, whether by examples, details, facts, or arguments.

REVIEW EXERCISE A. Select one of the topic sentences given below and expand it into a paragraph, underlining the connective words you use.[11]

[11] Additional instruction and practice in paragraphing will be found on pages 254-61. There you will learn how to divide a composition into paragraphs and how to join paragraphs in a composition by using linking or transition words and phrases.

told his son that they had not long to wait. Over in a dim corner a talkative woman kept asking questions of her unfortunate victim and followed every question with a silly grin. At last, with a short blast of its whistle, the train came slowly into the station. Conversation increased in volume and rapidity as the people pushed forward toward the gates.

3

My Aunt Myra is strangely like a thunderstorm when she's angry. Like a bright, sunny day that is usually the prelude to a storm, Aunt Myra's normal disposition suddenly begins to cloud. As the day darkens and a few thunderclaps roll out, so Aunt Myra darkens and begins to explode. The bolts get more and more frequent until finally the rain begins. With Aunt Myra, however, it is a torrent of words punctuated with frequent roars of thunder. The end of her wrath, like the end of a storm, is usually sudden. The words end abruptly; the clouds linger for a while; then the sky clears.

4

During the first part of my three-hour trip through Mammoth Cave, I tried to imagine the effect on the first lone discoverer of the place of such a spectacle as I was witnessing. My imagination could not hold out, however, under the increasing pressure of man's complete commercialization of this monster. The guide was continually boasting of the marvelous attendance records the cave had enjoyed during the last one hundred years. Our party was subjected to photographing by a corporation which, through high-pressure salesmanship, practically forced us to buy a picture. All through the cave's many miles of winding tunnels and chambers, the walls were covered with the signatures and addresses of our predecessors. In fact, the guide seemed to consider these abrasions one of the cave's main attractions, as he pointed out historic signatures dated as far back as 1820. These many signs of commercialization make it virtually impossible for an imaginative soul to gain any adventure out of the Mammoth Cave.

5

Although I think my little sister talks too much, I must admit that she displays a great deal of personality. Her actions reveal her enormous vitality and her over-vivid imagination. I have yet to see her when she is not ready to go anywhere or do anything which might prove to be fun. She's always afraid that she will miss something. She never gets or will get left behind. The minute anyone even starts or considers going somewhere, you can hear that same sweet voice questioning, "Where are you going? Can I come?" Sometimes I am convinced that she is psychic. It makes no difference in what part of the house she is, you just can't mention a plan without being quizzed, or sneak out without a third degree. She actually gets excited about going to the store or even the station. Before each of these little jaunts, she spends several minutes of primping before a mirror. "Gosh! my hair looks awful, doesn't it, Mother?" That is Mother's cue for a compliment.

6

In one-design racing the first boat to cross the finish line wins, but not so in the handicap class. The handicap and one-design classes start the same way, but there the resemblance ends because the winner is not always the first boat to finish. The faster boats have to give the slower boats "time." For example, we will say that *Boat A* has given *Boat B* an allowance of five minutes. Suppose *Boat A* finishes first; if *Boat B* can finish within five minutes after *Boat A*, it wins. This system keeps the local math wizards busy all week figuring handicaps for a Sunday race. It isn't as much fun racing in the handicaps division because of the fact that the first boat over is not necessarily the winner. In one race last summer the winning boat came in forty minutes after the first boat to finish. Needless to say, the owner of the boat which finished first was very bad company for several days afterward.

7

The audience is as amusing as the film. For instance, the heroine is praying in church and the hero is trying to

slip her a note of warning that the villain is the organ
pumper in disguise. The audience rises in a body, frantically pointing to the hero and screaming, "Look! Right
in back of you!" If, on the contrary, the hero is being
bested by the villain, there are protests of, "Foul, foul!"
The audience, which is always two jumps ahead of the
story, sees the hero about to be killed, and all laugh un-
sympathetically. They know the bullet will be stopped
by a bag of gold in the right place, a medal of valor, or
some such trinket. The tale ends satisfactorily to everyone except a few callous souls like myself, who would like
to see our curly-headed boy left for buzzard-fodder for a
change.

8

As for the romantic picturesqueness of ranch life —
that comes in the evening. The cowboy with his guitar
(you'll seldom find one without some musical instrument)
stations himself at some point not far from the ranch
house and starts to play and sing. Pretty soon the ladies,
just out of curiosity, wander out to investigate and, as a
rule, stay out there for at least two hours. There is a
special appeal in a cowboy song, mostly in the way it is
sung. The songs are usually about ill-fated love and the
"gal who was untrue to me." The cowboy invariably
glances up at each member of his audience in turn, singing the words as though that particular part were meant
for her alone; and when the ladies finally retire, slightly
chilled and bitten but very satisfied, each one feels that
he was singing to her and no one else and that this is
going to be a nice summer after all. The cowboy retires,
smiling to himself and wondering idly whether it will rain
tomorrow so that he won't have to work.

9

*(The following paragraph is a revision of the poorly written
model on page 210.)*

The Army Air Force had a quantity of obsolete airplane
engines which they offered to schools. Our industrial arts
department asked for one of the engines, and one day a

large truck drove up to the school and in no time at all dumped two massive boxes on the drive. The generous army had sent *two* engines! After the shop classes had worked for hours unpacking the motors, the teachers beamed with pleasure, for now they really had something to show their students. With the help of nearly everyone, they began to move the heavy motors toward the door. There the shock came! Neither motor would go through! It took several days of outdoor work to tear down the motors, move them part by part into the shop, and finally reassemble them there. Before they had finished, the boys had learned more about airplane engines than they had ever expected to know.

II. PLANNING A COMPOSITION

The purpose of all your work in this book is improvement of your writing and speaking. Understanding sentences and how to make them clear, correct, and interesting is an important help, but being able to write good *sentences* is not enough. Nor is it enough to know how to organize a paragraph. You must be able *to plan a whole composition*, to *organize* your ideas for writing. Study of the suggestions made in this chapter should make it easier for you to write good compositions.

11a. Choose a subject you know something about.

Really good writing is possible only when you know well the subject you are writing about. If you choose to write on a subject about which you have only a small amount of information or in which you are not interested, the result of your work will be of little value even though the writing is technically correct.

When your teacher gives you a choice, choose a subject about which you know more than the average student knows. If you are expected to look up information on a subject before writing, don't be satisfied until you have gathered enough information to make an interesting composition. In other words, you can always write better if you are convinced that what you are saying is going to be worth reading. Avoid saying over again the same old things that everyone always says about the subject. No matter how *correctly* you write, your work will be unsatisfactory if what you say is commonplace.

POOR PARAGRAPH — CORRECTLY WRITTEN
BUT COMMONPLACE IN CONTENT

Everyone with normal ability should have a high school education. In high school you learn how to make a living, and since you are going to have to do some kind of work after you leave school, it is important that you have enough education to get a job. The first thing any employer asks you when you apply for a job is how much education you have had. Then, too, you live in a very complex civilization. To understand the world and to live properly in it, you must be able to understand what you read in the papers and hear over the radio. Furthermore, you cannot be a good citizen unless you know enough to vote wisely. Finally, a high school education will increase your enjoyment of life. Appreciation of good books and good music makes your life more enjoyable and makes you a better person. Certainly everyone should have the benefits of a high school education.

11b. Limit the subject.

Another way to make sure that your compositions are worth writing is to limit the subject enough so that you can cover it in the space and time allowed. For essays of two or three pages, you do not need a big subject. In fact, you should learn to choose a *part* of a subject to write about. Before choosing a subject to write on ask yourself first, *Do I know enough about this subject to write a worthwhile composition on it?* Second, *Is the subject narrow enough for a short theme? If not, how can I limit it?*

Notice how the following general topics may be subdivided into more limited topics.

General Topic: HIGH SCHOOL ATHLETICS

    Specific Topics
    The Value of High School Athletics
    Dangers of High School Athletics
    How to Succeed in High School Athletics

General Topic: GOOD HOUSEKEEPING

    Specific Topics
    Spring Cleaning
    The Care of Rugs
    An Efficient Kitchen
    Time-Saving Aids in Housekeeping

General Topic: CITY GOVERNMENT

    Specific Topics
    Are We Paying Enough for Our Schools?
    Is Our City Government Democratic?
    A Needed Change in Our City Government
    The Duties of the Mayor

11c. Determine the purpose of your composition.

When you set about narrowing a broad subject, you must usually decide exactly what is to be your purpose in writing. The topic *High School Athletics* is not a good topic because it does not indicate the purpose of the writer. *Values of High School Athletics* is a better topic because it does indicate the writer's purpose. The writer has taken a particular attitude toward his subject. He has a purpose. In this case the purpose is to show in what ways athletics in high school are valuable. The writer may even state his purpose at the beginning of his composition: "High school students learn many valuable things from taking part in athletics."

EXERCISE 1. Below are 10 composition subjects. Of these, 5 are too general; 5 are properly limited. Decide which of these subjects could be discussed in a short paper. For each of the 5 general subjects write out 3 narrower topics which show clearly your purpose in writing and can be covered adequately in a few pages. The following are subjects or topics, not titles.

1. Pioneer life in America
2. Necessary instruments in a small dance orchestra
3. Swing music
4. The qualities of a good umpire
5. Advice to a jaywalker
6. Modern education
7. Study habits I have developed
8. Fishing
9. Recent contributions of science
10. I like the *Post* (or any other magazine).

HOW OUTLINING HELPS

11d. Plan your composition before writing.

(1) List your ideas.

The first step in planning a composition is to list on paper all the ideas you have on the subject you have chosen. Write them down as they come to you as rapidly as you can, without worrying too much at this time about the value of the ideas or where you would include them in your composition. Later, when you are organizing, you can cut out those which you decide not to use. The important thing is to see what material you have to work with.

FIRST LIST OF IDEAS FOR A COMPOSITION
ON "OCTOBER"

Purpose: to tell why October is the best month of the year.

football	the welcome change from
soccer	summer heat
the county fair	clear and crisp days
big football games	invigorating air
the colorful outdoors	first-of-term hopefulness
school again	new subjects and teachers
new acquaintances	hiking
old friends	Halloween

(2) Group related ideas under headings.

The second step is to group related ideas in this list so that your plan will gradually develop into a few larger divisions. When you have grouped your ideas together according to the phase of the subject they deal with, you will be able to decide on the principal headings in your composition.

IDEAS FOR THE COMPOSITION ON "OCTOBER"
GROUPED UNDER HEADINGS

   I. fall sports
      football
      soccer
      hiking
  II. events
      county fair
      big football games
      Halloween

III. school again
    new acquaintances
    old friends
    new subjects and teachers
    first-of-term hopefulness
IV. weather
    welcome change from summer heat
    clear and crisp days
    invigorating air
    colorful outdoors

(3) Arrange ideas in order; make an outline.

The third step is to arrange the ideas in the order in which you will discuss them in your composition. Some subjects will require a certain order. If your composition contains happenings which follow one another in story form, you will have to follow a chronological order. If the various headings are of varying importance, you may arrange them with the most important coming last and the least important first. The material under one heading may be necessary for understanding the material under one of the other headings. Then you will have to put that first heading before the one which depends upon it.

If the ideas themselves do not determine the order in which they should come, you may decide yourself upon the most interesting and clearest arrangement.

Arranging your ideas in a definite order is the first step in making an outline. Besides showing the order in which the ideas come, an outline shows their relative importance. You will have main headings and subheadings under them. If you acquire the habit of making an outline *before* you write a composition, you will find the writing much easier and the result much clearer. *It is always a good thing to have a plan. Your outline is your plan.*

For most of the compositions you will write, a *topical* outline will be satisfactory. A *topical* outline is one in which the various items are *topics*, not complete sentences.

TOPICAL OUTLINE

OCTOBER

(The title is not included within the outline.)

Purpose: to tell why October is the best month of the year.

I. Weather
   A. Clear and crisp days
      1. Welcome change from summer heat
      2. Invigorating air
   B. Colorful outdoors
II. School again
   A. First-of-term hopefulness
   B. New acquaintances
   C. Old friends
   D. New subjects and teachers
III. Fall sports
   A. Football
   B. Soccer
   C. Hiking
IV. Events
   A. County fair
   B. Big football games
   C. Halloween

11e. Observe rules for form in making an outline.

(1) Place the title above the outline. It is not one of the numbered or lettered parts of the outline.

(2) Use Roman numerals for the main topics. Subtopics are

given capital letters, then Arabic numerals, then small letters, then Arabic numerals in parentheses, then small letters in parentheses. Study the outline form.

CORRECT OUTLINE FORM

I.
  A.
  B.
    1.
    2.
      a.
      b.
        (1)
        (2)
          (a)
          (b)

II. etc.

(3) Indent subtopics. Indentations should be made so that all letters or numbers of the same kind will come directly under one another in a vertical line.

(4) There must always be more than one subtopic because subtopics are divisions of the topic above them. When you *divide* you must have at least two resulting parts, because you cannot divide anything into less than two divisions.

INCORRECT OUTLINE

I.
  A.
    1.
II.
  A.
    1.

If you find yourself wanting to use a single sub-topic, rewrite the topic above it so that this "sub idea" is included in the main topic.

WRONG   D. New subjects
           1. New teachers
RIGHT   D. New subjects and new teachers

(5) For each number or letter in an outline there must be a topic. Never place an *A*, for instance, next to *I* or *1* like this: *I A* or *A 1*.

(6) A subtopic must *belong* under the main topic beneath which it is placed. It must be closely related to the topic above it.

(7) Begin each topic with a capital letter. You may place a period after each topic or you may not, as you wish. But be consistent. If you use a period after one topic, use a period after all of them.

EXERCISE 2. Copy carefully the skeleton outline given at the right below and place each of the topics in the list at the left in its proper position in the outline. The title is included among the topics.

	(TITLE)
Working indoors	I. . . . .
Mowing lawns	A. . . . .
Delivering newspapers	B. . . . .
Baby-sitting	C. . . . .
Working outdoors	D. . . . .
Clerking in a store	E. . . . .
Ways to earn spending money	II. . . . .
	A. . . . .
Delivering groceries	B. . . . .
Clerking in an office	C. . . . .
Waiting on table	D. . . . .
Washing cars	
Shoveling snow	

EXERCISE 3. The items in the unsorted list of ideas below can be grouped under the 4 main headings given before the list. On your paper write these main headings; then under each list the topics which properly belong there. Number, letter, and arrange in a correct outline.

CHARACTERISTICS OF A GOOD DRIVER

Main Headings
   maintains a courteous attitude
   obeys the law
   keeps his car in good condition
   drives carefully

Unsorted List
   stops at red lights
   courteous to other drivers
   keeps brakes in good condition
   keeps tires in good condition
   drives at moderate speed
   courteous to pedestrians
   signals clearly
   keeps lights in good condition
   parks only where parking is permitted

EXERCISE 4. Select a subject of interest to you and write a sample outline of a composition you could write on it. Mix up the topics in your outline and arrange them in a list. Bring this list to class for one of your classmates to rewrite in outline form.

EXERCISE 5. Below is a list of unsorted topics for a composition on *Producing a Play.* Study the list, group related ideas together, and supply suitable main headings. Write a neat, correct outline for the composition.

Finding a play with the right number of characters
Rehearsing the lines
Making scenery
Deciding on a serious or light play
Arranging the lighting
Rehearsing the acting
Getting properties

INTRODUCTION, BODY, AND CONCLUSION

11f. Every composition has a beginning, a middle, and an end.

This simple fact is called to your attention so that you will plan your composition with an introduction (the beginning), a body (middle), and a conclusion (end). As you may have noticed, the terms *introduction*, *body*, and *conclusion* do not belong in your topical outline. They are words which refer to the plan or organization of your paper; they are not topics to be discussed *in* the paper. Nevertheless, always have these three parts of an essay in mind as you plan your work.

The *introduction* is always important. It must be interesting enough to make the reader want to read more. It must state clearly the purpose of your composition. It should include any facts or pieces of information which the reader will have to know in order to understand your composition.

The *body* is really the composition itself. It must fulfill the purpose you have set out to accomplish. The body will usually be about three-fourths or more of your paper.

The *conclusion* may summarize what you have said. A summary should not, as a rule, be a listing of the main points. It should be a restatement of the main idea of your paper and should leave the reader with a feeling of completeness, as of a job now finished.

Very often in a short article one paragraph for the introduction and one paragraph for the conclusion will be enough.

EXERCISE 6. Read the composition *Eating in Bed* on page 260. Be able to show that the composition fulfills the requirements just given regarding the introduction, body, and conclusion of a composition.

11g. Divide your composition into paragraphs.

In Chapter 10 you can learn how to write a paragraph, but there the paragraph is considered as a unit by itself. Usually, however, a paragraph is part of a larger composition. Now is the time to consider the paragraph used in this way.

It may be that in the body of your composition you can devote one paragraph to each main heading in the outline. If so, the problem of dividing your work into paragraphs will be solved as soon as you have made an outline. On the other hand, you may have more paragraphs than main headings, if your paper is long enough, or you may have fewer paragraphs than main headings. In any case, *each of your paragraphs must be centered around one idea.* Every time you take up a new idea, begin a new paragraph. *Do not start a new paragraph without having a good reason for doing so.*

EXERCISE 7. When the passage below was originally written by Mr. Akeley, it contained four paragraphs. Read the passage through and, on the basis of what you have learned in Chapter 10 about paragraphs, decide where paragraph divisions should be made. Be ready to defend your decisions.

The elephant's trunk is the most remarkable organ any animal possesses. The arm of a man is notable because it may be swung about at any angle from the shoulder, but the elephant's trunk may be twisted and turned in any direction and at any point in its entire length. It is just as powerful in one position as in another. It is without bone — a great flexible cable of muscles and sinew, so tough that the sharpest knife will scarcely cut it. It is so delicate that the elephant may pluck the tenderest blade of grass, yet so strong that he may lift a tree weighing a ton and toss it about easily. With his great height and short, thick neck, the elephant would find it difficult indeed to feed if it were not for his trunk. However it enables him to secure the choicest morsels on the ground or in the treetops and to strip a whole forest of bark and branches, if he feels like it. With his trunk he has a most extraordinary ability to detect the faintest scent and to punish or kill an enemy. Since the elephant has something like a fair chance, elephant hunting, unlike a good deal of the shooting that is done in the name of sport, always seems to me a legitimate game. This splendid animal wields a pair of heavy weapons — his mighty tusks — each one of which may weigh as much as the average man; and they are backed by several tons of brute strength. With an agility and a sagacity not to be rivaled by any other beast of his size today, he is a worthy opponent for any sportsman. Elephant hunting is always a game full of interest and excitement, because the elephant is such a wise old fellow that the hunter never learns all of his tricks. Swiftly and surely the white man and the white man's rifles are getting the better of old Tembo. Everywhere is he compelled to retreat before the advance of civilization. But occasionally the African elephant has his innings; and when he does, he winds up the episode with a dramatic flourish of trunk and tusks that the most spectacular handling of a gun cannot rival. Every elephant hunter has known moments of nerve-torturing suspense — moments when his wits, his courage, and his skill with a gun have stood between him and an open grave. His opponent is adroit, fearless, resourceful, and possessed of tremendous strength. Of course, no one can put himself in the elephant's place and imagine the animal's feeling when it faces a rifle, but I am convinced that this great beast's attitude is one of supreme confidence. A man is handicapped, when he confronts a charging elephant, by his own state of mind. He knows he has "picked the fight." He knows he is the intruder. And he has a guilty feeling that creates in him a demoralizing fear that could never affect one who enters a contest with an absolute conviction of right.[1]

11h. Use *linking expressions* to bridge the gap between paragraphs.

One problem which arises in a composition of several paragraphs is the problem of bridging the gap between paragraphs. *The thought of your composition should flow steadily from paragraph to paragraph.* It should not be so abruptly shifted at the beginning of a new paragraph that the reader cannot see the connection between the idea in the paragraph he has just read and the one he is just beginning.

Writers frequently use *linking words*, therefore, to link paragraphs.

Familiarize yourself with this list of linking words. Using one of them in the opening sentence of a paragraph will show the reader the relationship between the paragraph he is starting and the one that he has just finished.

[1] From *Adventures in the African Jungle* by Carl and Mary L. Jobe Akeley. Copyright, 1930, by Mary L. Jobe Akeley. Reprinted by permission of Dodd, Mead and Company, Inc.

LINKING EXPRESSIONS

therefore	likewise
in spite of this	furthermore
consequently	in the next place
accordingly	however
as a result of this	as might be expected
similarly	an example of this
besides	finally
nevertheless	lastly
on the contrary	also
on the other hand	meanwhile
after all	soon
such	in spite of this

in other words

Read the 4 paragraphs which follow, and note
how the author has used linking words to bridge the
space between the ideas in one paragraph and the
ideas in the next.

1

Through the friendly aid of Harold Bixby, of St. Louis,
a businessman much interested in aviation, a number of
St. Louis citizens supplemented the fund that Lindbergh
had saved from his earnings and thus enabled him to set
about the purchase of a plane. He investigated various
types of machines and decided that the one best suited
for his purpose was a monoplane with a single motor.
The monoplane he considered more serviceable than the
biplane because of the lack of interference between the
wings, which enabled it to carry a greater load for each
square foot of surface at a higher speed. The single-
motored machine had much less head resistance and therefore possessed a greater cruising range.

2

Lindbergh *therefore* placed an order for *such a machine*
with the Ryan Airlines, of San Diego, California. The

plane was to be equipped with a Wright Whirlwind 200 horsepower radial air-cooled motor. It also was to have a small cabin to protect the pilot from storms, with a periscope for vision ahead and side windows for looking right and left. He watched the building of the plane and when it was completed found that it flew perfectly on its first test flight. In compliment to the men who had helped him to buy the plane he christened it the *Spirit of St. Louis.*

3

A number of accidents occurred *during this time* to aviators who were planning to compete for the Orteig prize. In April Lieutenant-Commander Noel Davis and Lieutenant S. H. Wooster were killed when their biplane *American Legion* crashed to earth in Virginia. The Fokker monoplane *America,* built specially for the flight across the Atlantic, was wrecked in New Jersey and its captain, Lieutenant-Commander Richard E. Byrd, and its pilot, Floyd Bennett, together with two others of the crew, were injured. In May, Lindbergh heard that the celebrated French war ace, Captain Charles Nungesser, and Major François Coli were preparing at Le Bourget Flying Field, outside Paris, to take off for New York. On May seventh the two French aviators started; storms were encountered; and although search was made of their route across the water and of lands where they might have landed, no trace was discovered of them or their plane.

4

Meantime, at Long Island Clarence D. Chamberlin was waiting for news of the French aviators before making his start. Richard E. Byrd was also working on his plane in preparation for the transatlantic flight. Then arrived Lindbergh in the *Spirit of St. Louis.* He made the journey from San Diego to St. Louis in a single flight and from there had sped to Roosevelt Field. He reached that place on the afternoon of May twelfth. Little was known about him as an aviator; he was said to be a skilled and daring western air-mail pilot. To those who greeted him he said he intended to try to fly from Roosevelt Field to Paris.[2]

11i. In the first sentence of a new paragraph, you may refer to the thought in the preceding paragraph.

A common method of bridging the gap between paragraphs is to refer in the beginning of a paragraph to what you have just said in the paragraph before. You may do this by using a pronoun — *this, these, that, those, such, it, them,* etc. — which reminds the reader of what he has just read. Suppose, for instance, that you have been writing about the accomplishments of a prominent athlete. You have said that he was a star in football. Then you begin your next paragraph by saying, "But *this* was not Bill's only sport. He was as fast and skillful on the basketball court as on the football field." The pronoun *this* refers to *football,* a key word in the preceding paragraph.

An even surer way of making the change to another idea in a new paragraph is to refer directly to the preceding paragraph, not by a pronoun but by mentioning again the principal idea in the preceding paragraph. In the case of Bill, you might say, "But outstanding as he was in football, Bill played basketball even better."

EXERCISE 8. Read the following informal essay written by a high school sophomore.

1. Select the sentence in the first paragraph which states the purpose of the essay.

[2] Adapted from *Historic Airships* by Rupert Sargent Holland. Used by permission of the publishers, Grosset & Dunlap, Inc.

2. Select the topic sentence of each paragraph.

3. Note that the concluding paragraph restates the idea of the entire essay.

4. Select the expression (word or phrase) at the beginning of each paragraph which links the thought with the paragraph below it.

EATING IN BED

There is no doubt that eating your meals from a tray is your greatest problem when you are sick in bed. Unless you have a table especially constructed to hold the tray, you encounter the greatest difficulty in putting yourself and your tray in a position which is comfortable yet practical for eating. During your illness you try all sorts of ways to hold your tray, none of which ever seem successful.

The first way you try is sitting up straight with your back held up by pillows and the tray lying on your lap, but there are numerous drawbacks to this position. For instance, if you have a cold, and during the meal you feel that irritation in your air passages which foretells a cough, your whole body involuntarily shakes. This turbulent eruption forces the milk and soup upward against the force of gravity, forming a display equal to that of Old Faithful at Yellowstone. During the following seconds you get the sensation of being under a waterfall. First you feel the burning soup splashing over your body, streaming down your neck, and running over your stomach. Accompanying this scalding spray are small droplets of milk which tingle and tickle your skin. By this time your anger has reached its zenith. You jump out of bed, throwing back the soaked covers, which carry the tray, food, and dishes to their destruction.

Another objectionable feature of this method of eating is that your back is not perpendicular to your legs but slants backward. In order to see your food, you must press your chin into your neck. Moreover, when you finally manage to adjust your body to this position, you discover that there is a great distance between your mouth and your food. However, you gamely try to transport your food to your chewer. This is not so difficult until you make a sad attempt to convey a spoon of soup over the vast area. No one can realize how unsteady his hands really are until he has tried this. When the bowl of soup is empty, you find that one-third of it has entered your mouth. The rest has been absorbed by that towel which you had so cautiously placed over you. If you are a frugal person, you can wring out the towel over your mouth and thus enjoy all your soup.

Another slight disadvantage of placing your tray on your body is that, during your meal, you will undoubtedly have that uneasy sensation in the skin which makes you want to scratch the affected spot. It is always impossible to reach this irritated part because of your awkward position. Thus you begin that tiring process of carefully removing the tray and gently placing it on some firm surface. By the time you have satisfactorily scratched yourself and again placed your tray back on your lap, your food is cold and your itching begins again.

Other ways of posing yourself on the bed for eating usually make you dependent upon your elbows for support. You may lie on your side supporting yourself with one elbow and shoveling your food with the other arm. Or you may be flat on your abdomen, raising yourself with both elbows. When in this position you carry the food upward as far as your wrists will stretch and then lower your head to meet the food. However, these methods also inflict torture. Your elbows and neck muscles become sore. When your right hand tires, you must clumsily eat with your left. When eating with your left hand, you encounter great difficulty in making the fork hit its target squarely.

These are some of the ways in which I have suffered in trying to discover a satisfactory manner of eating in bed. I hope others may profit by my experience.

— ED BUSH

EXERCISE 9. Examine a magazine or news-paper article. Mark any linking words or expressions which serve to connect paragraphs.

EXERCISE 10. Examine one of your assignments in history or some other subject and find the topic sentence in each paragraph.[3] Note how it helps you to grasp the thought of the paragraph. Topic sentences in your own paragraphs will help your readers too.

EXERCISE 11. Choose one of the following topics and write a three- to five-paragraph composition on it. Be sure that each paragraph contains a topic sentence. Include a linking word or expression in the opening sentence of all paragraphs except in the first.

1. On Never Knowing What Time It Is
2. Breakfast at Our House
3. The Tricks of Advertisers
4. My Favorite Comic-Book Characters
5. On Passing a Lifesaving Test
6. Juvenile Fiction
7. On Taking Care of Children
8. Our Neighbors
9. Getting Out the School Newspaper
10. On Being a Junior Counselor
11. If Advertisements Came True
12. The Traits of a Good Citizen
13. Classical vs. Popular Music
14. The Values of Being a 4-H Club Member
15. My Favorite Elementary School Teacher
16. On Learning to Dance
17. Me
18. How I Do My Homework

[3] For discussion of topic sentences, see pages 214–19.

COMPOSITION MATERIALS

The way to learn to write is to write. Before you write, you must have something to write about. The following six assignments will suggest subjects.

The check list below is for use *before* and *after* you write. Use it *before* to remind you of the *techniques* of good writing. Use it *afterward*, before you write the final copy of your composition, to help you detect *weaknesses* in your writing.

COMPOSITION CHECK LIST

1. Logical organization?
2. Proper division into paragraphs?
3. Complete sentences?
4. Clear sentences?
5. Varied sentences?
6. Correct punctuation?
7. Topic sentences?
8. Choice of words?
9. Spelling?
10. Interesting and appropriate title?

1. A Character from Life

Just because you like to talk about others doesn't mean that you are a gossip. Everyone knows that there is nothing more interesting in the world than people; it's human nature to think about their peculiarities, their beauty or homeliness, the strange things they do. Maybe you don't talk about the people you know. If you don't, then you're different, and not talking about others is certainly one of *your* own peculiarities.

But have you tried your hand at *writing* about someone, putting him down on paper exactly as he is, and then taking a good look at him? You'll find it an entertaining experience, sometimes a very helpful one, for afterward you'll be sure to understand him better.

Remember Aunt Jane, who for forty years refused to eat breakfast? She said breakfast didn't agree with her. But after having lunch with her a few times, you discovered how she made up for the meal she missed. You know Mr. Timeline, the social studies teacher? He's always in a fog, you say. Well, is he really? Maybe he's thinking about that new development in Europe or what Lincoln said to McClellan. You know how much fun his classes are, too. Remember the time he got so excited pointing out local geography that he nearly fell out the window?

Of course, if you think it's safe, you can write a word picture of Joe Blair. He's a pretty good friend, but he surely does bother you sometimes. That voice that always seems to be changing, that crew haircut, that grammar!

Somebody you know will make a good subject for a sketch. Try your hand at writing one. Can you make your reader know the subject of your sketch as you know him? Can you make your subject as interesting to others as he is to you?

SUGGESTIONS

1. You can show what a person is like in several ways.

    a. By telling what he says and how he says it
    b. By describing typical actions
    c. By describing the person's appearance

2. Include some incidents (actual happenings) in your sketch. Select incidents which will show the character

traits you want to show. Your reader will be much more interested in reading of actual occurrences in which your character had a part than he will be in a formal description of your character's personality.

3. Begin with an incident, or, if you wish, with an arresting fact. Above all, do not begin by saying, "The person I am going to write about is ....." The following beginnings would be good:

   a. "Duck, everybody! Here comes Self-Importance."

   b. Two hundred pounds of pure fat may not appeal to you, but it is the physical structure of the best-natured man that ever forgave an icy snowball.

   c. She's pretty, she's graceful, she's charming, she's smooth!

2. A Character from Literature

In the same way that most of us spend a good part of our conversational hours learning *about* our friends *from* our friends, so we spend a good part of our reading hours reading about other people in books. Indeed the characters we read about are often more vivid than the people we actually know. Very often we know so much more about the novelist's or the biographer's characters because the writer has told us more things about this character than we know even about the members of our own family.

In your memory you cherish the acquaintance of many people whom you have read about. Some you admire; some you hate; some you love; some you can't understand. How many of the following do you *know?*

PEOPLE FROM FICTION

Winnie the Pooh	Jo
Sue Barton	Old John Silver

   David Copperfield Penrod
   Scrooge   Captain Bligh
      Sidney Carton

PEOPLE FROM REAL LIFE

   Orville Wright   Theodore Roosevelt
   Richard Byrd   Robert E. Lee
   Dwight Eisenhower Louis Pasteur

Perhaps you have recently read about a character who made a deep impression upon you. Maybe he was a fictional character; maybe he was a hero of World War II, or a hero of science or medicine. Plan a sketch of this character. Lift him right out of the book. Make him appear to be as real to others as he is to you.

SUGGESTIONS

1. Summarize by giving your general impressions. Don't try to write the whole book over again. Determine the two or three main qualities, or even only the one main quality, of the person. Build your composition around these qualities. Was your character brave, clever, ruthless, cruel, selfish, funny, brilliant, strong? Make your character's *outstanding* quality *stand out*.

2. Tell incidents in your character's life which will illustrate the truth of what you are saying about him. You will be able to include only three or four such incidents; therefore, select them carefully. Make the reader see why this person interested you so much that you chose to write about him.

3. Do not write a book report. Leave out the *whole* life story. Never mind all the interesting things you found in the book unless they are important to the points you are making about this one person.

4. Don't begin by saying, "Robert E. Lee was born at Stratford, Virginia, on January 19, 1807."

Better: "A noble gentleman first, a skillful general second — that was Robert E. Lee."

5. Polish up your adjectives. One well chosen adjective is worth ten poorly chosen ones. This composition will test your fund of adjectives.

Now, let's hear about your hero — or your favorite villain!

3. A Look at Ourselves

How good is your sense of humor? Can you laugh at yourself? Can you see some of the crazy things you and your crowd do, as your parents or your teachers may see them? How well do you know the modern adolescent? After all, you are one.

Put yourself and your friends into writing. Take a good look at *all* of you as you really are. Do you think the radio programs about boys and girls your age are true to life? Are the movies doing wrong by our high school students? What *are* you like, anyway?

This is not an assignment requiring you to write a serious essay about teen-agers. Rather it is an assignment to give a word picture of them in action. *Show,* don't *tell* what they do, how they talk, where they go, what they look like.

To do this you must decide two things first of all. (1) What is the *scene* of your picture to be? The locker room? the soda fountain? the study hall? the lunchroom? the movies? a dance? a pajama party? Pick a place where your characters will be seen just as they are, talking as they really do talk — pull no punches here — looking as they actually do look.

(2) You must have a chain of actions for your characters to perform. Maybe the best way would

be to look around you today. Watch them with an author's eye. What exactly do they do?

SUGGESTIONS

1. Don't have too many characters. Three or four will be enough for a short composition. Identify your characters early by giving a distinguishing characteristic of each. Betty has blonde hair and big blue eyes. Jack thinks he's funny. (He certainly wasn't funny the afternoon he tried to make his own soda. Mr. Krip's mirror still has spots on it!)

2. Make the setting clear in the beginning.

3. Start out with the action, not with a general description.

POOR BEGINNING   I am going to describe some of the things I saw in the cafeteria the other day.

BETTER BEGINNING   "Hi, Mary!" Sam Ingalls dropped from nowhere into the chair beside me. The mouthful of potato salad I had just taken in nearly exploded on my tray. "What's up?" he beamed.

4. The dialogue may very well make or break your composition. Make it natural. Perhaps you'd better look over pages 440–43 before you write any conversation, just to get the punctuation and paragraphing right.

Get busy on adolescents in action, as they really are!

4. How They Do Talk

Yes, how *do* they talk? Who are *they?* Anybody you want them to be — that couple that sat in the seat ahead of you in the bus the other day, for instance. You weren't eavesdropping. You just couldn't help hearing them. Yes, they certainly "had it bad." Try, if you wish, to reproduce their conversation. Maybe you and your family trying to get started in the morning, or the fateful hour when you met *her* parents on that first big date, would provide a more interesting dialogue. The purpose of this assignment is to give you practice in writing *dialogue* — conversation which will reveal the personalities of people who do the talking.

Did you listen in when your mother had callers a little while ago? Could you tell what each woman was like from what she said and the way she said it? Did you hear your father chatting about politics with the neighbor the time Dad got so excited? Maybe you can imagine two seniors talking about their boy friends or two freshmen talking about whatever two freshmen talk about. Did you ever think that two of your teachers might talk about *you?* Your task is to show, through what your characters say and how they say it, what kind of people they are.

SUGGESTIONS

1. Choose characters whose manner of talking you really do know — people that have distinct personalities — people that are "characters."

2. Let the dialogue carry the whole composition. The less you have to describe, the better. Most people describe themselves when they talk.

3. Make your dialogue natural. Let your people interrupt each other occasionally. Let them speak in words and phrases. We seldom use complete sentences in conversation.

4. You needn't use *said, replied, added*, etc., after every speech. Occasionally, give the speaker's action.

    a. "So I says to her, I says, 'You've got a lot of nerve.'" *Mamie's eyes burned with the memory.*

    b. "Look here, Al, I don't know where you get such crazy ideas." *Mr. Martin emphasized the remark by crushing in his fist the tomato he had just proudly picked in his garden.*

c. "Well, if *he* isn't a fresh customer!" *Arlene snapped her gum a little to show her indignation, and leaned over the showcase.*

d. "Where did you get that hat?" *Father dropped his newspaper.*

"Don't you love it, Carl? I just bought ....."

"You just *bought* it? You mean you paid money for ....."

"Now, Carl, you know I needed a hat." *Mother began her defense.*

5. Begin by setting the scene. Your first sentences may be dialogue and also give the *time* and *place*.

"Look, Helen, here are two seats." I was startled out of the first scene of the second feature by a high-pitched voice at my elbow.

6. Review the rules for punctuating and paragraphing dialogue on pages 440–43.

5. *Have You an Heirloom in Your Home?*

Now that you've looked up *heirloom* to find out what it means, you are ready to begin work on an heirloom assignment. Somewhere in nearly every home there is an article that is cherished and preserved year after year because it has a story behind it. This is called an heirloom assignment because such an article usually is an heirloom — handed down through the family for generations. But the article need not be an heirloom at all. As long as it has a story, it's material for this assignment.

It might be a pair of silver candlesticks, an old-fashioned home candle mold, a pair of hand carved earrings, a beautiful shawl (smelling of moth balls!), a big case watch, a hickory cane, a set of combs brought over from the old country by great-grandmother Wiggins. It might be a letter from great-great-grandfather to great-grandfather, written when the country was young and great-grandfather was pioneering on his new land. Or it might be a discharge paper from the Army, a silver loving cup, a beribboned medal, a mellow violin, a miniature portrait, or one of those amazing pictures from the family album with beards on the men and hoopskirts on the women.

You can see that this is one composition in which it will be all right for you to get your parents' help. Ask at home whether there is some article in the house — the attic usually yields any number of them — that has behind it an interesting story. When you've found something that will do, write a composition describing the article briefly and then telling its history. Interview your mother on this. She probably knows a lot of things that you can use, if you can draw them out of her.

When you have written your composition, bring the article you've written about to class, and show it to your classmates when you read your paper. Your teacher may wish to divide the class into smaller groups for this reading. It will take less time that way, and everybody will have a chance to read. Perhaps the best paper in each group can be read before the whole class.

Don't give up too easily in your search for an heirloom. Of course, if all you can find is the six-foot grandfather's clock that hasn't run for years, you'll not do very well at bringing it to class, but you can write a good account of it anyway. Should you be completely baffled, however, in your search for an heirloom, you may choose some object of modern interest provided it has a story. Something you made, perhaps, or bought the summer the whole family took an automobile tour in Canada. You need not limit yourself to heirlooms. They were suggested because they usually have a story behind them.

SUGGESTIONS

1. A good way to begin would be to describe the article you're writing about. See page 222 where the descriptive paragraph is discussed. On the other hand, you may prefer to begin at the beginning of the story, producing the article at the end as a kind of climax.

2. Your composition will be largely explanatory and narrative — explanatory when you're telling how the article was used, and narrative when you're giving the story behind it. (For discussion of explanatory and narrative writing, see pages 225 and 229.)

3. Plan carefully so that the events will come in order, and you won't have to insert "afterthoughts." If the rusty pistol you found was used by a great-uncle when he went hunting in the Rockies, don't wait until the end of your story to say that this was in 1890. Keep a *time* order.

4. You may, quite properly, add any comments of your own. If it occurs to you that the girls in other days must have been very uncomfortable in those heavy shawls and hoopskirts, say so. You can add spice to your composition by giving it this personal touch. Or, if you think Aunt Sarah, whom you, of course, never knew, looks like the sourest old lady in the picture, say so. There'll be no harm done, either, if you improve your story by an occasional dash of imagination. It will be a better story.

All right, let's hear about the key-winding watch that belonged to Great-Grandfather Stewart, who was never late to an appointment in his life!

6. What's Your Idea?

Every thinking person has a head full of ideas. Some of them aren't worth much; some of them are very good. You probably have a few pet ideas that, at times when you're alone, you think about and develop and criticize. Take out one of these ideas and write it down for this composition.

Be serious about it. Don't waste your time on a trifling notion, but try seriously to explain the idea you really believe in. Do you think the marking system is fair? That's an old chestnut, but you may have strong feelings about it. Do you approve of radio commercials? Granted that business concerns give us good entertainment in return for a chance to advertise, have you a better idea for their commercials? Maybe you think school should be held in July and August and the usual vacation time distributed evenly through the year. Could you suggest something to make Sunday School or church more attractive to young people? What's the greatest need of the world today? What's *your* idea?

In case your head may not be bursting at present with an important theory, you may find material in the daily newspaper, a magazine, or on the radio. Wherever you go, whatever you read, you are always forming opinions. These opinions can often be developed into really important ideas which you can easily sign, seal, and deliver as an English composition.

SUGGESTIONS

1. Before you begin to write, plan in detail what you are going to say.

    a. Define your purpose.

    b. List the ideas or arguments that will support your purpose.

    c. Organize these ideas into a brief outline.

2. Convince your reader that your idea is a good one. You can judge your success by the reactions of your classmates to your composition.

3. Don't be entirely critical. Spend most of your composition building up your theory. If you are proposing a better way for the city to keep its young people off the streets and out of trouble, devote most of your composition to explaining this better way — not to criticizing the present unsatisfactory method.

TOPICS FOR COMPOSITION

The topics collected in this list are intended as suggestions. If you find one that you could write on if it were changed a little, change it to suit your wishes. Word your own title.

People

1. The people who wait at our bus stop
2. Our druggist
3. My favorite old lady
4. Betsy is charming
5. Little Joe
6. My doctor
7. Our pet policeman
8. The postman knows everything
9. Mother is the president this year
10. Personally, I like the English (French, etc.)
11. Robin Hood is my favorite character
12. Patty's name just fits her
13. Aunt Jane was never young
14. An American ace
15. Father remembers when he was a boy
16. A champion
17. The school nurse
18. Emil drives our school bus
19. Jack is a picture when he is studying
20. Midge learns to skate
21. My favorite movie star
22. Brats
23. A teacher I'll never forget
24. My best friend
25. My favorite radio entertainer

26. My favorite radio news-caster
27. My little brother (sister)
28. A hero I know
29. A hero I have read about
30. The typical baseball fan

Personal

1. What happened to our dog
2. My kid brother struggles
3. I applied for a Saturday job
4. By their hats shall ye know them
5. The best party we ever had
6. My most memorable bus ride
7. The innocent often get caught
8. How to be unpopular
9. They called it initiation!
10. On keeping busy
11. Earning my own spending money
12. On being interrupted
13. My favorite meal
14. Getting along with my family
15. I remember a childhood experience
16. Breakfast at our house
17. My moods
18. Daydreaming
19. A chapter from my autobiography
20. Our family customs
21. Our family traditions
22. The family album
23. My afternoon in the beauty shop
24. I pack my own trunk
25. My first corsage
26. On dresses — past and present
27. Then my voice broke!
28. How to be a good friend
29. How to keep healthy
30. The movies taught me this
31. We train our puppy
32. I wish I knew . . . . . (any person)
33. I like to knit
34. I can't resist new shoes!
35. Why I want to be a nurse
36. The family clutters up my closet
37. What I plan to do with my savings bonds
38. My greatest mistake
39. My conscience is very alert
40. How to become a good hostess
41. My fluctuating bank account
42. I never could get away with anything
43. It turned out to be measles!
44. Saturday is the best day of the week
45. I'd rather live in the country (in the city)
46. I tried mental telepathy

47. My struggles with my diary
48. On being a big sister (brother)

Occasions

1. When I earned my first Scout badge
2. I learn to milk a cow
3. My first violin lesson
4. The dust storm
5. Did my hair curl!
6. Pete masters the art of conversation
7. Our cuckoo clock and the minister
8. The last pep rally
9. And *I* came in overalls!
10. My only visit to Ye Olde Antique Shoppe
11. *There* was a pillow fight!
12. My sister learns to drive
13. Quarantined — with no food in the house!
14. What the hurricane did
15. Sunday morning at our house
16. The tennis tournament
17. And the darned monkey *bit* me!
18. We planted a new lawn
19. The day I kept house
20. I misread the timetable
21. And then the fuse blew out!
22. Our church dresses up for Christmas
23. We moved to a farm

24. I found five dollars
25. Emily makes the debating team
26. The family all helped cook
27. When I walked on air
28. I'll never lend my bike again
29. When we ran over the suitcase
30. Don said *anyone* could make brownies
31. Now I avoid revolving doors
32. Driving in a sleetstorm
33. When Cue had puppies
34. And I was unprepared
35. The neighbors' child comes to call
36. When I got into the wrong house
37. My first big fight
38. I repair the plumbing
39. I fixed *him*
40. My first date

School

1. On being a good cheerleader
2. I imagine King Arthur
3. Louie's first sight translation
4. I believe in trying
5. My Latin book and I
6. When to start preparing for college
7. Systematic vs. random reading
8. How to use the library
9. Getting out the school paper

10. English — my native tongue
11. How words get into our language
12. We plan a radio program
13. How to study your lines for a play
14. Fascinating quicksilver
15. For once, I won't blame the teacher
16. What vitamins do for you
17. Once I tried to bluff
18. The future of uranium
19. How to study for a test
20. Streptomycin and what it cures
21. How to memorize
22. We see a Shakespearean play
23. Why we study mathematics
24. My first experience with stage fright!
25. Our club was in the red
26. On homework in general
27. And *I* was in charge of the lights!
28. Stage make-up
29. Arranging an exhibit
30. Now I understand algebra
31. How to make a poster
32. Teachers are funny
33. Father said he knew the answers
34. Building a vocabulary
35. I finally have a homework system
36. Our school paper
37. Fifth period lunch
38. Wonderful thing, the dictionary
39. What do teachers do in their spare time?
40. Why read?
41. Spanish finally makes sense
42. The typical student in our school
43. Petty thievery at school
44. You should see our locker room
45. Our class visits a factory
46. My chemistry project
47. The breaks of the game
48. Sportsmanship in our school
49. The football season
50. On being a second-string player
51. Needs of this school
52. School politics
53. Qualities of a good public speaker
54. Courtesy in school

Places

1. The lake in the moonlight
2. Main Street at 9:00 Saturday night
3. Our classroom was a shambles
4. We went to Washington!
5. My first sea voyage
6. The kitchen on Saturday morning

7. The view from our cabin
8. Dad's study — or the Den of Dollars
9. The hot dog roast on the beach
10. Our cabin was unbelievably tiny
11. The zoo on a rainy day
12. The cabin at the lake
13. The drugstore at 4:30 in the afternoon
14. The old Indian village
15. The Alcan Highway
16. A hotel lobby
17. Bargain basement sale
18. Our library
19. The story of Old Faithful
20. The doctor's waiting room
21. The harbor
22. The place I like best
23. Our town
24. A room with a view

Out of Doors

1. My encounter with a bull
2. On riding a horse
3. Never use a suitcase for a picnic lunch
4. The compass that didn't
5. I took to the air — on my bike
6. Growing my favorite flowers
7. We decorate for Christmas
8. The pageant
9. After Taps at camp

10. Painting Rover's doghouse
11. Chopping down the old apple tree
12. The overnight hike
13. Have you ever slept outdoors?
14. My first try at ice-skating
15. An hour watching the panda at the zoo
16. I'll never do a half-gainer
17. The mosquitoes *like* me
18. I imagine the Wild West
19. The campfire at Lake Winonaga
20. Caught in a blizzard
21. Advice to a young camper
22. The values of scouting
23. On being a tenderfoot
24. The art of trout fishing
25. My first hunt
26. Trapping

Hobbies

1. Did you ever raise guinea pigs?
2. How we changed our back yard
3. Painting the kitchen
4. My first experience with card tricks
5. We make our own costumes
6. Make-up — good and bad
7. Snakes are interesting
8. We made our own canoe

9. Collecting old labels (or anything else)
10. How to care for goldfish
11. I save my picture postcards
12. One summer I caddied
13. How to learn the crawl stroke
14. I knit for the Red Cross
15. Some day I hope to be a pianist
16. Make your own
17. My hobby is educational
18. Tips for stamp collectors

Miscellaneous Informal Subjects

1. Telephone manners
2. Teen-agers and the telephone
3. Radio quiz programs
4. Kids' programs on the radio
5. On radio commercials
6. Radio thrillers
7. Keeping up with baseball
8. We go to the attic on rainy days
9. My favorite ghost story
10. The county fair
11. Adventures in our bird bath
12. The slang we use
13. On making friends
14. Privileges that come with being trusted
15. The Boy Scouts
16. I pretend I am a famous person
17. Comic books
18. What's wrong with the movies
19. We never found out who it was
20. On "casting bread upon the waters"
21. The contents of his pocket
22. Parents are human, too
23. My latest discovery
24. Why we are taught good manners
25. I correspond with a French girl
26. And then the old sailor told his story
27. On introducing a stranger to your friends
28. The first Fourth of July
29. Southern customs
30. Anticipation is greater than realization
31. Some advertisements are silly!
32. On courtesy
33. Virtue is rewarded
34. The missionary told his story
35. How to wash a sweater properly
36. Honesty *is* the best policy
37. Superstitions and their effects on us
38. Making habits work *for* you.

12. USING THE LIBRARY

Few of the things you learn in school will be of more value to you than learning how to use the library. An educated person, someone has said, is a person who knows where and how to find out what he wants to know. If this is true, a thorough acquaintance with the library is an important part of your education, for the library contains the information you want to know. This chapter will help you to find your way in the library.

HOW A LIBRARY IS ORGANIZED

Since a library is a collection of books on all sorts of subjects, there must be a method of organizing or arranging these books so that it will be easy to find any volume you want. Most libraries today arrange their books according to the Dewey system, a system developed by Melvil Dewey, an American librarian. Anyone who wishes to find his way around a library using the Dewey system of classifying books should be familiar with the general nature of that system.

FICTION

In most libraries fiction books (novels and stories) are arranged alphabetically by the authors' names, and the books are placed on the shelves in this alphabetical order. If you wish to find a novel by John Tunis, you will find out first on which shelves the fiction books are standing. Then you will locate the books whose authors' names begin with T, and among these you will find the books by Tunis.

NONFICTION

But books of fiction are only a part of the total quantity of books in a library, and the other books (nonfiction) are arranged according to a number system. Whenever a new book is added to the library, the librarian writes on the back of the book its proper number. As a result, all books on the same subject will be placed together, making it easy for you, once you have found the proper number of the subject you are looking up, to find all the books the library owns on this subject. For example, all books about radio are given the number 621.38.

The classifications with the numbers that stand for them are as follows:

DEWEY DECIMAL SYSTEM

According to this plan, all books are grouped in ten subject classes.

000–099	General Works (includes encyclopedias, periodicals, etc.)
100–199	Philosophy (includes psychology, conduct, etc.)
200–299	Religion (includes mythology)
300–399	Social Sciences (includes economics, government, law, etc.)
400–499	Language (includes dictionaries, grammars, etc.)
500–599	Science (includes mathematics, chemistry, physics, etc.)
600–699	Useful Arts (includes agriculture, engineering, aviation, etc.)

700–799   Fine Arts (includes sculpture, painting, music, etc.)

800–899   Literature (includes poetry, plays, orations, etc.)

900–909 ⎫
            ⎬ History
930–999 ⎭

  910–919   Travel

  920–929   Biography

THE SUBDIVISIONS

Within each of these classifications there is an unlimited number of subdivisions. As an example of how the numbering is done, let's take a book of poetry by the American poet, Robert Frost, and see how it would be classified. Poetry falls in the 800 (literature) classification. Since the numbers 810–819 are reserved for American literature, the book's number will begin with the two digits 81. The third digit in the number indicates the classification of the book — in this case, poetry. The number for poetry is the number 1, and so with this added to the number 81, the classification number becomes 811. (Small libraries class American and English poetry together under 821, the classification number for English poetry.) Added to this is the letter F, for Frost. Your librarian can explain further details of this remarkable, but complex, system of classifying books; the principal facts given here are enough to show you how the system works.

THE CALL NUMBER

The number by which the book is classified is known as the *call number*. To find the call number of a book you look up the book in the card catalog. The call number is located in the upper left hand corner of the catalog card.

The call number is useful to you in two ways.

1. You can find out where on the library shelves the books of any particular number classification are located. By going at once to the shelves containing books with the number of the one you want, you can, in a few moments of looking along the shelves, find your book.

2. In a large library where books are kept in the "stacks" so that you cannot look for the book yourself, you tell the librarian the call number of the book you want, and he will send for it.

HOW TO LOCATE A BOOK IN THE LIBRARY: THE CARD CATALOG

In every library there is a chest of small drawers containing cards. These cards represent the books in the library. In the average well-indexed library there are usually three cards for each book. They are the *author card*, the *title card*, and the *subject card*.

THE AUTHOR CARD

The author card, as its name suggests, has the author's name at the top. You may find any book by looking it up under the author's name, and this way of locating the book has the added advantage of leading to all the books the library owns by this author. For instance, if you have read one book by Robert Louis Stevenson and you would like to know what other books of his the library owns, you will find cards for all of them arranged in alphabetical order of their titles, all with *Stevenson, Robert Louis* at the top of the card.

551.5
F

Finch, Vernor Clifford, 1883–

Elementary meteorology, by Vernor C. Finch ... Glenn T. Trewartha ... M. H. Shearer ... and Frederick L. Caudle ... New York and London, McGraw-Hill book company, inc. ₍1942₎

x, 301 p. illus. (incl. charts) diagrs. 23½ᶜᵐ.

"The authors have taken a substantial portion of the opening chapters of ₍their₎ The earth and its resources as a basis for this book."—Pref.
"References" at end of each chapter.

1. Meteorology.   I. Trewartha, Glenn Thomas, 1896–   joint author.   II. Shearer, Merle H., joint author.   III. Caudle, Frederick L., joint author.   IV. Title.

Library of Congress   ◯   QC863.F47   42—25429

₍45z5₎   551.5

AUTHOR CARD

Biographies are arranged on the shelves according to the person they are written about. Cards for books *about* an author are placed in the catalog *behind* the cards for books written *by* this author.

THE TITLE CARD

At the top of the title card is the title of the book. If you wish to find out whether a certain book is in your library and what its call number is, you may thumb through the card catalog in which title cards are alphabetically placed. In its proper alphabetical position as determined by the first word of the title, you will find the card. (If the first word of the title should be *the*, *an*, or *a*, the book will be listed under the second word in the title.)

Much useful information is given on a card in the card catalog. Not only can you find the call number and the author's name, but sometimes the date of his birth (and death), and occasionally a very brief statement about what is in the book. In many cases

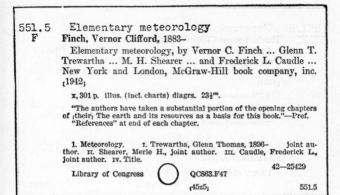

TITLE CARD

the card will also tell you the number of pages in the book and the illustrator, if the book is illustrated. You can also find the name of the publisher and the date the book was published.

THE SUBJECT CARD

Books are also catalogued according to the subjects they deal with. If you want to find out what books your library has on *model railroads*, you could look up *model railroads* in the card catalog. There you will find in one place a card for each book in the library on this subject.

"SEE" AND "SEE ALSO" CARDS

Occasionally when using the card catalog you will find what is known as a "see" card or a "see also" card. A "see" card is one which refers you to another part of the catalog for the information you are seeking. For instance, suppose that you are looking up material on various vocations. You look

---

551.5   Meteorology
F   **Finch, Vernor Clifford, 1883–**
        Elementary meteorology, by Vernor C. Finch ... Glenn T.
Trewartha ... M. H. Shearer ... and Frederick L. Caudle ...
New York and London, McGraw-Hill book company, inc.
₁1942₎

        x, 301 p. illus. (incl. charts) diagrs. 23½ᶜᵐ.

        "The authors have taken a substantial portion of the opening chapters
of ₍their₎ The earth and its resources as a basis for this book."—Pref.
        "References" at end of each chapter.

        1. Meteorology.   I. Trewartha, Glenn Thomas, 1896–   joint au-
thor. II. Shearer, Merle H., joint author. III. Caudle, Frederick L.,
joint author. IV. Title.

                                                   42—25429
    Library of Congress   QC863.F47
                     ₍45z5₎   551.5

SUBJECT CARD

for a subject card marked "Vocations." Perhaps
the card will say "see *Occupations.*" This means
that books in your library on the subject of vocations
are catalogued under the subject heading "Occupations."

A "see also" card refers you to other subjects
closely related to the one you are looking up. If,
for example, you should be looking up "radar," you
might find a card saying "see also *Electronics.*"
Looking under electronics, which is a subject to
which radar is closely related, you would quite
possibly find more books of help to you.

SUMMARY

The card catalog, then, is the place to find out
what books the library owns. Since books are
catalogued in three ways (by title, author, and subject) you can use the catalog as follows:

1. To find out whether a certain book is in the
library.

2. To look up the call number of a book whose title you know.

3. To look up the call number of a book whose author you know.

4. To look up call numbers or titles of other books by an author one of whose books you have enjoyed.

5. To find out what books on a certain subject the library owns.

6. To find the publisher, date of publication, and a general idea of the contents of a book, provided, of course, the book is in the library.

HOW TO FIND MAGAZINE ARTICLES AND OTHER REFERENCES

THE *READERS' GUIDE TO PERIODICAL LITERATURE*

To locate a magazine article on any subject, you use a most valuable book known as the *Readers' Guide to Periodical Literature*. The *Readers' Guide* indexes all the articles, poems, and stories in more than 100 magazines. A list of these magazines is given in the front of the *Readers' Guide*. The *Readers' Guide* is kept so closely up-to-date that every two weeks your librarian receives copies of the *Readers' Guide* for magazines published only a few weeks before. Furthermore, the *Readers' Guide* has been published since 1900, so that by using back volumes of it, you can find what articles have been published on a subject over a period of many years. It is published every two weeks from September through June, and monthly in July and August. Every year the numbers are combined into one volume, and every three years into a larger volume.

The *Readers' Guide* lists magazine articles by

subjects and authors. It gives information about each magazine article listed, using abbreviations which are easy to read. A key to these abbreviations is given in the front of the *Readers' Guide*.

Study the accompanying sample entries taken from the *Readers' Guide*. Can you "read" the abbreviations? Stories are listed in the *Readers' Guide* by title as well as by author. Poems are listed by title under the general heading POEMS, and by authors.

"See" and "see also" references are used in the *Readers' Guide*, just as they are used in the card catalog. See page 285.

Of course, finding out what articles have been published on a certain topic will be of little help to you unless you can get the magazine in which the articles appeared. Whether you can do so depends upon whether your library takes the magazine and whether it keeps back numbers of it. Usually you will find on or near the *Readers' Guide* table in your library, a list of the magazines which the library takes. The list will tell you, too, whether back numbers are available and if they are, exactly which ones.

EXERCISE 1. Using the card catalog and the *Readers' Guide* in your school or town library, look up the answers to the following questions.

1. What books by Commander Edward Ellsberg are in the library?
2. List three books the library owns on aviation. Give the call numbers.
3. List two books in the library about Abraham Lincoln. Give the call numbers.

MACHARG, William Briggs
Plenty of hats; story. Collier's 107:26 Ja 25 '41
Red silk; story. Collier's 107:23 Mr 15 '41
MODELS
America's five favorite hobbies. E. Teale. il Pop Sci 138:102 My '41
Little giants of industry. il Pop Mech 75: 328-31+ Mr '41
Structural models of atoms. Science ns 93: sup8 My 2 '41
Toothpick modeling is fast-growing hobby. il Pop Mech 75:534 Ap '41
　　See also

Anatomical models	Historical models
Engine models	Mechanical models
Firearm models	

MODELS (persons)
Campus queens, inc. il Am Mag 131:76-7 Ap '41
MODELS, Fashion
Shapely model is cast in plaster to make a master manikin mold. il Life 10:53+ Mr 3 '41
MODELS, Railroad. See Railroad models
MODELS of cities, towns, etc.
Backyard city: W. Murray's midget city. Littleville, Chesterton, Ind. il Pop Sci 138: 113-14 F '41
MOON, Harold P.
Development of a plastic molded airplane. Aviation 40:44-5+ Ja '41
MOON
All aboard for a trip to the moon. W. H. Barton, jr. Sci Digest 9:56-8 Je '41
Lunar shroud; mantle of volcanic ash which serves as insulation from the sun's great heat. il Science N L 39:139-40 Mr 1 '41
Paschal full moon. J. Stokley. Science N L 39:202-3 Mr 29 '41
Swarming sea worms living buried in rocks and dark, swarm at certain phases of moon and lay their eggs. Science N L 39: 219-20 Ap 5 '41
　　See also
Eclipses, Lunar
MOONFLOWERS
Catch the moonflower. House B 83:122 My '41
MOOR, Anthonis. See Moro, A.
MOORE, Anne Carroll
Three owls' notebook (cont) Horn Bk 16: 265-7, 338-40, 429-31; 17:24-6, 98-100 Jl '40- Mr '41
MOORE, Grace
Grace Moore picks up a home: Far away meadows, near Newton, Conn. B. Stillman. il por Arts & Dec 53:16-19 Ap '41
Portrait
　　Etude 59:289 My '41

4. Does the library own a copy of the *Adventures of Sherlock Holmes*, by Sir Arthur Conan Doyle?

5. When was *Penrod*, by Booth Tarkington, published?

6. Choose one of these topics and look up in the *Readers' Guide* three recent articles on it. Give complete information: title and author (if given), magazine, date, page numbers.

   The U. S. Army   Atomic Energy   Swing Music
   The U. N.   Cooking   Medicine

7. List the titles and authors of those articles you found in Question 6 which can be found in your library.

8. Select a prominent government figure — the President, Vice-President, Secretary of State, Ambassador to England, etc., and find in the *Readers' Guide* an article about him. On your paper copy the listing from the *Readers' Guide*.

9. Suppose you are writing an essay on General Dwight Eisenhower. Have any articles about him been published recently? If so, list them and give the information from the *Readers' Guide*.

10. How many articles on commercial aviation are listed in the volume of the *Readers' Guide* you are using?

REFERENCE BOOKS

In every library there is a section known as the reference section. Here the librarian keeps together those ready reference volumes which are designed to help you look up brief articles giving various kinds of information. You will find acquaintance with certain of these reference books to be very valuable.

THE DICTIONARY

The dictionary of the English language is probably the most useful of all the reference books you will encounter. So common is the dictionary and so much is it a part of the daily work of high school students that you should know it in detail. You may regard a dictionary as nothing more than a big book which gives the meaning and spelling of all the words in the language. It is, however, much more than that. You may be surprised to know all the various kinds of information the dictionary contains.

1. *Differences among dictionaries:*

Webster's New International Dictionary is the best known of the *unabridged* dictionaries. Your library undoubtedly has one or more copies. The unabridged — complete — dictionary contains all the words in the language and gives more detailed information about them than does the abridged — or shortened — dictionary which you are accustomed to use. For most purposes your smaller dictionary is adequate.

There are several popular dictionaries. The one you own or have been provided with for class study may be arranged in a way different from certain others, but it probably contains essentially the same information as all the others. What these differences among dictionaries are will be clearer to you as you gain experience in using various dictionaries. Eventually, you will be able to tell at a glance how the dictionary you are using is arranged; you will be able to use any dictionary efficiently. No one can use a dictionary efficiently unless he is familiar with the order of letters in the alphabet. On this and the following pages you will find exercises in alphabetizing. Working through these exercises will increase your efficiency in using the dictionary.

2. *Alphabetizing:*

How well do you know the alphabet? Since all reference books (encyclopedias, dictionaries, etc.), the card catalog, the fiction books, and the *Readers' Guide* are arranged in alphabetical order, you must be thoroughly familiar with the order in which the letters of the alphabet come. You may wonder why space in this book is given to alphabetizing, but any librarian will tell you that a great many students have only a vague idea as to whether *H* comes before *K,* or *S* comes before *R.* Try your speed on the following exercises.

EXERCISE 2. Arrange the following words in alphabetical order.

alarm	consent
base	hatred
safety	celery
motor	giant
radio	violet

EXERCISE 3. Arrange the following words in alphabetical order.

sprain	solo
sky	stingy
song	sample
stars	spare
split	simple

EXERCISE 4. Your teacher will time you on the following quiz. Accuracy is more important than speed, but speed *is* important.

Some of the statements below are true; others are false. Number from 1 to 20 on your paper. When the teacher gives the signal, place a + on your paper for each true statement, a 0 for each false one.

1. *S* comes before *W*
2. *N* comes before *P*
3. *R* comes after *S*
4. *F* comes after *E*
5. *J* comes after *G*
6. *L* comes before *K*
7. *N* comes before *M*
8. *I* comes before *K*
9. *J* comes after *I*
10. *U* comes before *W*
11. *Q* comes before *O*
12. *O* comes after *P*
13. *E* comes before *F*
14. *H* comes after *I*
15. *O* comes after *N*
16. *Q* comes before *R*
17. *U* comes after *S*
18. *W* comes before *V*
19. *S* comes after *R*
20. *W* comes after *U*

EXERCISE 5. Using last names only, make an alphabetical list of all the members of your English class. If two members have the same last name, arrange them according to their initials or the letters of their first name.

Samuels, Jane
Samuels, Joan

Names beginning with *Mc* (like *McKay*) are listed as though spelled *Mac* (*MacKay*). In a list of several *Mc* and *Mac* words, the letter following the *Mac* will determine the order.

When you have a long list of names to alphabetize, you will find your task easier if you write each name on a separate slip of paper and then arrange the slips in order.

EXERCISE 6. Using the dictionary provided for you, look up the following words. This is merely a test of your knowledge of alphabetical order and your speed in applying it. Save time by using the key words at the top of the pages to help you. When you have found the word, jot down the number of the page on which it appears.

1. gamble	7. comedy	13. record
2. quick	8. commotion	14. head
3. bend	9. immortal	15. heart
4. garage	10. niece	16. hitch
5. sentence	11. noise	17. knob
6. image	12. normal	18. miracle

WHAT THE DICTIONARY TELLS ABOUT A WORD [1]

As you study the following pages, keep the excerpt on page 295 from *Webster's Students Dictionary* before you so that you can refer to it easily.

1. *Spelling:*

The dictionary is the authority on correct spelling. If there are two spellings for a word, the dictionary gives the preferred spelling first (judgment, judgement).

If there might be some question as to the spelling or formation of the plural of a noun, the dictionary shows you how to spell the plural. *Gas*, for instance (see sample page), is spelled *gases* in the plural, not *gasses*. In the case of a verb, the past forms may offer a spelling problem. The past form of the verb *gas* is given, therefore. It is *gassed*, with two *s*'s.

2. *Capital letters:*

If you are in doubt as to whether a word is capitalized, the dictionary will help you. On the ac-

---

[1] To the teacher: the dictionary on which this section is based is *Webster's Students Dictionary* (1945). The material, however, will be found to apply to any good student dictionary, but the teacher will do well to check the drills and tests with the book his students are using. The most noticeable differences among dictionaries are the differences in indicating pronunciation of words. The work in this book is based on the Webster system, since the Webster unabridged is the most frequently used in schools.

gar·ri·son (găr'ĭ·sŭn; -s'n), *n.* [OF. *garison*, fr. *garir*; see GARRET.] *Mil.* **a** A fortified place in which troops are quartered. **b** A body of troops stationed in a fort. — *v. t. Mil.* **a** To furnish with soldiers, as a fort. **b** To secure with fortresses, as a frontier.

gar·rote' (gă·rōt'; -rŏt') *or* **gar·rotte'** (-rŏt'), *n.* [Sp. *garrote.*] **1.** A Spanish method of execution by strangulation with an iron collar tightened by a screw; also, the collarlike device. **2.** Throttling as if with the garrote, esp. for robbery. — *v. t.;* -ROT'ED *or* -ROT'TED; -ROT'ING *or* -ROT'TING. To strangle with a garrote; hence, to throttle and rob.

gar·ru'li·ty (gă·rōō'lĭ·tĭ), *n.* Talkativeness.

gar·ru·lous (găr'ŭ·lŭs; -ōō·lŭs), *adj.* [L. *garrulus*, fr. *garrire* to chatter, talk.] Talking much, esp. about trifles; wordy. — **Syn.** See TALKATIVE. — **gar'ru·lous·ly,** *adv.* — **gar'ru·lous·ness,** *n.*

gar'ter (gär'tẽr), *n.* [ONF. *gartier*, fr. *garet* bend of the knee.] **1.** A band or strap worn to hold up a stocking. **2.** [*usually cap.*] The blue badge of the **Order of the Garter,** the highest order of British knighthood; also, this order or membership in it. — *v. t.* To bind or support with a garter.

garter snake. A harmless agile American snake with yellow stripes along the back.

gas (găs), *n.; pl.* GASES (-ĕz; -ĭz). [invented by the chemist Van Helmont of Brussels (d. 1644); — suggested by L. *chaos*, Gr. *chaos*, chaos.] **1.** An airlike fluid, having neither independent shape nor volume, but tending to expand indefinitely. **2.** In popular usage, any gaseous mixture except air; specif.: **a** Any gas used as an anesthetic. **b** Any combustible mixture of gases for illuminating or fuel. **3.** Any substance used to produce a poisonous atmosphere, as in warfare. **4.** *Slang.* Empty, boasting, or humbugging talk. **5.** *Colloq.* Gasoline. — *v. t.;* GASSED (găst); GAS'SING. **1.** To affect or treat with gas; as, to *gas* lime with chlorine in making bleaching powder; to poison with gas, esp. in warfare. **2.** To supply with gas. — *v. i.* **1.** To give off gas. **2.** *Slang.* To indulge in idle or empty talk.

Gas'con (găs'kŏn), *n.* [F.] One of the natives of Gascony, in France, who were noted for boasting; hence [*not cap.*], a boaster. — **Gas'con,** *adj.*

gas'con·ade' (găs'kŏn·ād'), *n.* [F. *gasconnade.*] A boast or boasting; bravado. — *v. i.* To boast.

gas'e·ous (găs'ē·ŭs; *Brit. usually* gā'zĕ·ŭs *or* gā'sĕ·ŭs), *adj.* **1.** In the form of, like, or relating to, gas. **2.** Lacking substance or solidity.

gas fitter. A workman who installs or repairs gas pipes.

gash (găsh), *v. t.* [fr. OF. *garser, jarser*, to scarify.] To make a long deep cut in. — *n.* A deep and long cut, esp. in flesh.

companying sample, the word *Gascon* is defined as,
"One of the natives of Gascony, in France, who
were noted for boasting; hence [*not cap.*], a boaster."
The [*not cap.*] means that when the word is used
merely to mean a boaster, it should not be capitalized. "For what he said about his own successes,
he was called a *gascon*." Of course, when used to
mean a native of Gascony, the word is capitalized as
the dictionary shows.

3. *Syllables:*

Sometimes, for purposes of dividing a word at the
end of a line, you may wish to know how to split it
up into syllables, for words should be divided only
between syllables. The dictionary divides all words
into syllables: *garrulous*, for instance (see sample
page) is divided into three syllables — *gar ru lous.*

Between syllables the dictionary places a dot or a
small dash unless there is an accent mark between
the syllables. Do not confuse the dot or small dash
which shows the syllables with the longer, heavier
dash which indicates a hyphen. The noun, *go-be-
tween*, for instance, is hyphenated as indicated by
the long dash. Between the second and third syllables only a dot is used to show the syllables —
go'-be·tween'.

4. *Pronunciation:*

The dictionary shows the correct pronunciation of
a word. In order to show how a word is pronounced
the dictionary uses markings, called *diacritical mark·
ings*, which indicate the sound of vowels, and it
respells the word using certain consonants to mean
certain sounds. Time and experience are required

to master the dictionary's method of showing the correct pronunciation of a word. A pronunciation *key* is usually given at the bottom, or the top, of each page. Dictionaries differ somewhat in the marking system they use, but if you understand one system, you will probably be able to understand all of them. In the front part of some dictionaries there is a chapter on the whole subject of pronunciation, but this is usually too detailed to be of interest to the average person.

Your teacher may wish to have you learn the common pronunciation markings now so that in your dictionary practice you will be able to understand how to pronounce a word you have looked up. At your teacher's direction, you should turn to page 303–10, where you will find a more detailed account of this subject and exercises to give you practice.

5. *The part of speech:*

After each word listed in the dictionary, an abbreviation tells what part of speech the word is. These abbreviations are:

noun	*n.*	adverb	*adv.*	adjective	*adj.*
verb	*v.*	pronoun	*pron.*	preposition	*prep.*
		conjunction	*conj.*		
		interjection	*interj.*		

Since many words may be used as more than one part of speech, you will find the part of speech given before the definitions. Referring again to the sample page from a dictionary, you will see that *gas* is given first as a noun (*n.*). Then it is given as a transitive verb (*v.t.*) and then as an intransitive verb (*v.i.*).

6. *Derivation:*

The derivation of a word is, briefly, the history of the word. The dictionary tells you either the origin of a word or the language from which a word has come. To indicate the languages, abbreviations are used. For instance, L means Latin; F, French; AS, Anglo-Saxon, etc. The meaning of other abbreviations can be found by consulting the page of "Abbreviations Used in This Dictionary" which appears usually in the front of the book.

A glance at *garrulous* on the sample page will show you how derivation is indicated. There you see that the word is derived from the Latin adjective *garrulus* which in turn is formed from the Latin verb *garrire*, meaning *to chatter, to talk*. Hence the meaning of *garrulous* is "Talking much, especially about trifles; wordy."

The dictionary gives other types of information about the origin of words. The word *gas*, you are informed, was "invented by the chemist Von Helmont of Brussels," who died in 1644. It was suggested to him by the Latin word *chaos*, which in turn was based on the Greek word *chaos*.

7. *Meaning:*

The basic purpose of a dictionary is to give the meanings of words. You understand this well enough. You should realize, however, that most words have many different meanings; and since the dictionary gives them all, you must seek out the particular definition you are looking for. *Gas*, as a noun, has five meanings. These are indicated by number. The verb *gas* has two meanings. The dictionary usually places the oldest meaning first.

Because this old meaning is not necessarily the meaning you are looking for, you will have to run your eye over the many definitions until you find the one that fits the sentence in which you have found the word.

8. *Slang, colloquial, obsolete, etc.:*

Gas in its fourth meaning is labeled *slang.* The word may be used to mean "empty, boasting, or humbugging talk." People do use it this way commonly, but the dictionary tells you that the word, used in this sense, is not considered good usage. It is slang.

Used to mean gasoline (fifth meaning) *gas* is *colloquial*, which means that the word is used this way in conversation and informal writing, but not in formal speech or writing.

A word marked *obs.* is no longer in common use; it is *obsolete.*

There are many other special classes of words; for example: *archaic* (old-fashioned), *Mil.* (military meaning limited to military use), *Gram.* (grammar), *Bib.* (Biblical), *Dial.* (dialect), etc.

9. *Synonyms and antonyms:*

For some entries in the dictionary synonyms or antonyms, or both, are given. A synonym is a word having nearly the same meaning as the word being defined: *brave — courageous.* An antonym is a word having the opposite meaning: *brave — cowardly.*

Sometimes when there is only a slight difference in meaning among several words, the dictionary explains these shades of meaning.

"Gaze, gape, stare, glare, glower, peer, gloat. Gaze implies prolonged attention, esp. [especially] in wonder. *Gape* implies stupid and openmouthed wonder; *stare,* esp. insolence or vacant fixedness; *glare,* fierceness or anger; *glower,* scowling ill temper. To *peer* is to look curiously, esp. through or from behind something. To *gloat* is to gaze with profound, often malignant, satisfaction."

By permission. From *Webster's Students Dictionary,* copyright, 1938, 1943, 1945, by G. & C. Merriam Company.

10. *Illustrations:*

If the meaning of a word can best be shown by a picture, the dictionary may give an illustration. While you, of course, cannot depend on finding a picture of the thing you may be looking up, there is a chance that you might find one, especially if the object cannot be easily described.

WHAT THE DICTIONARY TELLS ABOUT FAMOUS PERSONS

Who was Clara Barton? When did Edison die? What was Chopin's nationality? What were the dates of Queen Elizabeth's reign? For what is Anthony Van Dyck famous? What was George Eliot's real name? How do you pronounce Hippocrates? The answers to such simple fact questions about famous persons can probably be found in your dictionary.

Some dictionaries devote a special section to famous persons. It is called a *Biographical Dictionary.* Others give names of persons and places in a section called *Proper Names.* Sometimes these names are included in the body of the book. You can easily discover which method your dictionary uses.

The following common pieces of biographical information are usually given in a dictionary:

1. *Name:* spelling, pronunciation, first name.
2. *Dates* of birth and death and of reign if a king or queen, or term of office if head of a government.
3. *Nationality.*
4. *Why famous.*

The following is a typical dictionary account of a famous person.

Byrd (bûrd), Richard Evelyn, 1888–   .   American rear admiral and explorer.   Airplane flights over North Pole (1926), South Pole (1929).

Mythological and Biblical, as well as some literary characters, are usually listed in the body of the dictionary: *Odysseus, Lancelot, Naomi, Romeo, etc.*

WHAT THE DICTIONARY TELLS ABOUT PLACES

Like the biographical entries in the dictionary, the geographical entries are sometimes given in the body of the book and sometimes in a special section. This section may be called a gazetteer — a geographical dictionary.

In general the following information is given about a place:

1. *Name:* spelling, pronunciation.
2. *Identification:* whether a city, country, lake, mountain, river, etc.
3. *Location.*
4. *Size:* population, if a city or country (usually given in thousands—225 = 225,000); area in square miles, if a country or territory or body of water; length, if a river; height, if a mountain, etc.
5. *Importance:* If a city is capital of a state or country, this will be indicated by a star or an asterisk. The capital city of a country or state will also be given under the name of the country or state.

6. *Historical or other interesting information of importance:* Thus for Hampton Roads, Virginia . . . . . "battle of *Merrimac* and *Monitor*, March 9, 1862." For Lake Mead, formed by Hoover Dam in the Colorado River, the dictionary says "the largest man-made lake in the world."

7. *Governed or controlled by what country:* for Wake Island, the dictionary says "belongs to U.S.A."

OTHER INFORMATION IN THE DICTIONARY

Most good dictionaries include the following kinds of information, either in separate sections or in the body of the dictionary itself.

1. *Foreign words and phrases:* spelling, pronunciation, meaning.

2. *Abbreviations:* a list of abbreviations of all kinds, giving the words in full.

An unabridged dictionary and some of the larger student dictionaries include:

3. *Signs and symbols:* Not all dictionaries include a section of this kind, but some do, and if yours does, you should study the section to familiarize yourself with its contents.

4. *Spelling rules.*

5. *Punctuation rules.*

6. *New words.*

SPEED AND ACCURACY TEST A. When your teacher gives the signal, look up the answers to the following questions in the dictionary you have. Write the answers on your paper. Accuracy is more important than speed, but speed *is* important. Your speed will show to some extent your knowledge of the dictionary.

1. Who was Nebuchadnezzar?   (Biblical)
2. When did Shakespeare live?
3. Give the meaning of the abbreviation B. P. O. E.
4. Write out the pronunciation and the meaning of the Latin phrase *carpe diem.*
5. Who was Arachne?   (mythology)
6. What is the derivation of *curfew?*
7. What is the height of Mt. McKinley?   Where is it?
8. What is the area of Lake Michigan?
9. What is the capital of Albania?
10. What country owns the Azores?

SPEED AND ACCURACY TEST B.   At the direction of your teacher look up in your dictionary the answers to the following questions.

1. Give the pronunciation and meaning of *laissez faire.*
2. Who was Persephone?   (mythology)
3. Give the preferred pronunciation of *ration.*
4. Of what country is Bangkok the capital?
5. What is the population of Buenos Aires?
6. What is the length of the Danube River?
7. What is the derivation of *calculate?*
8. What country governs Sicily?
9. Who was Sir John Falstaff?   (literature)
10. What is the meaning of the abbreviation *ms.?*

PRONUNCIATION

DIACRITICAL MARKS AND HOW TO READ THEM

VOWEL SOUNDS

The two commonest vowel sounds are indicated in the dictionary by the markings known as the *macron* and the *breve.*

The *macron* (ˉ), the long, straight mark over a vowel, indicates that the vowel is pronounced as it is named.   For instance, the name of the letter *a* is the sound of that letter when it is written ā as in *mācron* itself. Pronounce the following: ā, ē, ī, ō, ū. The sound of *ū* is *yew* as in *cūbe*, not *ōō* as in *cōōl*.

The dotted macron (ᐧ) means that the sound is still that of the name of the letter, but in pronouncing the letter you speak somewhat more rapidly. The dot "shortens" the long sound a little: *ėvent′*, *ȯbey′*.

The *breve* (˘), pronounced *brēve*, is the curved mark over a vowel, and it indicates that the sound is "shortened." Study the sounds indicated by the breve:

ă	ădd	ĭ	ĭll
ĕ	ĕnd	ŏ	ŏdd
	ŭ	ŭp	

OTHER VOWEL SOUNDS

While understanding the meaning of the macron and the breve will help you considerably to get the correct pronunciation of a word from the dictionary, you will need to know the markings used for other vowel sounds. To interpret these markings, all you need do is refer to the key which is printed at the bottom (sometimes at the top) of each page of the dictionary. This key is given below. Read aloud the key words, noting the markings as you do so.

āle, chȧotic, câre, ădd, ȧccount, ärm, ȧsk, sofȧ; ēve, hẽre, ėvent, ĕnd, silĕnt, makẽr; īce, ĭll, charĭty; ōld, ȯbey, ôrb, ŏdd, sŏft, cȯnnect; fōōd, fŏŏt; out, oil; cūbe, ūnite, ûrn, ŭp, circŭs.

CONSONANT SOUNDS

Whereas there are only five vowels in the language, there are twenty-one consonants. Most of these are pronounced just as they are named. A few, however, do present special difficulties, such as the sound of *th* in *then* and in *thin*. Notice how these two sounds are shown in the key below.

The dictionary uses respelling to indicate the sounds of some consonants. According to the key, how does the dictionary show the difference in sound between *c* in *can* and *c* in *certain;* between *g* in *germ* and *g* in *good;* between *ch* in *chain* and *ch* in *character;* between *s* in *loose* and *s* in *lose?*

KEY TO PRONUNCIATION OF CONSONANTS

chair; go; sing; then, thin; natŭre, verdŭre; ĸ = ch in G. ich, ach; yet; zh = z in azure.

By permission. From *Webster's Students Dictionary*, copyright, 1938, 1943, 1945, by G. & C. Merriam Company.

Pronunciation markings not given in the key may be looked up in the "Guide to Pronunciation" in the front of the dictionary.

ACCENT

In words of several syllables, one syllable is accented or stressed more than the others. This accented syllable is shown by an accent mark (′) placed immediately after and above it. For instance, *be lieve′, de cide′, un doubt′ed ly,* etc. In long words there may be two accented syllables, one of which receives greater stress than the other. The accents of these two syllables are shown in the words *man′u fac′ture, gen′er a′tion.* The main, heavier accent is marked by the heavier accent mark. The secondary, lighter accent is indicated by the lighter accent mark. Some dictionaries use a double accent mark printed lightly (″) for the secondary accent: generation, *jĕn″ ẽr ā′shŭn.*

Sometimes the same word may be accented in different ways, depending upon how the word is used. The listed words are examples of how the accent shifts when the words are used as different parts of speech.

com′pact (noun)	com pact′ (adjective)
con′duct (noun)	con duct′ (verb)
con′tent (noun)	con tent′ (adjective)
pro′test (noun)	pro test′ (verb)

The meaning may change completely with a change in accent: *ref′use, re fuse′*.

EXERCISE 7. Using the key on page 304, write the vowel markings above the vowels in these common words. Place accent marks in the words of more than one syllable. Final silent *e*, of course, cannot be marked.

1.	stop	11.	un til
2.	old	12.	de cide
3.	lame	13.	re make
4.	like	14.	mo lest
5.	rib	15.	rob in
6.	peek	16.	al i bi
7.	send	17.	a long
8.	use	18.	sum mer
9.	us	19.	trop i cal
10.	doom	20.	look ing

EXERCISE 8. Using the key, rewrite with diacritical markings, respelling, accents, etc., the following words as you think the dictionary might rewrite them to show their pronunciation. When you have finished, check your work with the dictionary.

1. guide	6. ac tive
2. Cu pid	7. mi crobe
3. rul er	8. pep per mint
4. pan cake	9. in ten tion
5. cir cus	10. book mark

EXERCISE 9. The following words are frequently mispronounced. Look up the pronunciation of each in a dictionary and copy each word onto your paper with the diacritical markings as shown in the dictionary.

Practice pronouncing the word yourself. Your teacher will tell you whether you have read the markings correctly. Note the meaning of any unfamiliar words.

A

1. arctic	6. coupon
2. bade	7. grimy
3. cache	8. often
4. café	9. ogre
5. chasm	10. via

B

1. admirable	6. mischievous
2. condolence	7. municipal
3. gigantic	8. museum
4. height	9. preferable
5. infamous	10. theater

C

1. athlete	6. diphtheria
2. bicycle	7. genuine
3. biography	8. government
4. blackguard	9. Italian
5. culinary	10. stomach

EXERCISE 10. Ability to understand the pronunciation markings will be valuable to you. Through no other means will you be able to learn from the dictionary how to pronounce a word. The following exercise will test your ability to read dictionary markings. The exercise assumes that you know the correct pronunciation of the words; it is designed merely to test your ability to interpret the markings.

Of the pronunciations written after each word, one is correct. Try pronouncing each as it is marked. Decide which is correctly marked.

1. because	bĕ kŭz′	bĕ kôz′	bē′kôz
2. hundred	hŭn′dērd	hŭn′drĕd	hŭn′dēr ĕd
3. diploma	dĭp lō′mȧ	dī plō′mȧ	dĭ plō′mȧ
4. pretty	pērt′ĭ	prĭt′ĭ	prĕt′ĭ
5. faucet	fȧ′sĕt	fä′sĕt	fô′sĕt
6. bicycle	bī′sĭk′l	bĭ′sīk′l	bĭs′ĭk′l
7. orchestra	ôr kĕs′trȧ	ôr′kĕs trĭ	ôr′kĕs trȧ
8. champion	chăm pē′ŭn	chăm pēn′	chăm′pĭ ŭn
9. perspiration	pûr′spĭ rā′shŭn	prĕs′pĭ rā′shŭn	
10. experiment	ĕks pĕr′ĭ mĕnt	ĕks pûr′ĭ mŭnt	

WORDS COMMONLY MISPRONOUNCED

The words in the following list are commonly mispronounced. The correct pronunciation of each is given here. By means of the diacritical markings, figure out how the word should be pronounced. Practice saying the word aloud, correctly.

Many of the words in the list below are included because, in pronouncing them, many persons enunciate poorly. *Enunciation means pronouncing with distinctness.* Such errors as "jography" and "jometry" for jḗ·ŏg′rȧ·fĭ and jḗ·ŏm′ḗ·trĭ are errors in enunciation rather than in pronunciation. As you know, pronunciation refers to letter sounds and accent.

across ȧ·krŏs′
alias ā′lĭ·ȧs
almond ä′mŭnd
alumnae ȧ·lŭm′nē
alumni ȧ·lŭm′nī
architect är′kĭ·tĕkt
arctic ärk′tĭk
athlete ăth′lēt
attacked ȧ·tăkt′
auxiliary ôg·zĭl′yȧ·rĭ

bade băd
because bē·kôz′
blackguard blăg′ärd
cabaret kăb′ȧ rā′
cache kăsh
cafe kȧ·fā′
calliope kȧ·lī′ō·pē
cello chĕl′ō
cement sē·mĕnt′
champion chăm′pĭ·ŭn

chasm kăz′m
column kŏl′ŭm
combatant kŏm′bȧ·tănt
communique kŏ·mū′nĭ·kā′
comparable kŏm′pȧ·rȧ·b′l
coupon koo′pŏn
creek krēk
culinary kū′lĭ·nĕr′ĭ
deaf dĕf
diphtheria dĭf·thĕr′ĭ·ȧ

dirigible dĭr′ĭ·jĭ·b′l
discretion dĭs·krĕsh′ŭn
docile dŏs′ĭl
drowned dround
elm ĕlm
extraordinary ĕks·trôr′dĭ·
   nĕr′ĭ
faucet fô′sĕt
film fĭlm
futile fū′tĭl
genuine jĕn′û·ĭn

geography jē·ŏg′rȧ·fĭ
geometry jē·ŏm′ē·trĭ
gesture jĕs′tŭr
gibberish jĭb′ĕr·ĭsh
gigantic jī·găn′tĭk
grimy grīm′ĭ
handkerchief hăng′kĕr·chĭf
height hīt
ignoramus ĭg′nō·rā′mŭs
impious ĭm′pĭ·ŭs

incomparable ĭn·kŏm′pȧ·
   rȧ·b′l
indicted ĭn·dīt′ĕd
infamous ĭn′fȧ·mŭs
influence ĭn′floo·ĕns
Italian ĭ·tăl′yȧn
italics ĭ·tăl′ĭks
just jŭst
length lĕngth
library lī′brĕr·ĭ
mischievous mĭs′chĭ·vŭs

mortgage môr′gĭj
municipal mŭ·nĭs′ĭ·păl
museum mŭ·zē′ŭm
pathos pā′thŏs
perhaps pēr·hăps′
perspiration pûr·spĭ·rā′-
    shŭn
poem pō′ĕm
preferable prĕf′ẽr·à·b′l
probably prŏb′à·blĭ
raspberry răz′bĕr·ĭ

recognize rĕk′ŏg·nīz
scion sī′ŭn
solace sŏl′ĭs
stipend stī′pĕnd
strength strĕngth
suite swēt
superfluous sŭ·pûr′floō·ŭs
telegraphy tĕ·lĕg′rà·fĭ
theater thē′à·tēr
wrestle rĕs″l

SPECIAL DICTIONARIES

In addition to the standard type dictionary of the English language which you have just finished studying, there are many special dictionaries written to help you with special problems of word choice, correct usage, etc. Very often a writer has some trouble thinking of the exact word with which to express his meaning. Often, too, he has used the same word so many times in a composition that he wishes to find a synonym for it to avoid repeating. The three books listed below, as their names suggest, will help a writer to find the words he needs.

FERNALD: *ENGLISH SYNONYMS AND ANTONYMS*

This book contains most of the words in common use and gives a number of synonyms (words which mean almost the same thing) for each. The words are arranged in alphabetical order.

ROGET: *THESAURUS OF ENGLISH WORDS AND PHRASES*

A *thesaurus* is a collection. The word is derived from a Latin word meaning *treasure*, so that literally a thesaurus is a treasury or storehouse. Roget's

Thesaurus is a book of synonyms and is used for the same purpose as Fernald's book. The latest edition is arranged in alphabetical order.

WEBSTER'S: *DICTIONARY OF SYNONYMS*

This is the most recently published of the synonym dictionaries. It is especially valuable in explaining the fine differences in meaning between words whose meanings are somewhat, though not exactly, alike.

ENCYCLOPEDIAS

As you have already discovered, an encyclopedia is a collection of articles, arranged in alphabetical order, on almost all subjects in the many fields of knowledge. It is useful to you especially in looking up information for history, science, and English classes. Biographies of great men of the past, historical events, information on countries, cities, etc., industrial and scientific processes — these are only a few of the subjects for which the encyclopedia is usually consulted.

FINDING A REFERENCE IN THE ENCYCLOPEDIA

Use the guide letters and the index to find an encyclopedia article. You may find an article in an encyclopedia in much the same way that you find a word in the dictionary; that is, by looking it up in its alphabetical position, using the guide words at the top of the page. Since encyclopedias consist of many volumes, guide letters are printed on the back of each volume. However, there may be several articles in an encyclopedia which would be of use to you in your search for material on a certain subject. Arranged alphabetically, these articles would appear under different subject headings at different places in the various volumes. In the index of the *Encyclopædia Britannica*, for example, you will find that there are articles on "Radio" in eleven of the twenty-three volumes. You probably would not have found all of these, if you had merely looked under "Radio" in the R volume. But using the index, you found them listed all together. To do a thorough job and to save time, use the index of an encyclopedia. If an encyclopedia has an index, you will find it in the last volume or at the back of each volume.

HOW ENCYCLOPEDIAS ARE KEPT UP TO DATE

Most encyclopedias, like dictionaries, are rewritten and revised occasionally. Such a big task requires many years of work. Probably the encyclopedias in your library were published several years ago. This does not mean that you cannot find up-to-date information in an encyclopedia, for some encyclopedias publish each year an *Annual* or *Yearbook* containing articles on important events in all fields of knowledge which occurred during the past year. If your library buys any of these yearbooks, you will find them useful additions to the wealth of information in the encyclopedia itself.

The following are the best-known general encyclopedias:

Encyclopedia Americana
  30 volumes
  Index in Volume 30
  Publishes the *Americana Annual*

Encyclopædia Britannica
  24 volumes
  Index and atlas in Volume 24
  Publishes *Britannica Book of the Year*

New International Encyclopedia
   25 volumes
   Publishes *New International Yearbook*

FOR YOUNGER READERS

Compton's Pictured Encyclopedia
   15 volumes
   One third of space is devoted to pictures
   Fact index (an index which itself gives information) at
      end of each volume
   Yearbook and annual supplement

World Book Encyclopedia
   19 volumes
   Reading and Study Guide in Volume 19
   Publishes an *Annual*

BIOGRAPHICAL REFERENCE BOOKS

There are many reference books, besides the standard encyclopedias, which will give biographies of important persons.

DICTIONARY OF AMERICAN BIOGRAPHY

This twenty-volume set contains excellent lives of famous Americans no longer living.

CURRENT BIOGRAPHY

Published monthly in pamphlet form, *Current Biography* is the best source of information about persons prominent in the news. The monthly pamphlets are bound into a book each year. By using the cumulative index in each issue, you can locate biographies of persons in the news in previous months. There are frequently pictures of the persons whose lives are given.

These are important volumes giving only the main facts about famous *living* persons. *Who's Who* contains information about famous Englishmen and some world figures from countries other than England. *Who's Who in America* contains information about famous Americans. Parentage, dates, positions held, principal achievements, books written, names of members of family, and present address are the sort of information given about a man or woman in the *Who's Who* volumes. Remember that these particular books contain information on *living* persons only and that they give only the essential facts of a person's life. *Who's Who* is published annually; *Who's Who in America* is published every two years.

REFERENCE BOOKS ABOUT AUTHORS

If your library has any of the "authors" books by Kunitz, you will find them valuable sources of "human-interest" information about authors. So far as possible, these books contain a picture of each author.

Living Authors, by Stanley J. Kunitz [Since this book was published in 1931, it is no longer a complete collection of biographies of *living* writers.]

Authors Today and Yesterday, by Stanley J. Kunitz

The Junior Book of Authors, by Stanley J. Kunitz and Howard Haycraft

British Authors of the Nineteenth Century, by Kunitz and Haycraft

American Authors 1600–1900, by Kunitz and Haycraft

Twentieth Century Authors, by Kunitz and Haycraft

ATLASES

You should know where in the library the atlases are kept, and you should take time to familiarize yourself with at least one good atlas. An atlas is much more than just a book of maps. It contains a vast amount of information about the cities and countries of the world. Population, resources, industries, natural wonders, climate, exports and imports, history, and many other kinds of information are easily found in an atlas. One or more of the following atlases are commonly found in high school libraries.

Hammond's *New World Atlas* Goode's *School Atlas*
Standard Atlas of the World *The Britannica Atlas*

THE WORLD ALMANAC AND BOOK OF FACTS

For factual information on the world today, this is the most useful of all the reference books in your library. Published annually, it is a book full of information and statistics on current events. Frequently in the *Almanac* the statistical tables give data for many years back as well as for the last year. You should become well acquainted with the *World Almanac*, for it is a book that will be useful to you every year and it cannot be adequately described in a few words. An index appears in the front of the *Almanac*. Typical items of information the *Almanac* gives are: batting averages of professional baseball players; exports and imports of principal countries; population statistics; government officials of states and countries; Nobel prize winners; accounts of important events of the year, etc.

LITERATURE REFERENCE BOOKS

BARTLETT'S *FAMILIAR QUOTATIONS*

Most famous of all "quotation books," Bartlett's *Familiar Quotations* is useful when you wish the following information: (1) the author of a quotation; (2) the source or literary work in which a quotation appeared; (3) the complete quotation of which you know only a part; (4) a few famous lines from any author.

This book is arranged chronologically by authors and contains alphabetical indexes of authors and quotations. To find a number of quotations from an author, you look up his name in the alphabetically arranged author index in the front of the book, then turn to the page where quotations from this author are given. If you know the quotation or a part of it and wish to find its author or the full quotation, you will use the index in the back of the book. This index is arranged alphabetically by the first word of the quotation. For instance, if you wish to find out who said

"The night has a thousand eyes,
The day but one ....."

you would look under the word *night*.

STEVENSON'S *HOME BOOK OF QUOTATIONS*

Used for somewhat the same purpose as Bartlett's book, Stevenson's *Home Book of Quotations* is, however, arranged differently. The quotations in this book are arranged by subjects. You can also find the author of a quotation although, since the book is not arranged by authors, you will find the book less efficient for this purpose than Bartlett's. Stevenson's book is especially helpful if you want a quotation on a certain subject. For instance, if you want one on *love* or *happiness* or *Christmas*, you will find many listed under each of those topics.

GRANGER'S *INDEX TO POETRY AND [RECITATIONS*

Granger's *Index* contains no poems or recitations. It tells you in what books you can find almost any poem or recitation (popular prose passage) you wish. If you know the title of a poem or its author, yet do not know in what books you will find the poem, look it up in Granger's. There you will find a list of books in which the poem can be found. By checking this list with the books in your library (use the card catalog), you will probably find that one or more of these books are available in your library. Since the titles of the books containing the poem you want are not written out in Granger's *Index* but are abbreviated to save space, you will have to refer to the list of abbreviations in the front of the book to find the title. Thus you might find that a poem you want is in a book entitled *Best Loved Poems of the American People*. Granger's refers to this book by the abbreviation *B L P A*. Granger's *Index* also contains listings of poems according to subjects. Since most poems and poets are listed in Granger's *Index*, the book is also a good place to find out who wrote a certain poem. Remember that Granger's *Index* will help you find a poem, but it does not itself contain any poems.

STEVENSON'S *HOME BOOK OF VERSE* AND STEVENSON'S
HOME BOOK OF MODERN VERSE

These books contain well known poems. Since the volumes are so large, you stand a fairly good chance of finding in them the poem you wish. At any rate you may save yourself time, when you are hunting for a poem, by looking in Stevenson first. The books are indexed in three ways: by author, by title, and by first line. The poems are classified under general headings; for instance, Poems of Youth and Age, Love Poems, Poems of Nature, Familiar Verse, and Poems, Humorous and Satiric, etc. This classfication helps you when you want a poem on a certain subject, but have no single poem or author in mind.

EXERCISE 11. Your teacher may assign you to give a brief description of those books in the following list with which he thinks you should be familiar. Tell what sort of material the book contains, how the material is arranged, and how to use the book.

SPECIAL DICTIONARIES

Fernald: *English Synonyms and Antonyms*
Roget: *Thesaurus of English Words and Phrases*
Webster's Dictionary of Synonyms

ENCYCLOPEDIAS

Compton's Pictured Encyclopedia
Encyclopedia Americana
Encyclopædia Britannica
New International Encyclopedia
World Book Encyclopedia

BIOGRAPHICAL REFERENCE BOOKS

GENERAL

Dictionary of American Biography
Current Biography

Who's Who
Who's Who in America

ABOUT AUTHORS

Living Authors
Authors Today and Yesterday
Junior Book of Authors
British Authors of the Nineteenth Century
American Authors 1600–1900
Twentieth Century Authors

ATLASES

Hammond's *New World Atlas*
Goode's *School Atlas*
Standard Atlas of the World
Britannica Atlas

ALMANAC

World Almanac and Book of Facts

LITERATURE REFERENCE BOOKS

Bartlett: *Familiar Quotations*
Stevenson: *Home Book of Quotations*
Granger: *Index to Poetry and Recitations*
Stevenson: *Home Book of Verse*
Stevenson: *Home Book of Modern Verse*

EXERCISE 12. Disregarding dictionaries and encyclopedias, decide what reference book would be the best in which to look up the following. Number on your paper from 1 to 10 and after the corresponding number write the title of the reference book. It is not necessary to use the same answer twice.

1. A picture of the modern author Carl Sandburg
2. The national tennis champion in 1940

3. A biography of someone recently risen to prominence in the news
4. The maiden name of the President's wife
5. The poem "A Visit from St. Nicholas "
6. Several quotations from Shakespeare
7. A number of quotations about *courage*
8. The title of a book containing Vachel Lindsay's poem "The Congo "
9. A good, brief biography of Benjamin Franklin
10. The poem "Birches" by Robert Frost, a modern poet

EXERCISE 13.   Disregarding dictionaries and encyclopedias, decide what reference book would be the best in which to look up the following.   Number on your paper from 1 to 10 and after the corresponding number write the title of the reference book.   It is not necessary to use the same answer twice.

1. An authoritative, brief biography of Stonewall Jackson
2. A list of the principal rivers of the world
3. The age of the British Prime Minister
4. Some interesting information about the modern author Sinclair Lewis
5. The rest of the quotation beginning "All the world's a stage . . . . . "
6. The author of the poem "The Charge of the Light Brigade"
7. A picture and biographical sketch of Walt Whitman, 19th century American poet
8. The name of the Chief Justice of the United States Supreme Court
9. Other important positions that the Chief Justice has held
10. The title of a book in which the poem beginning "The boy stood on the burning deck . . . . . " appears

EXERCISE 14. Name the reference book *best suited* for use in getting the following information You may include the dictionary and encyclopedia Be prepared to explain your choices.

1. A list of words meaning *cold*
2. An authoritative description of the open-hearth method of making steel
3. A good brief account of the life of William Jennings Bryan
4. A *complete* explanation of the differences in meaning among these words commonly used interchangeably: *desire, wish, want, crave*
5. A list of Senators and Representatives
6. A number of pictures of Chicago
7. The year Bobby Jones was both National Open and National Amateur golf champion
8. A brief biography of Charles Dickens
9. The title of a poem in which these lines appear:

    "And what is so rare as a day in June?
    Then, if ever, come perfect days ....."

10. The date of publication of Carl Sandburg's biography of Abraham Lincoln
11. The winner of the World Series in 1933
12. The height of Mt. Everest
13. The principal cities of Iran
14. The title of a book containing the poem "Casey at the Bat"
15. The meaning of the French phrase *raison d'être*
16. The capital of Vermont
17. Information about a man or woman prominent in the news recently
18. The title of a book containing the poem "The Battle of Blenheim"
19. The source of the quotation "A little learning is a dangerous thing"
20. A number of humorous poems

13. LETTER WRITING

When you hear the term "letter writing" you probably think of a friendly letter because most of your experience to date has been with that type of correspondence. This chapter provides you with a review of things to remember when writing a friendly letter and includes in addition instructions for writing the social note and the business letter.

LETTER WRITING IN GENERAL

Before you write any letter, plan what you are going to say and how you are going to say it. Remember that when your letter is read, you will not be there to explain what you mean. The letter must be clear. Furthermore, a letter represents *you*. Many times, especially in business, letters are received from people whom the reader has never met and never will meet. The writer is judged entirely by his letter. If you send a neat, correctly and clearly written letter, you will naturally be taken for an intelligent, educated person. If you send a letter which is not neat, which is filled with misspelled words and errors in writing, and which shows you do not know how to write a letter, the reader's opinion of you will drop accordingly. Be sure your letter makes a good impression.

In your letters, as in all your personal relationships, *be yourself*. Don't try to write like Jim because you think Jim is clever, or like Sally because she is so smart in everything. Write the way *you* can write. An original is always better than a poor imitation, and there are few better ways of reflecting your personality than a letter written by *you*, in *your own style*, saying what *you* want to say. If you write naturally, if your letter "sounds like you," it will be a much better product than if you try to mimic somebody else. Leave that to the experts.

THE FRIENDLY LETTER

This is the kind of letter with which you already have had a good deal of experience. It is a casual, informal sort of letter, the kind you write to your family and friends. The form of a friendly letter is rather elastic, but there are a few customs which you should follow.

APPEARANCE

Take pride in the appearance of your letter. Use letter stationery, preferably white, and always write in ink.

Space your letter so that it looks well on the page. Keep the margins as even as possible. Have at least three lines on the last page; never finish your letter on one page and put the leave-taking and signature alone on the next page.

If you use folded stationery and your letter is more than two pages long, use the page order of a book. Write page two on the back of page one. If your letter is only two pages long, write the second page on the third page of your stationery.

HEADING

It is customary to write your complete address (unless you are sure the receiver knows it) and the date at the top right-hand corner of the page, with a comma between the town and the state, and a comma between the day of the month and the year. Don't crowd this **heading.**

> *14 Brixton Road*
> *Dayton 3, Ohio*
> *September 17, 194–*

If you use abbreviations, be consistent — abbreviate the word "street" as well as the state. An abbreviation is always followed by a period. In general, it is better not to use abbreviations.

You may put your address and the date at the end of the letter, in the lower left-hand corner, instead of at the top.

SALUTATION (GREETING)

The **salutation** of a friendly letter is easy to learn. The usual form is "Dear . . ." followed by a comma.

> *Dear Dad,*
> *Dear Dr. Riley,*
> *Dear Bruce,*

COMPLIMENTARY CLOSE (LEAVE-TAKING)

After finishing the main part or **body** of your letter, you write a **complimentary close.** In a friendly letter there are many appropriate complimentary closes, such as, *Sincerely, Cordially, With love, Affectionately, etc.,* each of which is followed by a comma.

206 Rayburn Drive
Milltown, Oklahoma
August 8, 194–

Dear Babs,

I promised I'd write you about how our new cooking club turned out on Friday. Don't think I'll forget your mean chuckles when I told you what we were going to do, either! "So you six girls are going to cook, are you?"

Well, anyway, here's the story. We met at Jane's house after school on Friday and decided what we'd like to have for dinner. Then two of us shopped for it, two others set the table — and later did the dishes — and the other two did the cooking. Here's what we had: tomato juice, broiled lamb chops, mashed potatoes, fresh peas, lettuce and cucumber salad, chocolate tarts, and milk.

My conscience tells me I'd better admit that the chops were a _little_ burned, and the lettuce slightly wilted by the time we finally sat down to dinner, but outside of that, even Jane's dad (who had raised an eyebrow and suggested that he was doubtful about staying home — imagine!) admitted it was good.

Mother says she is delighted that we've finally found something to do that is worth while and fun at the same time. And speaking of Mother, right now she is giving me her if-you-don't-hurry-I-can't-wait-for-you look.

Do write soon and tell me what you're up to these days.

Love,
Marcia

Avoid endings such as "Yours till Niagara Falls." They don't ever look as well as you think they will, and they are in very poor taste.

Capitalize only the first letter of the complimentary close. Never write a business ending such as *Very truly yours* on a friendly letter. Don't use too many sentences beginning with *I*. The chapter on *Variety*, pages 198–212, will help you correct this fault.

Try not to write too many questions at the start of the letter. (How are you? Did you have a good time at the dance? What did your mother say?) The receiver wants a *letter* from you, not a questionnaire. Avoid the awkward close such as "I have to go now" and "Well, I guess I'll close."

Try to end your letter a little more originally and gracefully. For instance, if you are writing a friend whom you haven't seen in some time, perhaps you can suggest a visit to you. If the letter is going to someone to whom you have long owed a letter, you might assure him you will try to be a little more prompt next time. Make your closing appropriate to the person to whom you are writing as well as to the situation, and he will find your letter much more interesting.

Always remember that in friendly letters the most important things for you to think of are *to say what you mean* and *to be yourself*.

THE SOCIAL NOTE

The social note is a short letter usually written for one of the following purposes: (1) to extend an informal invitation; (2) to accept or decline an informal invitation; (3) to thank someone for a gift or for entertaining you.

The form of the social note is very much like that of a friendly letter, with the address and the date either in the top right-hand corner or the lower left-hand corner, the salutation *Dear* . . ., and the informal leave-taking.

The social note may be written on regular note paper, on correspondence cards if the note is a short one, or on personal note paper. White is preferred, although a pastel shade may be used. You may be proud of your violent-colored paper, and you may like to use white, red, or green ink on it, but don't use that kind of thing for social notes. It's likely to brand you as a person who doesn't know the proper thing to do.

THE INFORMAL INVITATION

Although the form and content of an invitation are very similar to those of a friendly letter, you do have to be careful to include the following:

1. Your full address.
2. The date, time, and place (if other than your home).
3. Any necessary explanation regarding the kind of affair it is to be.

REPLYING TO THE INFORMAL INVITATION

Still another kind of social note is the one you write when accepting or declining an invitation that is informal. Perhaps a friend of yours has invited you to his summer home for the day, or he and his sister have planned a party in your honor. If the invitation is a written one, your acceptance or re-

81 Waverly Place
New York 13, New York
May 14, 194—

Dear Dottie,

You remember how often I've spoken to you of Rachel Woods, the girl who went with us on our tour last summer. I've finally persuaded her to come for a week-end visit, and I'm asking a few of the girls to tea at four on Friday to meet her. I do hope you can come.

Cordially yours,
Alice

---

418 Fulton Avenue
Hempstead, Long Island
April 7, 194—

Dear Sam,

Bill Mercer came over the other night and we started talking about last summer at camp. That reminded us of canoeing. I remember how much you like canoeing, and Bill and I wondered if you'd like to go on a trip with us the last week end of the month — April 28th and 29th.

We could leave here before noon on Saturday, camp out at the end of the river that night (I've managed to get an extra bed roll for you), and mosey back on Sunday. Bill is already bragging about what a good chef he is, and I guess I can stand his cooking if you can.

There's a 9:18 train that leaves Penn Station, arriving in Hempstead at 10:15. I'll pick you up at the station. I hope you can make it.

Sincerely yours,
Bob

LETTER OF ACCEPTANCE

48 Williston Court
Manhasset, New York
May 15, 194–

Dear Alice,

I'll be delighted to come to your tea to meet Rachel. I've heard so much about her that it seems almost as though I knew her already.

It's always a treat to come to your house. I'll see you Friday at four.

Sincerely yours,
Dottie

LETTER OF REGRET

2132 Elkton Place
Greenwich, Connecticut
April 9, 194–

Dear Bob,

Your invitation for Saturday came in the morning mail, and how I hate to have to turn it down! A first-of-the-season canoeing trip sounds wonderful to me, but Dad had already bought tickets for the high school play that night, and we've all counted on going.

Give me another try, will you?

Cordially yours,
Sam

fusal should be written. Don't forget that it should be a gracious acceptance or a regretful refusal. Always remember the importance of politeness, even more particularly when you write than when you speak. Experience in writing letters will enable you either to accept an invitation gracefully or to decline one sincerely.

THE THANK-YOU NOTE

Most of the social notes you have had to write so far are thank-you notes for a gift you have received. A gift should never go unacknowledged as it represents a thoughtful gesture on the part of the person who gave it to you. Your thank-you notes should always be prompt, courteous, and appreciative. Go out of your way to make certain that the giver feels you enjoy the gift and that you will make use of it.

THE "BREAD-AND-BUTTER" NOTE

Another type of social note is the thank-you letter you write after you have been entertained at someone's home. Commonly called a "bread-and-butter" letter, this kind of social note is sent to your hostess, thanking her for her hospitality and saying what a good time you had. If you have been visiting a friend of your own age at his home, you should write your "bread-and-butter" letter to his mother (or whoever your hostess happened to be).

EXERCISE 1. Write a social note covering the following situation: You have received an unusual gift for Christmas. Thank the person who gave it to you and explain what you plan to do with the gift.

29 Kimberly Road
Glen Oaks, Wisconsin
June 22, 194–

Dear Jane,

You are a dear to remember my birthday! The beautiful white scarf you made arrived this morning, and it is already dated up with me for a trip tomorrow, where I'll show off your handiwork to some of my friends. How did you ever find time to do it? I particularly love the long fringe and the tiny hem-stitching that only you can do.

Today is really going to be celebrated in a grand way — Daddy is taking us to town for dinner and the movies. I can hardly wait for three o'clock.

Thanks again, Jane, for your marvelous gift.

Affectionately yours,
Sue

"BREAD-AND-BUTTER" NOTE

44 Appleton Road
Long Beach, California
August 2, 194–

Dear Mrs. Fairben,

Thank you a lot for having me at your home over the week end. You know what a good time Bruce and I had, and I hope I didn't make too much extra work for you. (Some time would you tell my mother how you make apple pie?) It was swell of you to invite me, and I enjoyed every minute of the week end.

Tell Bruce I'll write him soon.

Sincerely yours,
Larry

EXERCISE 2. You have been entertained for a week end at the cottage of your best friend. On Saturday it rained all day, but you all had a good time learning new card games and toasting marshmallows. Sunday the weather was perfect and you were in the water almost all day. Write your friend's mother a "bread-and-butter" letter, thanking her for her hospitality and also for having been resourceful about what to do to keep you entertained during the bad weather.

EXERCISE 3. Write a note to an out-of-town friend, asking him to spend the day with you during Easter vacation. Give him a choice of either of two days. Tell him what you plan to do (a bicycle trip, a baseball game, fishing — these are suggestions), and tell him to let you know what train he will come on.

EXERCISE 4. Answer the preceding invitation, either accepting or declining it. If you decline it, be sure to explain why you can't go.

THE BUSINESS LETTER

A business letter is written usually to a firm or an individual in a firm. It must be a combination of clearness, brevity, and courtesy.

APPEARANCE AND STATIONERY

Proper stationery is the first important consideration in a business letter. Businessmen much prefer that you type your letter if possible, on the usual $8\frac{1}{2} \times 11$ plain white paper. The typewritten letter is more legible and therefore more quickly read than a handwritten one. Business firms know that time is money to them; they do not want to have to decipher or decode your letter. If you write the letter by hand, use the same stationery as for a typewritten letter, if you have it; if not, any good-sized white writing paper will do. Also, remember to write carefully; your best penmanship is a courtesy you owe to anyone to whom you are writing.

FORM

The form of a business letter follows a certain pattern. Whether your letter is typewritten or handwritten, the pattern is the same. The semi-block form is used in the illustrations which you will find later in this chapter; however, the complete block form is also acceptable, and an illustration of that form is also given.

THE LETTER PICTURE

Before beginning your letter, judge the amount of space it will occupy on the page you are using. Center it as nearly as possible by making sure you have approximately the same margin at the top of your page as at the bottom, and the same margin on both the left- and right-hand sides. *Never* run your letter off the page at the right-hand side, and never finish the body of your letter at the end of a page so that you have nothing left for the second page except the complimentary close and your signature, or worse still, just your signature. For a model letter, see page 337.

1. *Heading:*

To begin your business letter, always put your *complete* address and the full date in the upper right-hand corner. It is better to write this **heading** without abbreviations.

EXAMPLES

49 Surrey Lane
Clinton, Iowa
June 4, 194–

or

R. F. D. 4
Cross Corners, Pennsylvania
September 27, 194–

2. *Inside address:*

The **inside address** should be placed at the left-hand side of the page, flush with the margin and several spaces (at least four, if the letter is type-written) lower on the page than the date. It should include the full name of the company to which you are writing, as well as its full address. If you are writing to an individual in the firm, use his full name and title, with a comma between the two if they are on the same line; if the name and title are too long to be put on one line, put the title on the next line.

The James Mills Company
220–224 Center Street
Waukegan, Illinois

Mr. James R. Joy, Vice-President
Newland and Company
40 Fifth Avenue
Dallas 8, Texas

Mr. Reginald B. MacPherson
Secretary to the President
Wilbur Field and Sons
218 South Street
Fort Hamilton, Virginia

Principal
Lakeview High School
Lakeview, Michigan

3. *Salutation (Greeting):*

The **salutation** is placed two spaces below the last line of the inside address and flush with the margin. The proper salutation for a letter written to a firm is *Gentlemen* followed by a colon. *Dear Sirs* is also used. When writing to an individual within the firm, the correct salutation is *Dear Mr. . . .* (or *Mrs.* or *Miss*) followed by a colon. If you are writing to a professional man or woman, use his title instead of *Mr.*

EXAMPLES   Gentlemen:
           Dear Mr. Bowne:
           Dear Dr. Grayce:
           Dear President Tyson:

Sometimes you may be writing to an officer in a firm without knowing his name. You may have just "Principal," "President," or "Secretary" on the first line of the inside address. The proper salutation then is *Dear Sir* followed by a colon.

4. *Body:*

The form of the **body** of a business letter is the form followed in the body of any letter. A double space is used between paragraphs of a typed letter. If your typewritten letter is short (7 lines or less), you may either put it on a smaller sheet of stationery or double space the entire body of the letter on 8½ × 11 stationery.

5. *Complimentary close (Leave-taking):*

The **complimentary close** of a letter is the leave-

taking that comes between the body of the letter and
the signature. In business letters, your complimentary closes are limited, and the same ones you use in
friendly letters will not do. *Very truly yours, Yours
truly*, and *Yours very truly* are the ones most frequently used. *Sincerely yours* and *Yours sincerely*
are also correct. The complimentary close is placed
just to the right of the center of the page, two spaces
below the last line of the body of your letter. It
is followed by a comma.

Avoid ending your letter with an outmoded phrase
such as "I beg to remain," "Hoping to hear from
you soon, I am," or "Thanking you in advance, I
am . . ." End the body of your letter with a *period*,
and then begin your complimentary close.

> Very truly yours,
> Yours truly,
> Sincerely yours,

6. *Signature*:

Sign your full name to your letter. Do *not* put
"*Miss*" or "*Mr.*" before your name. An unmar-
ried woman writing to a stranger should put *Miss*
in parentheses before her signature.

> *(Miss) Margaret Hoyt*

A married woman signs her full name (*Elise M.
Rhoad*), and if she wishes, she may put in paren-
theses and directly below her signature (*Mrs.
Robert L. Rhoad*).

> *Elise M. Rhoad*
> *(Mrs. Robert L. Rhoad)*

A signature should always be handwritten. If your
letter is typewritten, type your name below your

MODEL BUSINESS LETTER

1112 Rose Boulevard
Salt Lake City 2, Utah
June 1, 194—

Mr. George R. West, Director
Camp Winona
Sunrise Lake
Waban, Montana

Dear Mr. West:

Will you please send me the booklet
about your summer camp? I have heard about
your camp from several of my friends and it
sounds like just what I want.

If the booklet does not contain specific information about rates, will you
send me that also?

Very truly yours,

Gregory Jones
Gregory Jones

written signature, flush with the first letter of the complimentary close and far enough below to allow room for your signature.

7. *Envelope:*

For a letter on small stationery, use a small envelope (be sure the letter fits it). A letter on small single-sheet stationery is usually folded twice unless it fits into the envelope without any folding. The folds are made in this way: up from the bottom about a third of the way, then down from the top, so that when it is unfolded it will be right side up for the reader. Note paper or personal stationery is usually folded in half and inserted with the fold at the bottom of the envelope.

Either a small or a large envelope may be used for a letter on large single-sheet stationery. If a large envelope is used, the folding is the same as that of a small sheet for a small envelope. If the envelope is small, fold your letter up from the bottom to within a quarter of an inch of the top; then fold the right side over a third of the way; finally, fold the left side over. Insert in the envelope with the fold at the bottom of the envelope.

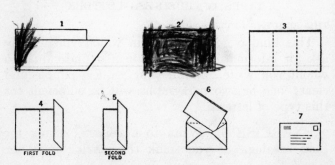

```
James Fairfield
188 Park Street
Bloomington, Illinois



                    Mr. Robert R. Sandless, Auditor
                    Field and Sons
                    215 North Avenue
                    Milwaukee 8, Wisconsin
```

Your envelope should carry both your full address and the same inside address as is on the letter. You may also include your name if you wish. You may put your return address on the back of the letter, but the Post Office prefers that you put the return address in the upper left-hand corner of the envelope on the same side as the address to which it is going. Unless the address to which a letter is being sent is very long, you should start it about halfway down the envelope and a little to the left of the center.

TYPES OF BUSINESS LETTERS

THE REQUEST LETTER

This kind of letter is one in which you usually ask for information from the firm or individual to whom you write. Make your request simple and clear; one or two paragraphs will be sufficient for this type of letter.

EXERCISE 5. Write to a college, asking for their catalog. If you think the catalog may not

MODEL REQUEST LETTER

76 Brixton Place
Phoenix 8, Arizona
July 8, 194—

Model Airways, Inc.
410-12 Second Avenue
Flagstaff 4, Arizona

Gentlemen:

    Will you please send me a copy of your
latest catalogue on model airplanes? I
have three of your models and would like to
add some of the later ones to my collection.

Very truly yours,
Frank Tyndall
Frank Tyndall

include all the information you need, ask specifically for whatever you wish to know.

Another type of request letter is the kind you write when you ask a firm to send a representative to your school for some purpose or other. This kind of letter is a little more complicated to write, because it is *you* who have to give the company information before they reply. Remember to include all the details necessary for the company's complete understanding of the situation.

EXERCISE 6. Copy in proper form the business letter given below.

420 Jackson Avenue, Far Hills, Texas, January 8, 194–. Mr. R. F. Hawkins, Business Manager, Perry and Company, 480–96 Dallas Street, Dallas 14, Texas. Dear Mr. Hawkins: Our junior class of 170 pupils in Far Hills High School is to decide this month on our class rings and pins. We expect to have representatives from several companies here on Monday, January 21, to show us samples of the rings and pins their firms make, together with price lists. We'd like very much to have someone from your company here on that date, if possible. Your representative should come to Room 31, any time after 2:45. Very truly yours, Sarah Porter, Secretary of the Junior Class, Far Hills High School.

EXERCISE 7. Using the following information, set up this material in the form of a business letter. You must compose the letter.

Miss Elsie Dowing of 222 Twin Oaks Road, Carlsburg, Ohio, writes on April 6, 1948, to the George C. Buckeye Company, 240 Lexington Avenue, Cleveland 2, Ohio, stating that while shopping there the week before, she lost a valuable gold ring. It contained a diamond and two pearls in an old-fashioned setting. She would like to know if it has been found and if so, where she may call for it.

EXERCISE 8. As student assembly-program chairman, you wish to have a neighboring high school send their glee club to perform in one of your assembly periods. Give the time, date, place, length of program, type of song selection (if you wish), details about transportation to your school, and any other information you think is necessary.

EXERCISE 9. You are interested in art. There is an exhibit to be given in the high school auditorium of a near-by city. Write to the art department of the high school requesting information. Ask specific questions about what you want to know — time, admission price, dates the exhibit will be displayed, etc.

EXERCISE 10. Write to the Cunard–White Star Steamship Company, asking them to send you their Travel Bureau booklets on the Lake Country of England. Request any information they can give you on sailings on their line from New York to either Liverpool or Southampton, England, for this next summer.

EXERCISE 11. You have failed your English course. Your principal has just told you that if you study through the summer you may be given a make-up examination in the fall. Your English teacher has already gone for the summer. Write to your teacher, explaining the circumstances and asking him to recommend an English textbook for you and perhaps suggest specific chapters in it which would help you most.

THE ORDER LETTER

If you are writing an order letter, you should list the items you wish, one below the other, with complete information (catalog number, style, size, price, etc.) about each item. The price should be put at the right-hand side (flush with the right-hand margin) and each amount should be placed directly under the one above, to make it easier to add the prices.

Also, in an order letter, be sure to specify how the articles you are ordering are to be paid for — check, money order, C. O. D., etc.

EXERCISE 12. Write a business letter to Marshall Field and Company, Chicago, ordering two size 14, long-sleeved cotton blouses, one plain white, the other French blue, at $3.98; 1 green "Betty Gaye" dress, size 13, @ $9.95. Have them sent C. O. D.

EXERCISE 13. Write to a stationer you know in a near-by city, asking him to make up for you 200 sheets of large personal stationery and 100 envelopes, both with your name and address printed on them. Give size, color, type of print, etc. Include information about how you will pay for this writing paper, and the approximate date you wish to have it sent.

EXERCISE 14. Pretend you have received a $50 check for your birthday and you wish to order

MODEL ORDER LETTER

58 Crane Street
Canton, Iowa
December 1, 194—

Webb and Sons
140–156 Seventh Avenue
Des Moines 11, Iowa

Gentlemen:

I should like to order the following articles, as advertised in the Des Moines Press of November 29.

2 white silk scarves, fringed, one with
   black initials A. J., the other with
   red initials M. W., @ $2.98 $5.96
1 size 15–34 man's white shirt, collar
   attached, @ $3.24   3.24
                  Total $9.20

I am enclosing a check for $9.20 to cover the total amount.

Very truly yours,

Amy Ladd

Amy Ladd

a complete outfit from your clothing store. Remember to include number, size, style, price (approximate, if you are not sure), and any other necessary information about each article you order.

THE ADJUSTMENT LETTER

An adjustment or a complaint letter is one which you write after an error has been made, either on your part or on that of the firm to which you have written.

Perhaps the wrong catalog has been sent to you, or you did not receive all the materials you ordered. Since this kind of situation is often a delicate one to handle, it calls for all the tact and diplomacy you can command. Even though it is a "complaint" letter, the tone need not necessarily be complaining. A courteous request to clear up the misunderstanding is more likely to meet with a courteous and prompt response than is a curt letter saying, "*This* time send me what I ordered in the first place!" Try to put yourself in the other person's place — the Golden Rule is still applicable — and let that be your guide in writing your adjustment letter. Be sure you give all information needed to clear up the situation.

EXERCISE 15. You have written to James B. Grayson, 20 Hill Street, Princeton, New Jersey, asking if you could borrow his vacant store at 401 Main Street for your club meetings. He has not replied. Write him again, explaining the circumstances. Before handing in your letter, read it over to see how you would feel if *you* were receiving the letter — would *you* lend *your* store?

MODEL ADJUSTMENT LETTER

2018 Lexington Avenue
Huntington, New York
October 3, 194—

Gimbel Brothers
33rd Street and Sixth Avenue
New York 1, New York

Gentlemen:

Two weeks ago I ordered from you, by
letter, a brown suede jacket, size 16,
Type 4-A, as advertised in the New York
Times for Sunday, September 15. I have
not heard from you to date and am wondering if my letter went astray or if you have
no more of the type of jacket I ordered.

Yours very truly,
Benjamin Rafter
Benjamin Rafter

EXERCISE 16. Revise the following letter as to form and content. Review this chapter before you attempt to do it. You should find 11 errors in form — the errors in content are uncountable!

---

14 Salisbury
Hampton, N. H.
July 5

Robert Berry and Co
State Street
Bridgeport 4, Connecticut

Dear Mr. Berry,

Last month I sent you an order and you haven't filled it yet. I ordered some white pine boards, 6 12x18x1 pieces, nails, a screw driver, and a hammer, and a saw. The whole bill came to $19.68 and I sent you a money order. I hope you take care of this immediately, if not sooner.

Angrily yours
Bert Dawson
Bert Dawson

THE LETTER OF APPLICATION

The letter of application is one with which you have no doubt had very little experience to date. However, you soon may find that it is one of the most important types of business letter, for it is in the application letter that you try to *sell yourself*.

When you apply for a position, your letter of application comes before your personal interview with your prospective employer. It is the first contact you have with him. Therefore, you must "put yourself across" in a way which will make him feel confident that you can do the job called for. You will also have an added advantage if you can put some original, personal touch into your letter (but only if it comes naturally to you), to distinguish you, favorably, from the rest of the applicants this employer may be considering.

There are certain things which should be included in every letter of application.

(1) Include a statement of the position you are applying for, and how you learned about it.

(2) Show that you know what qualifications are needed and that you believe you can fill them. State your age, experience, and education.

(3) Give references as to your character and ability.

(4) Request an interview at the employer's convenience.

EXERCISE 17. Write to a woman of your acquaintance who, you have heard, wants a girl during the month of July to take care of her children, ages 3 and 6, from 8:30 to 1:00 each day except Sunday.

State your qualifications, and try to make your letter interesting as well as informative.

EXERCISE 18. A drug store in a neighboring town needs a delivery boy from 4:00 to 6:00 after school and all day on Saturdays. Write your letter of application. Convince the druggist you are the best one for the job.

MODEL LETTER OF APPLICATION

---

                            98 Oxford Street
                            Clayton, Illinois
                            April 2, 194—

Mr. O. A. Lester, Director
Camp Carlson
Oneidaga Lake
Bloomfield, Illinois

Dear Mr. Lester:

   Ben Nichols, one of your regular campers, told me this week that you have a vacancy for a swimming counselor on your camp staff this summer, and I should like to apply for the position.

   I am a senior at Clayton High School and am eighteen years old. For the last two years I have been the junior swimming counselor at Camp Winnebega, Cauhoga Falls, Wisconsin. I have just received my Examiner's badge in lifesaving and am now certified for the position of senior swimming counselor. If you have junior or senior lifesaving classes, I am also qualified to direct them. Although I must admit I haven't had much experience in teaching lifesaving as yet, I feel right now as though I had been "worked on" plenty, both at camp and in our "Y" here at home.

The following men have given me permission to use their names as references:

Mr. J. B. Morse, Director, Camp Winnebega, Cauhoga Falls, Wisconsin.

Mr. Alexander B. Davis, Secretary, Y. M. C. A., Clayton, Illinois.

Mr. Chester Roberts, Principal, High School, Clayton, Illinois.

I shall be glad to come for a personal interview at your convenience.

Sincerely yours,
Frank Larson
Frank Larson

14. SPECIAL PROBLEMS IN GOOD USAGE

CHOOSING THE CORRECT WORD

The words grouped together in the list below are sometimes misused by persons who do not understand their meaning. Study the meaning of each so that in your speaking and writing you can choose the correct word.

Words whose *spelling* is hard to distinguish (words like *already, all ready; peace, piece; here, hear*) are explained in the spelling chapter. See pages 469 to 478.

accept, except. *Accept* is a verb; it means *to receive. Except* as a verb means *to leave out;* as a preposition it means *excluding.*

> I *accept* your apology.
>
> If you *except* the cost of materials, your estimate will be incorrect.
>
> Everyone *except* Dad gave his permission.

affect, effect. *Affect* is always a verb; it means *to influence. Effect* as a verb means *to accomplish. Effect* as a noun means the *result* of some action.

> Your story *affected* us deeply.
>
> The new principal *effected* several changes in the school.
>
> The *effect* of these changes was good.

allusion, illusion.   An *allusion* is a *reference* to something. An *illusion* is a *mistaken idea*.

> The speaker's *allusion* to the President was not flattering.
>
> Boris's ideas were impractical; he lived in a world of *illusions*.

alumni, alumnae.   *Alumni* (pronounced *à* lŭm′nī) is the plural of *alumnus* (male graduate). *Alumnae* (pronounced *à* lŭm′nē) is the plural of *alumna* (female graduate). The graduates of a co-educational school are referred to (as a group) as *alumni*.

> The girls were *alumnae* of many different schools.
>
> Yale has many famous *alumni*.
>
> The *alumni* of our high school frequently come back to visit us.

alumnus, alumna.   An *alumnus* is a *man or boy graduate*. An *alumna* is a *woman or girl graduate*.

> He is Harvard's most famous *alumnus*.
>
> Marie is an *alumna* of a distinguished girls' school.

beside, besides.   *Beside* means *by the side of* someone or something. *Besides* means *in addition to*.

> We will sit *beside* you.
>
> The school has several musical organizations *besides* the band.

EXERCISE 1. Number on your paper from 1 to 15. Choose the correct one of the two words in parentheses and write it after the proper number.

1. Please (accept, except) my congratulations.
2. His (allusion, illusion) to my brother disturbed me.
3. The Girls' Athletic Association of our school sent invitations to their (alumnae, alumni).

4. The coach has two good pitchers (beside, besides) Carl.
5. Under the (allusion, illusion) that the game was over, Gerald stopped playing.
6. Is she an (alumna, alumnus) of your school?
7. The dean refused to (accept, except) my excuse.
8. Everyone was noticeably (effected, affected) by the sudden change in temperature.
9. Both men and women among the (alumnae, alumni) contributed to the girls' gymnasium fund.
10. The Student Council (effected, affected) an improvement in student behavior.
11. I was surprised to find my father standing (beside, besides) me.
12. The (effect, affect) of the drug was miraculous.
13. Marilyn is an (alumna, alumnus) of a girls' school in the East.
14. The (effects, affects) of the storm were visible everywhere.
15. (Besides, Beside) her own children, Mrs. Frost takes care of her brother's child.

effect. See *affect, effect.*

emigrate, immigrate. *Emigrate* means *to go from a country* to settle elsewhere. *Immigrate* means *to come into a country* to settle there.

Thousands *emigrated* from Ireland during the years of famine.

Many Europeans *immigrate* to America every year.

except. See *accept, except.*

fewer, less. *Fewer* is used to refer to *number.* *Less* is used to refer to *quantity.*

There are *fewer* books in the school library than in the public library.

There is *less* carbon in this grade of steel.

good, well. *Good* is an *adjective*. Do not use *good* to modify a verb.

> WRONG The boys played good.
> RIGHT The boys played *well*.

Well is an *adverb* except in three uses: (1) When used to mean *healthy*, (2) when used to mean *neatly groomed* or *attractively dressed*, (3) when used to mean *satisfactory* — in all these instances *well* is an adjective. (See page 177.)

> She reads poetry very *well*. [adverb]
> Is your mother *well?* [adjective]
> You look *well* in blue. [adjective]
> All is *well*. [adjective]

imply, infer. *Imply* means *to suggest* something. *Infer* means *to interpret* or *get a certain meaning from* a remark or an action.

> In his comments, he *implied* strong opposition to our candidate.
> From your comments, I *infer* that you do not approve of my plan.

EXERCISE 2. Number on your paper from 1 to **12.** Choose the correct one of the two words in parentheses and write it after the proper number.

1. The Pilgrims (emigrated, immigrated) from England to escape the restrictions on freedom of worship.
2. There are (less, fewer) students in our school than in yours.
3. Jimmy can always be depended upon to play (well, good).
4. The teachers (implied, inferred) that they would excuse us.

5. In the first race, Harry ran (good, well).
6. There were (less, fewer) people in the stands than on the field.
7. Everyone thought you did very (good, well).
8. Most of the people who (immigrated, emigrated) to the United States in the nineteenth century came from northern Europe.
9. Helen did (good, well) in all her subjects.
10. The soccer team had (less, fewer) reserves than the football team.
11. I cannot help what others (infer, imply) from my remarks.
12. He always does his assignments (good, well).

illusion. See *allusion, illusion.*

immigrate. See *emigrate, immigrate.*

in, into. Careful speakers use *in* to mean *within a place*, and *into* to mean *movement from the outside to the inside of a place.*

> We waited *in* the lobby.
>
> I walked *into* the room.

learn, teach. *Learn* means *to acquire knowledge. Teach* means *to give out knowledge.*

> At an early age he *learned* to fly.
>
> I asked my brother to *teach* me how to dive.

leave, let. *Leave* means to go away. *Let* means *to allow* or *permit.*

> *Let* him *leave* when he wishes.

lie, lay. Do not confuse the various forms of these verbs whose meanings differ. *Lie* means *to recline, to rest, to remain in a lying position. Lay* means *to put, to place* something.

Lie never has an object. *Lay* may have an object.

The principal parts of *lie* and *lay* are:

	PRESENT	PRESENT PARTICIPLE	PAST	PAST PARTICIPLE
lie (to recline)	lie	lying	lay	(have) lain
lay (to put)	lay	laying	laid	(have) laid

WRONG I laid down for a rest.
RIGHT I *lay* down for a rest.
WRONG The book is laying over there.
RIGHT The book is *lying* over there.
WRONG We had laid there too long.
RIGHT We *had lain* there too long.

Exercises on the use of *lie* and *lay* will be found on pages 159–63.

like, as. *Like* is a *preposition*. *As* is usually a *conjunction*.

She plays *like* a professional. [prepositional phrase]
She plays *as* a professional plays. [subordinate clause introduced by a conjunction]

respectfully, respectively. *Respectfully* means *with respect* or *full of respect*. *Respectively* means *each in the order given*.

The ambassadors bowed *respectfully* before the king.
Ruth, Eleanor, and Polly will stand in first, second, and third places *respectively*.

rise, raise. Do not confuse the various forms of these verbs whose meanings differ. *Rise* means *to go in an upward direction*. *Raise* means *to force* some object *to move in an upward direction*.

Rise never has an object.
Raise may have an object.

The principal parts of *rise* and *raise* are:

	PRESENT	PRESENT PARTICIPLE	PAST	PAST PARTICIPLE
rise (to go up-ward)	rise	rising	rose	(have) risen
raise (to force upward)	raise	raising	raised	(have) raised

WRONG He raised from his chair reluctantly.

RIGHT He *rose* from his chair reluctantly.

WRONG The fog was raising rapidly.

RIGHT The fog was *rising* rapidly.

WRONG Clouds of dust had raised from the field.

RIGHT Clouds of dust *had risen* from the field.

Exercises on the use of *rise* and *raise* will be found on pages 166–67.

sit, set. Do not confuse the various forms of these verbs whose meanings differ. *Sit* means *to rest in an upright, sitting position.* *Set* means *to put, to place* something.

Sit never has an object. *Set* may have an object.

The principal parts of *sit* and *set* are:

	PRESENT	PRESENT PARTICIPLE	PAST	PAST PARTICIPLE
sit (to rest)	sit	sitting	sat	(have) sat
set (to put)	set	setting	set	(have) set

WRONG I set in the fresh paint.

RIGHT I *sat* in the fresh paint.

WRONG We were setting on the porch.

RIGHT We were *sitting* on the porch.

WRONG I have set in this chair many times.

RIGHT I *have sat* in this chair many times.

Exercises on the use of *sit* and *set* will be found on pages 163–66.

EXERCISE 3. Number on your paper from 1 to 20. Choose the correct one of the two words in parentheses and write it after the proper number.

1. At our approach he rushed (in, into) the house.
2. (Leave, Let) us go with you.
3. He (taught, learned) me all I know about riding.
4. With his usual courtesy, he signed the letter (Respectively yours, Respectfully yours).
5. We (lay, laid) the foundation yesterday.
6. "(Leave, Let) us stay a little longer," they pleaded.
7. I always wished I could play the violin (like, as) she does.
8. I crawled (in, into) the room through a small window.
9. The senator expected his audience to listen (respectively, respectfully).
10. Do (like, as) your father does.
11. (Leave, Let) him go when he apologizes.
12. Two dogs are (lying, laying) on the lawn.
13. He (rose, raised) up suddenly.
14. We (set, sat) there for an hour.
15. I (lay, laid) my glasses here an hour ago.
16. We are (sitting, setting) in the last row.
17. The teacher can't (teach, learn) you anything if you won't try.
18. When the fire siren blew, everyone ran (in, into) the street.
19. I offered to (teach, learn) him a few tricks.
20. You learn everything (as, like) I do — the hard way.

REVIEW EXERCISE A. Number on your paper from 1 to 20. Choose the correct one of the two words in parentheses and write it after the proper number.

1. Please (leave, let) her do as she wishes.
2. Many Italians have (immigrated, emigrated) to this country since 1900.

3. He reads French (good, well).
4. Go (in, into) the gym determined to win.
5. My father is an (alumna, alumnus) of Princeton.
6. (Besides, Beside) a Christmas party, we're having guests until New Year's.
7. How can anyone (teach, learn) you if you won't study?
8. Do (except, accept) my apologies for being late.
9. Mrs. Brown and Mrs. Stevens are (alumni, alumnae) of our high school.
10. I (infer, imply) from your letter that you are not interested in the position.
11. The decorated gymnasium gave one the (illusion, allusion) of being in a garden.
12. Try to do your homework (like, as) your sister does.
13. Where was it (laying, lying)?
14. We listened (respectfully, respectively) to the minister.
15. Bill got (less, fewer) people to vote for him this year.
16. Who is (sitting, setting) in the big chair?
17. The smoke (rose, raised) miles high.
18. How long has this been (laying, lying) here?
19. Where do you want to (sit, set)?
20. They have (lain, laid) here for days.

REVIEW EXERCISE B. Number on your paper from 1 to 20. Choose the correct one of the two words in parentheses and write it after the proper number.

1. She said she would (learn, teach) us to make fudge.
2. The culprits took their (respectful, respective) places one behind the other.
3. He (sat, set) on the broken chair.
4. Sheila is an (alumnus, alumna) of Girls Commercial School.
5. (Beside, Besides) going to school, he works at the post office.
6. Who has been (lying, laying) on this bed?

7. Are you (implying, inferring) that I can't spell properly?
8. I'm going (in, into) my room now.
9. Prices had (risen, raised) twenty per cent.
10. The soldier's speech (effected, affected) all of us deeply.
11. (Except, Accept) for two girls, the whole class was present.
12. Our ancestors (emigrated, immigrated) from Scotland in 1735.
13. Why are you (setting, sitting) here?
14. These boys are all (alumni, alumnae) of Brown University.
15. Please (leave, let) me do it my way.
16. I think Bill plays the piano (as, like) Mr. Bush.
17. He (lay, laid) his gifts under the tree.
18. What (affect, effect) did this have on you?
19. All the debaters did very (good, well).
20. Storm clouds were (raising, rising) in the west.

AVOIDING COMMON ERRORS

The words and expressions listed below are common errors in English. Ask yourself whether you ever use any of them. If you do, now is the time to eliminate them from your speech and writing.

ain't. Don't say it!

all the farther, all the faster. Poor English when used to mean *as far as, as fast as*

WRONG This is all the farther you can go .

RIGHT This is *as far as* you can go.

and etc. Since *etc.* is an abbreviation of the Latin *et cetera*, which means *and other things*, you are using *and* twice when you write "and etc." The *etc.* is sufficient.

anywheres, everywheres, nowheres. Use these words and others like them without the *s*.

RIGHT   *Everywhere* I looked, I saw mountains.

at.   Don't use *at* after *where.*

WRONG   Where were you at?
RIGHT   Where were you?

being as, being that.   Poor English. Use *since* or *because.*

WRONG   Being that there was no snow, we postponed our sleigh ride.
RIGHT   *Since* there was no snow, we postponed our sleigh ride.
WRONG   Being as he's the boss, we do what he says.
RIGHT   *Because* he's the boss, we do what he says.

bust, busted.   Use *broke* or *burst* instead.

WRONG   While skiing, he busted his ankle.
RIGHT   While skiing, he *broke* his ankle.
WRONG   The frozen pipes busted.
RIGHT   The frozen pipes *burst.*

bursted.   Incorrect past form of *burst.* The principal parts of *burst* are *burst, burst, has burst.*

WRONG   The gasoline tanks bursted into flame.
RIGHT   The gasoline tanks *burst* into flame.

EXERCISE 4.   The following sentences contain the errors just listed. Rewrite each sentence correctly. Practice saying *aloud* the correct sentences.

1. Being as we were tired of rising early, gulping our breakfast, catching the bus, and etc., we were glad to move nearer to school.

2. When I sat on the trunk, it busted wide open, and the contents flew everywheres.
3. Is this all the faster your car will go?
4. In Chicago where did you stay at?
5. A mob of children bursted through the doors.
6. I saw your sister somewheres downtown.
7. Being that the fog was heavy, we didn't know where we were at.
8. The bumper was busted and one of the tires had bursted.
9. Boards, bricks, window frames, and etc., were everywheres around the new house.
10. This is all the farther the road goes.
11. Terry busted his leash and we couldn't find him anywheres.
12. Being that the boiler has a safety valve somewheres on the top, it won't bust.

can't hardly, can't scarcely.   See *Double negative* (page 366).

can't help but.   See *Double negative* (page 366).

could of.   See *of*.

done.   Not the past form of *do*. *Done* always needs a helping verb: *has* done, *was* done, *will be* done, etc. The past form of *do* is *did*.

WRONG They done their best.
RIGHT They *did* their best.
RIGHT They *have done* their best.

don't.   A contraction of *do not*, *don't* should not be used with a singular noun or the third person singular pronouns (it, he, she). Use *doesn't*.

WRONG He don't mean what he says.
RIGHT He *doesn't* mean what he says.
WRONG It don't make any difference.
RIGHT It *doesn't* make any difference.

drownded. Incorrect past form of *drown*.

> WRONG No one was drownded in the flood.
> RIGHT No one was *drowned* in the flood.

had of. See *of*.

had ought. The verb *ought* should never be used with *had*.

> WRONG We had ought to have started earlier.
> RIGHT We *ought* to have started earlier.

> WRONG You hadn't ought to work so hard.
> RIGHT You *ought not* to work so hard.

hardly. See *Double negative* (page 366).

he, she, they, etc. Do not use unnecessary pronouns. This error is sometimes called the *double subject*.

> WRONG My sister she gets better marks than I.
> RIGHT My sister gets better marks than I.

kind of a, sort of a. The *a* is unnecessary. Leave it out.

> WRONG What kind of a book did you read?
> RIGHT What *kind of* book did you read?

might of, must of. See *of*.

nowheres. See *anywheres*.

of. Do not use *of* for *have*. Writing *of* for *have* (*should of, ought to of, might of, must of*) occurs because of faulty enunciation of *have*. Be careful that you do not *write* it as you sometimes *say* it.

> WRONG I could of beaten him.
> RIGHT I could *have* beaten him.

Do not use *of* unnecessarily. Avoid such expressions as *remember of, off of, had of*.

WRONG I don't remember of reading this before.
RIGHT I don't remember reading this before.

WRONG The boxes must have fallen off of the truck.
RIGHT The boxes must have fallen off the truck.

WRONG If I had of known, I'd of hurried.
RIGHT If I had known, I'd have hurried.

off of. See *of*.

ought. See *had ought*.

remember of. See *of*.

says. Commonly used for *said*. Avoid this usage.

WRONG When I saw Arnold he says, "I heard a story about you."
RIGHT When I saw Arnold, he *said*, "I heard a story about you."

WRONG I says to him, "Who told you the story?"
RIGHT I *said* to him, "Who told you the story?"

scarcely. See *Double negative* (page 366).

them. *Them* is not an adjective. Use *these* or *those*.

WRONG She bought one of them plastic handbags.
RIGHT She bought one of *these* plastic handbags.
RIGHT She bought one of *those* plastic handbags.

this here, that there. The *there* is unnecessary. Leave it out.

WRONG This here drawing won first prize.
RIGHT This drawing won first prize.

try and. The correct form is *try to*.

WRONG I will try and get the tickets for you.
RIGHT I will *try to* get the tickets for you.

ways, way. Use *way* in referring to a distance. Do not use *ways*.

WRONG He lives a long ways from here.
RIGHT He lives a long *way* from here.

when. Do not use *when* in writing a definition.

WRONG A foul ball is when the ball lands outside the playing field.
RIGHT A foul ball is *one that* lands outside the playing field.

where. Do not use *where* for *that*.

WRONG I read where the price of food is going up.
RIGHT I read *that* the price of food is going up.

Do not use *where* in writing a definition.

WRONG A lab is where a scientist does his experimenting.
RIGHT A lab is *a place in which* a scientist does his experimenting.

where . . . at. See *at*.

which, that, who. *Which* should be used to refer to *things* only. *That* may be used to refer to *both things and people*. *Who* should be used to refer to *people* only.

RIGHT He lived in one of the *houses which* were destroyed.
RIGHT There is a *man whom* (not *which*) I admire.
RIGHT There is a *man that* I admire.

you was. Don't say it. Say *you were*.

EXERCISE 5. The following sentences contain the errors just listed. Rewrite each sentence correctly. Practice saying *aloud* the correct sentences.

1. What sort of a hat do you want?
2. You must of come a long ways.
3. I don't remember of seeing that kind of a car.

4. A revolution is when the citizens rise up against their government.
5. You was going to try and collect some money for me.
6. The people which live on this here street must of lived here for years.
7. That there kind of a boat can go a long ways without refueling.
8. He fell off of one of them high fences.
9. I read where the mayor is going to try and raise taxes.
10. Some of them people which you was watching are wealthy immigrants.
11. I says to Peggy, "Get off of the running board." Then she says to me, "You don't own this here car."
12. I'll try and do them problems without your help.
13. It don't matter why he done it.
14. You hadn't ought to of said he was drownded.
15. My aunt she don't live here.

THE DOUBLE NEGATIVE

A *double negative* is a construction in which *two negative* words are used where one will do. Avoid using double negatives.

WRONG There isn't no time left.
RIGHT   There *is* no time left.
RIGHT   There isn't *any* time left.

There are several common double negatives; all are poor English.

can't help but

WRONG You can't help but like him.
RIGHT   You *can't help liking* him.

WRONG You couldn't help but doubt such a strange story.
RIGHT   You *couldn't help doubting* such a strange story.

hardly, scarcely, but, only should be used without a
negative word.

WRONG I can't hardly believe you.
RIGHT I *can hardly* believe you.
WRONG There weren't scarcely enough dishes for the
       crowd.
RIGHT There *were scarcely* enough dishes for the crowd.
WRONG I haven't but (only) a few more problems to
       solve.
RIGHT I *have but (only)* a few more problems to solve.
WRONG You hadn't no right to speak for me.
RIGHT You *had no* right to speak for me.

no, nothing, none

WRONG I haven't no excuse.
RIGHT I *have no* excuse.
RIGHT I *haven't any* excuse.   •
WRONG She hasn't done nothing all year.
RIGHT She *hasn't done anything* all year.
RIGHT She *has done nothing* all year.
WRONG I couldn't find none.
RIGHT I *couldn't find any*.

EXERCISE 6. The following sentences contain
the errors covered in Exercise 5 and those just listed
under the double negative. Rewrite each sentence
correctly. Practice saying *aloud* the correct sentences.

1. It could of been he who was drownded.
2. It don't matter whether I have the original or the
   copy because you can't hardly tell the difference
   between them.
3. My father he told me I hadn't ought to use poor
   English.
4. I can't help but wonder why she don't work harder.

5. My uncle and his family they always drop in when we haven't nothing in the house to eat.
6. If Jack had of been there, he wouldn't of been of no help.
7. It don't make no difference to me.
8. There wasn't scarcely time enough to finish our homework.
9. You hadn't ought to stay out so late.
10. The men drownded because we couldn't do nothing to help them.
11. We couldn't help but wonder where you was at.
12. Although it is a long ways to Houston, we'll try and be there by noon.
13. This here bike is not the kind of a bike I ordered.
14. He says to me, "I done my best."
15. The boys which live on our street formed a ball team, but they didn't win no games.
16. A lateral pass is when the ball is thrown back or across, not up the field.
17. I read in the paper where all them new houses had been sold.
18. They hadn't ought to swim so far out.
19. He done his best which wasn't hardly good enough.

REVIEW EXERCISE C.   The following sentences contain the common errors you have been studying.   Rewrite these sentences correctly.

1. He might of fallen from that there tree, for he can't hardly climb at all.
2. She don't know where she's at.
3. We certainly done our best to try and save her, but she was quite a ways out in the water and we couldn't scarcely see her from where we were.
4. I don't remember of seeing that movie; I must of seen it a long time ago.
5. Here is a boy which needs no introduction to you; you can't help but know him well.

6. Jim and Tom could of gone in Max's car, being as he had it for the day, if the fan belt hadn't busted.

7. Patsy couldn't of thought of anywheres else to go.

8. There wasn't hardly a place around this here town where she hadn't been at.

9. Hand me them shears, will you? I can't hardly reach them.

10. When you got off of the bus, you was nearly home.

11. As he pulled me out, my uncle says, "You might of drownded! You had ought to be more careful."

12. I can't hardly see the fire from here; most of it must be behind that there building.

13. An error is when a player makes a mistake.

14. Books, papers, magazines, and etc., littered the room; there wasn't nowheres to sit down.

15. If I had of gone with my aunt instead of my mother, there wouldn't of been nothing said.

REVIEW EXERCISE D. The following sentences contain the common errors you have been studying. Rewrite these sentences correctly.

1. We hadn't only fifty cents, so we shouldn't of started out anyway.

2. Our water pipes bursted, and some of the plaster busted off the ceiling.

3. My friends they always phone me before eight o'clock, being that they know I start my homework then.

4. A jackknife dive is when you spring, touch your hands to your knees, and then straighten out.

5. In the paper I saw where we're in for trouble in this here town.

6. Bruce must of gone quite a ways into the woods, since he didn't realize where he was at.

7. We looked everywheres for him; and when we finally found him, we couldn't hardly see him, as it was dusk by that time.

8. We done the only thing possible; we hadn't no compass, so we broke a trail to find our way back.
9. I says I didn't remember of doing that.
10. There was a man which we hadn't seen before.
11. Although we hadn't but two gallons of gas, we set out for the beach; we found it wasn't scarcely enough.
12. You really hadn't ought to be swimming in this here weather.
13. My pals they said they hadn't no suits, so they wouldn't go.
14. If we'd of been smart, we would of noticed the rain clouds.
15. It don't matter if the fender is busted.

15. CAPITAL LETTERS

The use of capital letters is a matter of habit and carefulness as well as of knowing the rules. Always read over your written work to check it for capitals.

TRY–OUT TEST. If you can make 100% on the following quiz, you may work through this chapter very rapidly. If you make a lower score, you should learn the uses of capital letters and do the exercises so that you will be able henceforth to use capital letters correctly.

Number on your paper from 1 to 25. In each of the following items you are to choose the correct one of two forms. After the proper number on your paper write the letter of the correct form (a or b).

1. a. We spent the summer in Maine.
   b. We spent the Summer in Maine.

2. a. the Mississippi River
   b. the Mississippi river

3. a. the Empire State building
   b. the Empire State Building

4. a. He lives on Pine Street.
   b. He lives on Pine street.

5. a. Lafayette college is in Easton.
   b. Lafayette College is in Easton.

6. a. Are you going to the Senior Prom?
   b. Are you going to the senior prom?

7. a. He will be a senior next year.
   b. He will be a Senior next year.

8. a. Amherst was his college.
   b. Amherst was his College.

9. a. I am taking Latin and Geometry.
   b. I am taking Latin and geometry.

10. a. the Atlantic ocean
    b. the Atlantic Ocean

11. a. our High School
    b. our high school

12. a. The Principal is in his office.
    b. The principal is in his office.

13. a. We heard the President speaking from the White House.
    b. We heard the president speaking from the White House.

14. a. Mr. Lewis, superintendent of schools
    b. Mr. Lewis, Superintendent of Schools

15. a. They worshiped god in their own way.
    b. They worshiped God in their own way.

16. a. The Rivoli Theater
    b. The Rivoli theater

17. a. Zeus was a Greek god.
    b. Zeus was a Greek God.

18. a. Is he a Frenchman?
    b. Is he a frenchman?

19. a. The cities of europe were destroyed.
    b. The cities of Europe were destroyed.

20. a. Harold owns a cocker spaniel pup.
    b. Harold owns a Cocker Spaniel pup.

21. a. Thirty-fourth Street
    b. Thirty-Fourth Street

22. a. We spent our vacation in the North.
    b. We spent our vacation in the north.

23. a. They drove South for ten miles.
    b. They drove south for ten miles.

24. a. the General Electric Company
    b. the General Electric company
25. a. Everyone feared a civil war.
    b. Everyone feared a Civil War.

15a. Capitalize the pronoun *I* and the interjection O.

WRONG "o boy!" i cried.
RIGHT "*O* boy!" *I* cried.

15b. Capitalize the first word in any sentence.[1]

WRONG Jefferson was an early champion of states' rights. on the other hand, Hamilton believed in a strong central government. it was a good thing to have these two views represented in the early days of our country.

RIGHT Jefferson was an early champion of states' rights. On the other hand, Hamilton believed in a strong central government. It was a good thing to have these two views represented in the early days of our country.

15c. Capitalize proper nouns and proper adjectives.

A proper noun is the name of a particular person, place, or thing.

How a proper noun differs from an ordinary, common noun, which is not capitalized, can be seen from the following lists.

COMMON NOUN	PROPER NOUN
city	Chicago
boy	George
lake	Crater Lake

[1] Failure to use a capital letter at the beginning of a sentence is almost always the result of failure to recognize the beginning of a sentence. For exercises in recognizing the beginning of a sentence see pages 101–103.

Do not confuse proper nouns, which are *names*, with nouns which merely state kind or type. For instance, *terrier* is not a proper noun because it is not the name of a particular dog; it is merely a kind or type of dog; similarly, *truck* is not the name of a particular automobile (like Chevrolet, Plymouth, etc.) but tells only the type of automobile.

RIGHT   Helen's dog is a cocker spaniel.
RIGHT   His name is Blackie.
WRONG   Jerry's ambition is to own a Ford Convertible.
RIGHT   Jerry's ambition is to own a Ford convertible.

A proper adjective is an adjective formed from a proper noun.

PROPER NOUN	PROPER ADJECTIVE
Spain	*Spanish* town
America	*American* citizen
Democrat	*Democratic* leader

Careful study of the classifications which follow will help you to recognize the most frequently used proper nouns.

(1) Capitalize geographical names.

CITIES AND TOWNS: Meadville, Kansas City
COUNTIES AND TOWNSHIPS: Nassau County, Sherman Township
STATES: Arkansas, New Mexico
COUNTRIES: Union of Soviet Socialist Republics, United States of America, Great Britain
CONTINENTS: Europe, Asia
ISLANDS: Fire Island
BODIES OF WATER: Columbia River, Great Salt Lake, Lake Erie, Pacific Ocean, Red Sea
MOUNTAINS: Appalachian Mountains, Bear Mountain

STREETS: Main Street, Fairmount Boulevard, Dover Parkway, Twenty-third Street. [In a hyphenated *number*, the second word begins with a small letter.]

PARKS: Yellowstone National Park, Deerfield State Forest

SECTIONS OF THE COUNTRY: the East, the Middle West

(2) Do not capitalize *east, west, north,* and *south* when they indicate merely directions. Do capitalize them when they refer to sections of the country.

RIGHT Go west for two miles and turn south.
RIGHT We enjoyed our winter in the South.

(3) Do not capitalize a common noun modified by a proper adjective unless it is part of a name.

RIGHT a Mediterranean *country*
RIGHT a Pacific *island*
RIGHT Catalina *Island* (*Island* is part of a name)

EXERCISE 1. Copy the following, using capital letters wherever they are required.

1. anderson park
2. the arctic ocean
3. washington avenue
4. a french village
5. glen lake
6. savannah river
7. staten island
8. bergen county
9. the kansas wheatfields
10. an indian canoe
11. a mile west of here
12. an american industry
13. birmingham, alabama
14. twenty-first street
15. in south america

16. living in the east
17. the west side of twelfth street
18. the ural mountains
19. some montana copper mines
20. a lake michigan steamer

EXERCISE 2. Copy the following sentences, inserting capitals wherever needed.

1. Heading west from new york, we drove down seventh avenue, under the hudson river and across the pulaski skyway in new jersey.
2. Crossing the delaware river at easton and the susquehanna river at harrisburg, we soon entered one of america's best superhighways.
3. In somerset county we crossed the allegheny mountains, which separate the east from the middle west.
4. At pittsburgh the allegheny river and the monongahela river come together to form the ohio.
5. After continuing our drive across ohio to buckeye lake and columbus, we headed west to visit our friends on an indiana farm near indianapolis.
6. Father wanted us to see chicago, which lies in cook county, illinois, at the foot of lake michigan.
7. We visited municipal pier, where we boarded a large lake steamer which had just arrived from mackinac island and a northern cruise into lake superior.
8. The meeting place of the great railroads of the east with those of the west, chicago has always been the greatest inland city of north america.
9. As there were no mountains on our route between the appalachians and the rockies, we had to wait until we reached denver, where we saw pike's peak towering to the south.
10. We spent a week in rocky mountain national park before continuing our journey toward california and the pacific ocean.

EXERCISE 3. Read the following paragraphs and list in a column all words requiring capitals. When two capitalized words belong together list them together: *West Main Street, Memorial Park,* etc. Before each word write the number of the sentence in which it appears. Do not list words already capitalized.

EXAMPLE

1. We moved recently from west main street to park boulevard. 2. Our new home looked out on memorial park and morgan's creek.

1. West Main Street
   Park Boulevard
2. Memorial Park
   Morgan's Creek

1. Our school is a consolidated school on the shores of greenwood lake in macy county. 2. The students come from farms and towns as far away as somerset to the west and bordenville to the east. 3. Yesterday our assembly speaker was a professor of economics from Western Reserve University in cleveland.

4. He was explaining to us our dependence upon all parts of the united states for products we use every day. 5. To her embarrassment, he called Betty, a junior from storm corners, to the platform and asked her where she thought her sweater had come from. 6. Betty told him her mother had bought it for her at Boyd's Department Store on franklin avenue, and this gave the speaker his chance.

7. He pointed out that the wool may have come from a farm in the middle west and been knitted by a machine in a new england factory, perhaps on the shores of the merrimack river in new hampshire. 8. He thought the sweater may have been designed on thirty-first street in new york city. 9. Dyes for the wool would at one time have come

from germany, but today probably were manufactured in the east. 10. As for Betty's blouse, made of rayon, there was little doubt that its source was pulpwood from trees grown in canada or in maine.

11. The speaker thought that the leather for Betty's loafers may have once roamed a ranch in wyoming. 12. He said that it could have come from argentina, by ship through the atlantic ocean, into the caribbean sea, and eventually via new orleans up the mississippi river to st. louis, which is the principal shoe manufacturing city of north america.

13. Noticing the textbook in Betty's hand, the speaker told of seeing trees growing along nipigon bay and nipigon river in ontario, canada, on the northern shore of lake superior, which were destined to be shipped as pulpwood down through lake huron to paper mills in michigan.

(4) Capitalize names of organizations, business firms, institutions, ships, planes, brand names of business products, special events, items on the calendar, races, and religions.

ORGANIZATIONS AND CLUBS: Independent Order of Odd Fellows, Masquers Club, North Shore Country Club

BUSINESS FIRMS: Harcourt, Brace and Company; Sperry Gyroscope Company, Hostage Book Stores, Inc.

INSTITUTIONS: Mercy Hospital, Woolworth Building, Waldorf-Astoria Hotel, Fantasy Theater, Harvard University, Dartmouth College, Belmont High School, Montclair Academy, Congress, the Supreme Court

NOTE: Do not capitalize such words as *hotel, theater, college, high school* unless they are part of a proper name.

Williams College	a college in Massachusetts
Commodore Hotel	a hotel in New York
Lakewood High School	a high school student, a high school in Ohio

SHIPS, PLANES, BUSINESS PRODUCTS, AND OTHER THINGS
HAVING PARTICULAR NAMES: the *Britannic* (ship),
a Constellation (plane), the Congressional Medal of
Honor

EVENTS: National Horse Show, National Tennis
Championships, Senior Prom

HISTORICAL EVENTS AND PERIODS: Dark Ages, Battle of
El Alamein, Reconstruction Period, World War II

CALENDAR ITEMS: Monday, January, Thanksgiving,
Memorial Day [2]

RACES AND RELIGIONS: Negro, Presbyterian

(5) Do not capitalize the names of seasons.

RIGHT summer, winter, spring, fall [Some newspapers
do not follow this practice.]

**(6) Do not capitalize *senior, sophomore, junior, freshman,* un-
less part of a proper noun.**

RIGHT A sophomore may go to the Senior Prom if escorted
by a senior.

15d. Do not capitalize the names of school subjects, except the languages. Course names followed by a number are usually capitalized.

RIGHT English, French, Spanish, Latin, German, Italian
RIGHT algebra, art, chemistry, domestic science, history
RIGHT Algebra II, History III

EXERCISE 4. Copy the following sentences, inserting capital letters wherever needed.

1. This novel was published on armistice day last year
by henry holt and company.

---

[2] The usual rule is that *day* is capitalized when it is a part of the
name; otherwise, it is written with a small letter: Memorial Day,
but Christmas day. This distinction, however, is not always
observed.

2. This day was chosen because the book describes the deeds of American soldiers in all the wars fought by America, including the civil war, the spanish american war, and both world war I and world war II.

3. I began to read the book on sunday afternoon, but it was wednesday before I finished it in english class.

4. Many of the heroes were boys just out of high school, while others had graduated from colleges in all parts of the United States.

5. One of them had been an employee of the wright aeronautical corporation and the ford motor company before he was drafted into the Navy.

6. A graduate of deerfield academy and the massachusetts institute of technology, he was an expert radio technician and had been sent to columbia university for further training.

7. His experiences began in the fall of 1944 when he was stationed at a base in the Pacific.

8. He went to sea in the spring and saw action in the battle of the philippine sea and the invasion of Leyte.

9. That summer he was given the navy cross for valor in action when his ship, the *Corsair*, sank, and he saved the lives of several men.

10. On his return after v-j day the rotary club of his home town gave a dinner in his honor at the bennett hotel and held a mass meeting in the savoy theater where he received a gift from the chamber of commerce.

11. On armistice day he was the principal speaker in assembly at his old high school where, as a representative of the navy's bureau of public relations, he told the juniors and seniors about his war experiences.

12. The other character I liked best in these stories was a hero of the confederate army in the american civil war.

EXERCISE 5. Copy the following sentences, inserting capital letters wherever needed.

1. A letter from the republic aircraft corporation announces that three planes will be sent to the national air show in cleveland, ohio, which will open on the fourth of july.
2. Is he a member of either the local masonic lodge or the elks club?
3. The american legion will have charge of the parade on armistice day.
4. The parade will form at the gate of the shelley electric company and march past the johnson memorial hospital and the sherman building to the united presbyterian church.
5. Jerry, whom I knew when we were in high school, resigned from his position with the general electric company in order to enroll at cornell university.
6. Although I don't do so well in social studies, mathematics, and chemistry, I enjoy them as much as english and french, which are my best subjects.
7. The stamp club, which meets at the community building once a week, probably has the quietest meetings of any club in our high school.
8. The park theater, which stands next to the new hayes-belmont hotel, shows pictures made by metro-goldwyn-mayer, damon brothers, and paramount.
9. On the morning of thanksgiving day the family went to municipal stadium for the game between madison high and southwestern.
10. Because he had studied only two years of latin in high school, he had to take latin I during his freshman year in college.
11. The juniors were invited to attend the senior prom the night before commencement, but freshmen and sophomores had to be escorted by a junior or senior.
12. Fred's description of costumes worn during the stone

age was naturally much shorter than Helen's account of dresses worn during the victorian era.

13. Because he failed both algebra and history last spring, my brother went to the freeport summer high school this summer.

14. The dramatic club meets every friday afternoon from december to march, but only on every other friday during the fall and spring.

15. The posters made by seniors in their art classes this fall, picturing the work of the red cross from the crimean war to world war II, were displayed from thanksgiving to christmas in the store windows of the C. G. Longmans company.

EXERCISE 6. As you did in Exercise 3, list all words requiring capitals in the following sentences. Do not list words already capitalized.

1. Mary Ann was a stranger here last october. 2. On memorial day, she had landed in detroit from dayton, but she had gone to dayton from washington and to washington from texas. 3. All this she had done in one year because she was the daughter of an Army officer who was apparently getting new orders about once a month.

4. Her first view of the city was from an airplane. 5. The penobscot building, she said, was clearly distinguishable, as were such places as cadillac square, grand boulevard, and briggs stadium.

6. So far as high schools are concerned, Mary Ann has seen all kinds. 7. Although she prefers smaller schools, she says she likes highland park high. 8. The trip downtown on a woodward avenue bus seems long to her, but any ride on land seems long to Mary Ann, who is used to flying her own aircoupe at the wayne county airport.

9. Her father, Colonel Bryan, taught her to fly last year in arizona. 10. Furthermore, she seems to be rather used to swimming in the pacific ocean one day and in the

atlantic ocean the next. 11. Perhaps now that she's living in the north she'll be having her summer swims in the detroit river at belle isle and her winter ones in our school pool. 12. She plans to fly to florida for Christmas and get acquainted with the gulf of mexico.

13. Mary Ann is taking english, social studies, trigonometry, chemistry, and commercial work. 14. She's had to give up her spanish because her frequent moves interrupted her work. 15. She says you have to keep at a foreign language to learn it at all and that when you know as little about spanish as she does you forget between moves. 16. She had the same trouble with french and latin last year. 17. With all the traveling around she seems to do, though, she'll probably end up in france or spain and learn her french and spanish that way.

18. I think Mary Ann is lucky to have seen so much, but she says to give her a home either north, south, east, or west, but not all four directions at once.

REVIEW EXERCISE A. Copy the sentences below, using capital letters wherever they are required.

1. The old school building at the corner of twenty-first street and carlton avenue has been sold by the greenville board of education.
2. The church street junior high school was built by the wagner construction company during the spring and summer of last year.
3. In junior high school I had better grades in english than in social studies and math.
4. The drama club tried to rent the peabody auditorium for its play, but the woman's club had reserved it for a concert by the minneapolis symphony orchestra.
5. His ship, the *Flying Gull*, sailed from lake michigan to the gulf of mexico via the mississippi river.

6. New factories in the south rival the industrial plants of the north.
7. On the west side of town lies coolidge park, and on the east side lies burnham park.
8. The countries of europe are not sure whether to turn their faces west toward the americas or east toward asia.
9. The great smoky mountains are the principal mountains in tennessee and north carolina.
10. Both seniors and juniors have been invited to the sophomore carnival in the gym on the eve of christmas vacation.
11. During the victorian age the british empire expanded into all corners of the world.
12. The american history classes of the three city high schools produced a pageant on memorial day honoring american soldiers and sailors.
13. A dodge coupe belonging to the gulf oil corporation was parked at foster's garage in the mechanical trades building.
14. On the north side of the street several indian and mexican villagers formed a small crowd.
15. The paramount theater was showing a french film with english subtitles.

15e. Capitalize titles.

(1) Capitalize titles of persons: General Marshall, Superintendent Jones, President Marks.

NOTE: Do not capitalize titles used alone or after the person's name unless they are titles of important government figures or titles of persons to whom you wish to show special respect.

RIGHT The President addressed Congress today.
RIGHT Mr. Harper is president of this company.
RIGHT Mr. Anderson, the superintendent of schools, introduced Captain Armstrong.

NOTE: Names of official positions, such as *senator, representative, admiral,* etc. are not capitalized unless used with a name or to refer to a particular person.

RIGHT Although he wanted to be a senator from his state, he ran first for the office of representative.

RIGHT The Senator will be glad to help you.

NOTE: Words of family relationship (mother, cousin, aunt, etc.) are capitalized when used with a person's name.

RIGHT Uncle George, Cousin Martha

Words of family relationship may be capitalized or not when used in place of a person's name.

RIGHT "Hello, *Father.*"   (*Father* is used in place of the man's name.)

RIGHT "Hello, *father.*"

When preceded by a possessive noun or pronoun, words of family relationship are not capitalized unless used with the person's name.

RIGHT The boy's *father* sent him to a private school.

RIGHT I visited my *uncle* in Denver.

RIGHT I am very fond of my *Uncle Bill.*

(2) Capitalize the first word and all important words in the titles of books, magazines, newspapers, articles, historical documents, works of art: *Atlantic Monthly, Madonna of the Chair, The Last of the Mohicans, Treaty of Paris, Mutiny on the Bounty.*

NOTE: The words *a, an,* and *the* written before a title are capitalized only when they are a part of the title. In the case of magazines and newspapers, they are usually not capitalized at all.

EXAMPLES Part of title   *A Tale of Two Cities*
                         The End of the Trail

Not part of title   the *Saturday Evening Post*
the *Adventures of Sherlock Holmes*

(3) Capitalize words referring to the Deity: God, Father, His will, etc.

NOTE: The word *god*, when used to refer to the pagan deities of the ancients, is not capitalized.

RIGHT   The Greek gods had human traits.

EXERCISE 7.   Copy the following sentences, inserting capital letters wherever needed.

1. A novel, *lost horizon*, by the English writer James Hilton, was recommended by Betty Swan, president of the Book Club.

2. The movie version of the play *ten little indians* was called *and then there were none*.

3. Mr. Briggs, principal of the high school, enjoys good biographies. He told me to read Carl Sandburg's *abraham lincoln: the prairie years*.

4. We asked professor Barclay, head of the art department in Burton College, to tell us about Leonardo's painting, *the last supper*.

5. My aunt Jane, who is my mother's sister, lives with grandfather Whiting in Nebraska.

6. Anderson's play, *the eve of st. mark*, describes the hardships of our soldiers before the loss of Bataan, but his best-known war play, *what price glory?*, was written about World War I.

7. The statue, *the returning warrior*, by professor Hall, is a better work of art than Miss Long's painting, *the veteran returns*.

8. The French painter Millet, who painted *the angelus*, should not be confused with the English artist Millais, who painted *the boyhood of raleigh*.

9. The reverend John Boardman, pastor of our church,

urged his congregation to do the will of god and to pray for his blessing.

10. After reading the *Saturday evening post* from cover to cover, dr. Bowles read the current issue of *reader's digest*.

11. Whenever I ask mother for money, she says, "Ask your father."

12. The first article in this month's *harper's*, "some facts about atomic energy," was written by doctor Owen Rand, chairman of the physics department and author of the book *how to smash an atom*.

13. Marilyn, who has read *gone with the wind* five times, never has time to read her homework.

14. The crowds greeted king George and queen Mary enthusiastically.

15. It was chancellor Jordan, formerly president of Fernall College, whom we heard lecture on *the values of a college education*.

REVIEW EXERCISE B. Copy the following sentences, inserting capital letters wherever needed.

1. "Learning to use capital letters," said professor quiz at his lecture in byrne hall, "is as important as it is easy."

2. They put in a call for dr. carter, the only doctor in geopolis, whose office on main street and maple avenue occupies the back part of the commercial building.

3. Although the united states is bounded on the east by the atlantic ocean, the south, by the gulf of mexico, and the west, by the pacific ocean, the state with the longest coast line is not florida or california, but michigan, which is bounded on three sides by the great lakes.

4. "Languages taught in american high schools are latin, which is a classical language, and german, spanish,

french and italian, which are modern languages," explained mr. bright of woodview high school in addressing the meadville chapter of the league of women voters last monday.

5. "Their native language, english," added the teacher, "often seems more foreign even to juniors and seniors, than do some of the other modern languages they learn in high school."

6. Around garden city, nassau county is very flat, but north of there, in the region of great neck and roslyn, there are hills which look out upon long island sound.

7. My friend peter blakely, president of the american cycle company, has an office in the empire state building, a home in the suburbs, and a summer home on the delaware river in the pocono mountains of pennsylvania.

8. Treasure island in san francisco bay was the scene of the golden gate exposition in 1939; and flushing meadow in the borough of queens was the scene of the new york world's fair which opened in 1938 and continued until the fall of 1939.

9. Many american citizens saw both fairs and a good part of north america that summer as they crossed the continent with brief excursions into mexico to the south or canada to the north.

10. The smith shoe company has factories in new england and in the south, but the main offices are in the smith building overlooking the hudson river in new york city.

11. The *great charter*, which was signed by king john at runnymede on june 15, 1215, was declared null and void by the pope in august.

12. The president closed his address before congress on memorial day with a request to god for his guidance.

13. Having read *a tale of two cities* by the famous english novelist charles dickens, I read *the old curiosity shop*

and *bleak house*, and then turned to some of the other victorian writers.

14. We went to the hollywood theater to see *the march of time* last evening and missed *information please*, one of our favorite radio programs.

15. Velasquez' paintings, *the forge of vulcan* and *portrait of the child don carlos*, which are hung in the prado museum in madrid, were moved to geneva, switzerland, during the spanish civil war.

REVIEW EXERCISE C. Copy the following sentences inserting capital letters wherever needed. In this exercise apply all the capital letter rules you have learned.

1. Fred Martin graduated from lincoln high school in seattle, washington, in june, and he entered washington state college the following fall.

2. In high school he was captain of the football team and majored in science and math, but in college he went out for cross country and majored in english and european history.

3. Since all school teams follow the rules of the american football association, the football played in the west is exactly like the football played in the east.

4. Our seats in bryce stadium were on the east side of the field so that we had to look west directly into the sun.

5. Between albany and buffalo the new york central railroad follows the mohawk valley, running alongside the mohawk river and the new york state barge canal.

6. On labor day we hurried back from baker lodge in the white mountains, where we had spent the summer.

7. The american holiday, the fourth of july, commemorates the signing of the declaration of independence at independence hall in philadelphia in 1776.

8. My mother and I went to father's office where we met uncle bill and my aunt.

9. My first book report this fall was on *the carolinian*, Sabatini's story of the south in the american revolution.

10. The committee asked commander lane of the american legion to speak on the subject *lessons learned from world war II*.

11. The board of directors elected mr. thomas marshall to the presidency of the eagle aircraft corporation, makers of the *cloudbreaker* and the *hi-flyer*.

12. A class in french for juniors was scheduled this fall at mayer high school for students who had not taken a foreign language in their freshman and sophomore years.

13. The minister prayed, "o god, teach us to do thy will at all times."

14. On saturday, december 3, we took off from newark airport in new jersey, in an american airlines plane.

15. It was principal Marks of the grove street school who opposed mayor walker when he forced the board of education to hold school on the friday after thanksgiving day.

CAPITAL LETTERS

SUMMARY STYLE SHEET

GEOGRAPHICAL NAMES

Dodge *City*	a *city* in Kansas
Chippewa *State Park*	a *state park*
Bear *Mountain*	a *mountain* stream
Arctic *Ocean*	an *ocean* liner
Main *Street*	a wide *street*
Missouri *River*	a navigable *river*
living in the *West*	facing *west*, the *west* side of the road

a *Western* cowboy   the *western* slope
the Mediterranean *Sea*   a Mediterranean *country*

ORGANIZATIONS, INSTITUTIONS, BUSINESS PRODUCTS,
SPECIAL EVENTS, CALENDAR ITEMS,
RACES, AND RELIGIONS

Varsity *Club*   a *club* for athletes
Elco *Electric Company*   an *electric company*
the Bijou *Theater*   a modern *theater*
Garfield *High School*   a large *high school*
Roosevelt *Hotel*   the newest *hotel*
the *Civil War*   a *civil war*
the *Middle Ages*   in *medieval times*
Labor Day   *Christmas day*
English, French, Latin, Ger-   algebra, art, domestic science,
  man, Spanish, Italian, Al-   science, history, math
  gebra II
the *Senior Prom*   a *senior* [*junior, sophomore,*
                                  freshman] in high school
                                  summer, winter, fall, spring

Negro
Roman Catholic

TITLES

Superintendent Jones ·   Mr. Jones, the *superintend-*
                                  ent
the *President* [the *Senator*,   a *senator's* power, the *presi-*
  the *Congressman*, etc. —   *dent* of the class
  high government offi-
  cials]
A Tale of Two Cities, The
  Casting Away of Mrs.
  Lecks and Mrs. Aleshine
the Philadelphia *Inquirer*
God made *His* will known.   the *gods* of the Greeks
Aunt Sarah   my *aunt*
I'll tell *Mother*.   my *mother*

16. PUNCTUATION

END MARKS

PUNCTUATION FOR CLEARNESS

The various marks of punctuation exist for the single purpose of making meaning clear. What this means may be seen in the following sentences where punctuation marks are necessary to make the sentence understandable.

CONFUSING Into the boiling stew she dropped the vegetables and Mary stirred them with a spoon.

CONFUSING My uncle Captain Leslie said James is a poor sailor.

CONFUSING The children munched happily on the various courses: soup vegetables and meat salad rolls and butter pie and ice cream.

CONFUSING He settled wearily onto the first chair which was not strong enough to hold him.

WHEN IN DOUBT LEAVE IT OUT

Modern writers use punctuation as much as is necessary to make clear what they want to say, but they use it only when it *is* necessary. Have a reason (either a definite rule or a matter of meaning) for every mark of punctuation you use. When there is no rule requiring a mark of punctuation and the meaning of the sentence is clear, do not insert any punctuation mark. This is a general principle which applies to most situations, though not to all; it does not mean that you can argue in favor of careless punctuation by insisting to the reader, "You know what I mean!" It's your business to punctuate so clearly that your sentences can have only one meaning.

The various punctuation marks are listed on the following pages, and rules are given for the use of each. Learn the rules; do the exercises. *Above all, apply what you learn to everything you write.*

PERIOD, QUESTION MARK, EXCLAMATION POINT

16a. A declarative sentence is followed by a period.[1]

RIGHT I went to South America by plane.
RIGHT Mr. Shafer left a fortune to his daughter.

16b. An interrogative sentence is followed by a question mark.

RIGHT Where have you been?

NOTE: Distinguish between a declarative sentence containing an indirect question and an interrogative sentence which asks a question directly.

EXAMPLES *I asked him* where he had been. [Declarative]
Did you know where he had been? [Interrogative]

16c. An exclamation is followed by an exclamation point.

RIGHT What a game!
RIGHT My heavens!

---

[1] For explanation of the kinds of sentences see page 40.

16d. An imperative sentence may be followed by either a period or an exclamation point, depending upon the purpose of the sentence.

RIGHT Hand me the hammer, please.
RIGHT Get out!

If you keep your wits about you, you will have little difficulty using the question mark and the exclamation point correctly. Failure to use a period at the end of a sentence, however, is a common error with writers who do not know what a sentence is and therefore do not know where a sentence ends. If you have studied Chapters 1–4 of this book, you should have learned what a sentence is; and knowing a sentence when you write it or see it, you will know where to place a period.

EXERCISE 1. In this exercise write on your paper only the final word of each sentence followed by the proper end mark. Add the first word of the sentence which follows.

EXAMPLE He went home during the fifth period did you see him leave he looked rather worried . . . . . etc.

period. Did
leave? He

1. What a day we were late to school because the icy roads slowed down the school bus my English teacher called on me because I was whispering to Betty what do you think he asked me he wanted me to tell the whole class what I had whispered to her was I embarrassed what could I do I just looked foolish and said nothing
2. In social studies Jane tried to pass me a note Miss Lang saw her and took the note she read it aloud did Jane

and I blush everybody teased us after class how we
suffered

3. Do you think this is all that went wrong today no, indeed lunch hour was terrible I had forgotten to bring
any money, and I couldn't borrow any talk about
starving they had hot roast beef sandwiches, too it was
awful

4. What luck Jimmie Clark offered to buy me a sandwich
if I'd let him copy my math homework of course, I
knew better, but I was so hungry Mr. Taylor quickly
discovered the copied lesson he sent both Jimmie and
me to the office did you ever hear of such a bad day

EXERCISE 2. Copy the following sentences, inserting the proper end marks — period, question
mark, exclamation point. Begin each sentence with
a capital letter. Whenever an end mark and quotation marks come together *in this exercise*, place
the end mark inside the quotation marks.

1. When Helen gets on the telephone, the rest of us
give up Helen is my seventeen-year-old sister what a girl
do you think she can talk less than half an hour every
evening she settles down at the phone, which is in the back
hall she doesn't seem to care whether anyone overhears
her perhaps she knows that no one would listen twice to
her silly patter the calls begin coming in about seven
o'clock Josie is usually first, but Josie isn't very long-
winded she lasts only about twenty minutes then Sally
takes over an hour later, when the conversation has passed
through the low-tone stage and the giggles have worn
everyone out, Dad emerges from his paper

2. "Good heavens" he explodes "Doesn't that girl
have anything else to do"

3. Mother lays down her sewing and leaves the room
we can hear her telling Helen the time is up

4. Helen is indignant "Oh, Mother, we've hardly said

anything yet listen, Sally, shall I call you back later g'by"

5. "Come here, young lady" Dad exclaims as Helen waltzes in "Do you know you have been on that phone for nearly two hours do you know that I had a letter from the telephone company yesterday asking me to shorten our calls a fine situation"

6. "Why, Dad" exclaims injured innocence "we were talking over our homework all the time"

7. At this point I let out one big howl

EXERCISE 3. Write a paragraph one page in length which calls for the use several times of *all three* end marks. Make a copy without any end marks and bring this copy to class. In class exchange papers with someone and put the end marks in the paper you receive.

EXERCISE 4. For further practice in the use of end marks turn to Exercises 7–10 on pages 100–103 in Chapter 4, "Writing Complete Sentences."

16e. An abbreviation is followed by a period.

adv.	adverb
Col.	Colonel, Colorado
Fla.	Florida
etc.	et cetera (Latin)
N.S.P.C.A.	National Society for the Prevention of Cruelty to Animals

NOTE: Abbreviations are capitalized only if the word they stand for is capitalized.

EXERCISE 5. Copy the following paragraph, inserting periods after all abbreviations. This is an exercise on punctuating abbreviations; it is not an example of the way abbreviations should be used in good writing.

1. Pvt Harry Bourne, U S M C, came back to the U S A with rows of ribbons on his coat. 2. His ship, the U S S *Morgan*, docked at the foot of Twenty-third St in New York, N Y. 3. After a few days at Ft Dix, N J, Pvt Bourne was on his way to Harrisville, Pa, his home town. 4. There the I O O F and the Am Legion had decorated the Grove Bldg with "Welcome Home" signs; the band, under the direction of Capt J O Staunton of the Natl Guard, was there to greet him. 5. To an admiring crowd in Pershing Sq Dr S E Burman, the mayor, introduced Harry. 6. Employees of the Eastern Candy Co and students from Harrisville H S jammed the square.

17. PUNCTUATION

THE COMMA

17a. Use commas to separate words, phrases, and subordinate clauses written in series.

WORDS WRITTEN IN SERIES

RIGHT Books, pamphlets, magazines, and newspapers cluttered the teacher's desk. [nouns]

RIGHT We played, swam, ate, sang, and danced. [verbs]

RIGHT He was a short, fat, good-natured man. [adjectives]

PHRASES WRITTEN IN SERIES

RIGHT Examinations will be given at the beginning of the term, at midterm, and at the end of the term.

SUBORDINATE CLAUSES WRITTEN IN SERIES

RIGHT He declared that the roof leaked, that the windows leaked, and that the plumbing leaked.

(1) When the last two items in a series are joined by *and,* you may omit the comma before the *and* if the comma is not necessary to make the meaning clear.

CLEAR WITH COMMA OMITTED: Telegrams, letters and gifts poured in upon him.

NOT CLEAR WITH COMMA OMITTED: The following courses will be offered by the art department this term: figure sketching, fashion design, interior decoration, advertising and commercial art. [How many courses will be offered, four or five? Is *advertising and commercial art* one course, or are there two courses, *advertising* and *commercial art?*]

CLEAR WITH COMMA INCLUDED: The following courses will be offered by the art department this term: figure sketching, fashion design, interior decoration, advertising, and commercial art.

NOTE: Some words usually appear in pairs and may be set off as one item in a series: *hat and coat, bread and butter, pork and beans,* etc.

RIGHT   The meal consisted of soup, bread and butter, pork and beans, and crackers and cheese.

(2) If all items in a series are joined by *and* or *or*, do not use commas.

RIGHT   Father and Chester and Jerry and I went to the movies together.

RIGHT   Harry or Bill or Joe will take us.

(3) When the last adjective in a series is thought of as part of the noun, the comma before the adjective is omitted.

RIGHT   He was a clever, fearless *little man.*
RIGHT   He was a fearless *little man.*

Consider *little man* as one word, like *policeman.* Then *fearless* does not modify *man;* it modifies *little man.* The comma is omitted before *little.*

RIGHT   I got the information from a polite, helpful *young man* at the hotel desk.

RIGHT   The stranger was a funny *little fellow.*

(4) Main clauses in series are usually separated by semicolons. If the clauses are short, however, commas may be used.

RIGHT   The huge ship rose slowly to the top of each mountainous wave; it poised there for a moment; it plunged sickeningly into the flowing valley of green water below.

RIGHT   Dogs barked, children shouted, adults applauded.

EXERCISE 1. Copy the following sentences, inserting commas where needed.

1. Frances Jane Alice and I organized a spinster club.
2. Mother had planned to serve frankfurters baked beans salad and ice cream and cake.
3. The clinic will be open this afternoon tonight and tomorrow morning.
4. We traveled by car bus train and plane.
5. The boys were expected to play and study and work in equal amounts every day.
6. Father snapped the switch tightened the plug tried a new bulb and finally called an electrician.
7. I had expected a tall handsome young man.
8. He handed me the paper thrust a pen into my hand and told me to sign on the dotted line.
9. He stopped he looked and he listened.
10. The following groups will be formed: freshmen sophomores juniors and seniors.
11. Diplomats Congressmen and reporters mobbed the President's office.
12. The winner will probably be Bayside or Rockville or Freeport.

EXERCISE 2. Copy the following, inserting commas where necessary.

1. Mary Carolyn Jane and I have been singing together for a year. 2. We have sung at school assemblies church socials and school parties. 3. Our quartet was formed one boring lazy fall afternoon at Jane's house. 4. We discovered that our voices were all different — first soprano second soprano contralto and alto. 5. Jane's radio phono-

graph and piano were at once brought into use to help us.
6. We began on such old favorites as *Who Sweet Sue Tea
for Two* and *I Been Workin' on de Railroad.* 7. Mary
and Jane and Carolyn have solo voices, but I stick to
harmonizing. 8. Through September October and November we practiced on Friday afternoons Sundays after our
young people's meeting at the church and occasionally
during lunch hour at school. 9. Mr. Sorrell, director of
our school chorus, asked us to sing at the fall concert.
10. We found we liked to sing classical religious and
popular selections equally well. 11. We sang some beautiful old French songs for our French class some Eliza-
bethan madrigals for English and some ballads and folk
songs for Miss Martin's history class. 12. All this took
our week ends free periods and lunch hours, but we had
so much fun getting together and practicing and per-
forming that we didn't mind.

EXERCISE 3.   Copy the following, inserting
commas where needed.

1. One afternoon in June we did some close harmonizing
at the Senior Picnic, and afterwards an impatient businesslike little man bustled up to us handed us his card and
introduced himself. 2. He was program director for a
chain of radio stations, and he wanted to try us on the air.
3. We listened to his offer scheduled a try-out and then
began really to work. 4. We thought a short sponsored
radio program would be a help this summer as we hadn't
decided what we'd do during July August and September.
5. Of course, the little radio man wanted popular songs.
6. We got the music went over to Jane's and began
practicing. 7. Jane provided us with sandwiches cookies
and cokes. 8. Mary made arrangements Carolyn played
them and we all sang them.
9. For days we did nothing but play the piano and
sing and listen to records on the radio. 10. Finally, the

important exciting long-awaited day for our audition arrived. 11. We were nervous eager and frightened as we rode down to the studio found it and took our places around the mike. 12. But after the first faint wavering notes, we got warmed up and made a recording. 13. From then on we had a regular job at four o'clock Mondays Wednesdays and Fridays. 14. The station found sponsors for us, and during the summer we advertised for Heartie's Wheat Flakes Primo Candy and Cremie Soap. 15. It has been rather hard nerve-racking work. 16. At this point we're slowly unwillingly breaking up. 17. Mary Carolyn and I are going to college, and Jane has a scholarship at a large well-known and popular music school.

EXERCISE 4. Write 5 sentences, each sentence illustrating one of the following uses of the comma.

1. Adjectives in a series.
2. Nouns in a series requiring a comma before the *and* between the last two items.
3. Phrases in a series.
4. Short main clauses in a series.
5. A series joined by conjunctions, requiring no commas.

17b. Use commas to set off expressions which interrupt the sentence.

There are seven kinds of "interrupters" which you should be able to recognize.

(1) Appositives with their modifiers are set off by commas.

An appositive is a word or group of words which follows a noun or pronoun and means the same thing. An appositive usually gives information about the noun or pronoun that precedes it.

EXAMPLES Bergen, *the fullback,* played a good defensive game.

Mr. Salt*,* **owner** *of the ranch,* offered me his own horse.

I sent for Joe*,* *the school's* **plumber.**

In these sentences *fullback, owner,* and *plumber* are appositives.

NOTE: When you set off an appositive you include with it all words which modify it.

EXAMPLES Mike Casella, *the **janitor** at our school,* is always good natured.

Arnold Wilcox, *the **boy** I met at the convention,* gave me some inside information.

NOTE: Sometimes an appositive is so closely related to the word preceding it that it should not be set off by commas. Such an appositive is called a *restrictive appositive.*

EXAMPLES My brother Bill

The composer Beethoven

Her old friend Betty

EXERCISE 5. Copy the following sentences containing appositives, inserting commas where needed.

1. Helen the leader of the group conducted the meeting a membership rally.
2. My sister Jean a sophomore at Briarcliff will be home for the holidays.
3. His new car a streamlined model attracted much attention.
4. Our friends the Moores built their new house a small bungalow very near to ours.
5. The dog a mongrel was purchased by Mr. Sayles mayor of the village.
6. We enjoyed the meals a combination of French and Italian dishes.

7. The stream a cataract of ice and debris gradually rose to flood height.

8. My younger brother Bill is working for Mr. Henry owner of a local drug store.

9. Our pastor the Reverend John Brooks works hardest on Sunday the "day of rest."

10. Joe Green the best guide in Maine was hired to take us on our canoe trip a 200-mile voyage.

11. The poet Longfellow enjoyed great popularity at home and abroad.

12. The book a novel about the Revolution was written by Kenneth Roberts an American author.

(2) Words used in direct address are set off by commas.

RIGHT *Frank,* please give us a hand.
RIGHT Yes, *my friend,* you are probably right.
RIGHT *Mr. Chairman,* I rise to a point of order.

(3) Parenthetical expressions are set off by commas.

Expressions commonly used parenthetically are: *I believe (think, suppose, hope, etc.), on the contrary, on the other hand, of course, in my opinion, for example, however, to tell the truth, nevertheless,* etc.

RIGHT You have, *on the other hand,* nothing to lose.
RIGHT The speech, *in my opinion,* was a failure.

NOTE: These expressions, of course, are not *always* used as interrupters.

> NOT USED AS AN INTERRUPTER: You must try *to tell the truth*.
>
> USED AS AN INTERRUPTER: He is, *to tell the truth,* dangerous.
>
> NOT USED AS AN INTERRUPTER: *I think* these are the best students.
>
> USED AS AN INTERRUPTER: These are, *I think,* the best students.

(4) Certain words, when used at the beginning of a sentence or remark, are followed by a comma. These words are *well, yes, no, why,* etc.

RIGHT *Yes,* your answers are correct.
RIGHT *Well,* we were certainly taken by surprise.
RIGHT *Why,* you little rascal!

EXERCISE 6. Copy the following sentences, using commas where they are needed to set off the interrupting expressions. Be prepared to give the rule for each comma.

1. One of the boys Joe Withers took his sister Mary to the dance.
2. No Janet I haven't met Mrs. Williams our new adviser.
3. My friend Raymond lives in Columbus the capital of Ohio.
4. Well it was Bill I believe who bought the decorations.
5. The answers on the other hand are incorrect.
6. Yes we can at least offer our services to Betty the president.
7. Come here Sally. Mother I think is looking for you.
8. Well when this liquid a salt solution touches the ice, the freezing point drops.
9. Yes these are in my opinion very good criticisms of this book *Silas Marner.*
10. Experience shows however that students do in general enjoy the book.
11. Well this class is indeed enthusiastic.
12. There is according to our teacher another book by the same author George Eliot that we should read.

(5) In dates and addresses every item after the first is *enclosed* by commas.

RIGHT After December 26, 1948, I may be addressed at 345 Hill Street, Ann Arbor, Michigan.

RIGHT My new address will be 70 Fifth Avenue, New
York 11, New York, until Christmas.

RIGHT My year in St. Louis, Missouri, was very successful.

RIGHT Write to John Mills, 450 Madison Avenue, New
York 17, New York.

RIGHT Tomorrow is Friday, December 13.

EXERCISE 7. Copy the following exercise, inserting commas wherever needed.

1. We are staying at 41 Meadbrook Road Summerville
Alabama.
2. On June 20 1949 the office at 31 Main Street Mount
Pleasant Michigan will be closed.
3. Please change my address from 18 Broad Street Newark
New Jersey to 421 Springfield Avenue South Orange
New Jersey.
4. He arrived on September 1 1946 and left on April 1
1947.
5. After several years in Columbus Georgia we moved to
Orlando Florida on March 1 1948.
6. The letter came from Boulder Colorado and was addressed to Mr. Harry Moore 231 Fifth Avenue New
York 10 New York.
7. June 6 1944 was D Day in Europe, and October 3 1945
had been scheduled as D Day in Japan.
8. Brownsville Texas is a winter resort across the Rio
Grande River from Matamoras Mexico 400 miles from
New Orleans Louisiana.

EXERCISE 8. Write 5 sentences of your own,
each of which illustrates the punctuation of a different one of the 5 types of interrupting expressions
you have learned.

(6) A nonrestrictive clause is set off by commas.

A *nonrestrictive* clause is a subordinate clause which
merely adds an idea to the sentence but is not neces-

sary to the meaning of the sentence. The opposite of a nonrestrictive clause is a *restrictive* clause, which *is* necessary to the meaning of the sentence.

NONRESTRICTIVE   Fred Bates, who is a sophomore, played all season on the varsity.

Since you know without the clause who it was that played all season on the varsity, the clause is not necessary to identify Fred, but adds information about Fred. It is a nonrestrictive clause and should be set off by commas. *Most adjective clauses which modify proper names* are nonrestrictive and require commas.

RESTRICTIVE   Boys *who skip school* must be punished.

The subordinate clause *who skip school* serves to identify the boys. It is necessary to the meaning of the sentence. If the clause is omitted, the sentence has a very different meaning. The clause is restrictive and does not require commas.

RESTRICTIVE   The book *that I want* is not in the library.

The clause *that I want* tells which book is not in the library; it identifies *book;* it is restrictive. A helpful guide to follow is that adjective clauses introduced by *that* are almost always restrictive. Hence, if you can substitute *that* for *who* or *which* at the beginning of a clause, you may usually assume that the clause is restrictive.

Study these examples of restrictive (no commas) and nonrestrictive (commas) clauses. Can you explain the punctuation?

EXAMPLES The girl whom you met this morning is my sister.

Marilyn, whom you met this morning, is my sister.

George Washington and Abraham Lincoln, who were born in February, were our greatest Presidents.

The Presidents who were born in February were George Washington and Abraham Lincoln.

A Tale of Two Cities, which we read last term, was written by Charles Dickens.

The Dickens book which we read last term was *A Tale of Two Cities.*

Sometimes the writer of a sentence is the only one who knows whether the clause he uses is nonrestrictive (commas) or restrictive (no commas). This is true because he has a definite meaning in mind for his sentence. For example, the clauses in the following sentences may be either nonrestrictive (commas) or restrictive (no commas), depending upon the meaning intended by the writer.

NONRESTRICTIVE My older brother, who goes to Cornell, will be home for the holidays. [I have only one older brother. The clause is not needed to identify him. It is unnecessary, nonrestrictive, and requires commas.]

RESTRICTIVE My older brother who goes to Cornell will be home for the holidays. [I have two older brothers. Only one goes to Cornell; the other goes to Dartmouth. The clause is necessary to tell which brother I am talking about. It is restrictive and does not require commas.]

EXERCISE 9. Punctuate the following sentences. Be able to explain orally the reasons for your punctuation. Some of the sentences could be interpreted in two ways.

1. Jean who is blonde always looks best in blue.
2. Of my three sisters the one who is blonde looks best in blue.
3. Philip who enjoys winter sports prefers to live in the North.
4. A man who enjoys winter sports prefers to live in the North.
5. The movie that we saw last night is a thriller.
6. I picked up the magazine which Harold had been reading.
7. The copy of *Life* magazine which Harold had been reading was all marked up.
8. The *Saturday Evening Post* which comes to us weekly is a large magazine.
9. The police caught the thief who had broken into the school building.
10. The thief who was a stranger in town confessed his crime.

(7) A nonrestrictive participial phrase is set off by commas.

A participial phrase (see page 68) is a group of words containing a participle. When nonrestrictive — not necessary to the sentence — the phrase is set off by commas. Present participles end in *–ing*. Most past participles end in *–ed*.

NONRESTRICTIVE PRESENT PARTICIPLE: Jimmy, *leaning lazily against the door,* fell into the room when the door opened.

RESTRICTIVE PRESENT PARTICIPLE: We watched carefully the stranger *leaning lazily against the door.*

NONRESTRICTIVE PAST PARTICIPLE: Bart and I, *deserted by our companions,* found our way home alone.

RESTRICTIVE PAST PARTICIPLE: Anyone *deserted by his companions* should sound a distress signal.

EXERCISE 10. Punctuate the following sentences. Be able to explain orally the reasons for your punctuation.

1. Will the people standing in the back of the room please come forward?
2. The referee who is wearing a striped shirt is very strict. (How many referees are there?)
3. No one liked the records which John brought.
4. The Sunday concerts of the New York Philharmonic which we always listen to are broadcast in the United States and Canada.
5. The concert which we heard yesterday was especially good.
6. Jack who is usually late didn't know how to set the alarm clock which he received for Christmas.
7. This clock which is a new type got him up an hour too early.
8. Mr. Olds seated in the front row was able to hear every word.
9. The brunette whom George took to the dance was too popular with the other boys.
10. Helen Boyd whom George took to the dance is the most popular girl in school.
11. Planes which were built for military purposes cannot be easily converted to commercial use.
12. The people waiting for the bus grew impatient.

EXERCISE 11. Write 5 sentences containing a nonrestrictive clause (commas) and 5 sentences containing a restrictive clause (no commas).

EXERCISE 12. Copy the following sentences, inserting commas where needed. Be prepared to give the reason for each comma. This exercise covers the use of commas with expressions which interrupt the sentence (**17b**).

1. Buenos Aires which has a population of more than two million is I believe the largest city in South America.
2. Situated on the south bank of La Plata River which is formed by the Paraná and Uruguay rivers Buenos Aires is the capital of Argentina the second largest South American country.
3. The pampas large treeless plains in the center of the country provide good grazing for cattle raising a major industry.
4. Most of the meat which is produced in Argentina is exported to England which does not produce enough for its own needs.
5. Argentina a largely agricultural country must on the other hand import manufactured goods from Europe and our own country the United States.
6. Its climate which is temperate differs very little according to the atlas from that of the United States.
7. Henry bring me the atlas which is on my desk and turn to the page which gives a map of South America.
8. There is I believe no map of Argentina in the atlas which you have brought, but this map a physical map of the continent will do.
9. My friend Esteban who lives in Buenos Aires sent me his address which is if I remember correctly 423 Avenida de Mayo Buenos Aires Argentina.
10. Well Esteban urged my brother Jim and me to go to Argentina this summer, but Father on the contrary advised us to wait until we are older.
11. My Spanish teacher Mr. Peron sailed for Buenos Aires on June 21 1947 and returned to New Orleans Louisiana on September 5.
12. He brought me a fine pair of rancher's boots which he had bought in Argentina and several books large illustrated volumes describing the country.

13. Mr. Peron having nothing to do one day called on my friend Esteban who showed him some parts of the city which a foreigner usually doesn't see.
14. The teacher pleased by such kindness entertained Esteban at a party given by South Americans.
15. No Don I have never been abroad, but I hope to go to South America after graduation.

17c. Use a comma before and, but, or, nor, for, yet, when they join main clauses.

RIGHT In the morning the janitor cleans the walks in front of our apartment house, and his wife straightens up the lobby.

RIGHT There are few islands in the Eastern Pacific Ocean, but there are thousands of them in the Western Pacific Ocean.

RIGHT I'll go and I will not return. [clauses too short to require commas]

Do not be misled by compound verbs which often make a sentence look as though it contained two main clauses.

COMPOUND SENTENCE [main clauses requiring commas]:

RIGHT They toured Colonial Williamsburg, and they visited historic William and Mary College.

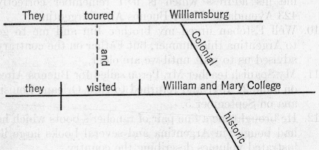

COMPOUND PREDICATE [no clauses, no comma]:

RIGHT They toured Colonial Williamsburg and visited
historic William and Mary College.

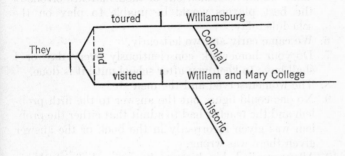

EXERCISE 13. The sentences in this exercise
contain main clauses joined by the conjunctions *and,
but, or, nor.* Do not copy the sentences. Number
on your paper 1–20. Decide where the commas
should come, and write on your paper after the
proper number the word preceding each comma;
add the comma and the conjunction following it.
Do not be misled by compound verbs.

EXAMPLE Williams got a two-base hit but Bernstein hesitated at third and the throw beat him to the
plate.

hit, but
third, and

1. The audience was composed of hundreds of formidable
   looking thugs and Commissioner Wright felt that
   these men would appreciate his strongest language.
2. The champion was serving viciously and he managed
   to keep the upper hand throughout the first two sets.
3. For Friday's dance I made a date with Jane and Jim
   made a date with Belle.

4. Janie got a bad cold and Belle sprained her ankle playing hockey; we all stayed home and felt glum.
5. Our golf team had consistently bad luck this spring. They would be rained out of their matches or one of the best players would be unable to play on the scheduled day.
6. We came early and we left early.
7. Do your homework conscientiously every day or I shall have to keep you after school until it is done.
8. The women served and the men ate.
9. No one could figure out the answer to the fifth problem and the teacher had to admit that either the problem was given incorrectly in the book or the answer given there was wrong.
10. Allan studied his history lesson and finished his English theme before going to bed but did not do his math.
11. The noon train was an hour late but the passengers had been warned beforehand that they wouldn't get into Denver until one o'clock.
12. Dinner was served on the plane and it was the best meal we had eaten in weeks.
13. The boys couldn't figure out why Beth was laughing at them so hard nor did they realize that several other girls had just gone around the corner, holding their sides at the ludicrous picture the boys presented.
14. We could not find our tickets or we would have been at the theater earlier.
15. The farmer's wife banged on a big kettle and shouted in her loudest tones but the men were late to dinner.
16. She said the dinner would be cold but it was steaming hot.
17. Sarah Wilkins had her youngest son run all the errands for the family and she often said she did that because his legs were newer and hadn't had a chance to get tired.

18. Keith and Sally couldn't decide whether to go to the movies or stay home; if they went to a movie, they'd have to walk a mile each way and they were in a lazy mood that night.
19. The wave rose menacingly as it approached the shore and it spilled over a hundred sand castles on the beach.
20. The motor sputtered and died and left an ominous stillness but our driver leaped out and began to make repairs.

17d. Use a comma after an introductory adverb clause, an introductory participal phrase, or a succession of introductory prepositional phrases.

An introductory clause or phrase is a clause or phrase coming first in a sentence or preceding a main clause.

INTRODUCTORY ADVERB CLAUSE: *Whenever Mother sees the telegraph boy approaching the house,* she assumes that bad news is coming.
As soon as you finish, your dinner will be ready.

INTRODUCTORY PARTICIPIAL PHRASE: *Leaving the dishes for me to do,* my sister Helen dashed gaily out.

A SUCCESSION OF INTRODUCTORY PREPOSITIONAL PHRASES: *On the morning after graduation,* Jack began looking for a job.

A short introductory phrase does not require a comma.

RIGHT At the movies we forgot our troubles.

EXERCISE 14. The sentences in this exercise contain introductory clauses and phrases. Decide where a comma should be used. Copy on your paper the word preceding each comma and place the

comma after it.   Number your answers to accord
with the numbers of the sentences.

EXAMPLE With a clatter of hoofs and a blare of trumpets
        the white charger galloped into the center ring.

                        trumpets,

1. When the people realized that the hurricane was
   headed in their direction they had little time left to
   prepare for it.
2. After the warning had been passed by word of mouth
   to all who could be reached preparations were made
   to withstand the storm.
3. Since the Everglades are low and hold a great deal of
   water high winds and rain bring floods.
4. For most of a day, while people huddled in the few
   strong buildings available the storm tore down their
   houses and carried off their possessions.
5. Although the center of a lake would seem to be a very
   dangerous spot in a hurricane a large barge anchored
   there rode out the storm, carrying 211 persons safely
   through.
6. While the hurricane lasted many acts of great courage
   were performed.
7. By midnight the storm had reached its height.
8. On the morning following the storm rescue crews
   made their way through a ruined world.
9. After a thorough inspection of the area had been made
   the country realized that it had suffered one of its
   greatest tragedies.
10. Receiving news of the disaster the Red Cross rushed
    help to the scene.
11. Although thousands had lost everything the people
    of the Everglades bravely set about their heart-
    rending job of restoration.
12. For years signs of the destruction caused by the high
    wind could be seen.

13. At last the land was made productive, and at the present time it is second to none in the entire country.
14. Traveling through the region today one would never suspect how devastated it had once been.

EXERCISE 15. Write compound sentences using each of the following conjunctions and requiring a comma before the conjunction: *and, or, but, nor.*

Write 5 sentences, each introduced by an adverb clause followed by a comma.

EXERCISE 16. Decide where commas should be used in these sentences. Copy on your paper the word preceding the comma in each sentence. Place the comma after the word. Be on the alert for commas in all uses and for sentences which do not require commas. Number your answers to accord with the numbers of the sentences.

EXAMPLE If he insists on an immediate decision have him call me.

decision,

1. As long as you and he are such good friends you ought to be able to tell him the truth.
2. Since the pay was small and the hours very long one after another the men quit the job.
3. As the flag was carried past the reviewing stand the mayor and his party removed their hats.
4. Standing in the arched doorway two guards held their guns stiffly.
5. At last we had won the big game of the year.
6. Although we begged them to leave the boys hung around for hours.
7. When he is left alone in the house Laddie usually curls up on the best furniture.

8. Production has been stepped up rapidly but it has never been able to meet the demand.

9. Although water forms between the threads of the weave it does not soak into the thread and the ground does not really get wet.

10. The fiber was combed and spun into yarn and the yarn was woven into cloth.

11. If a crime is considered to have national importance it is briefly reported in the *Times*.

12. When he had looked over the housing situation rather thoroughly Mr. Banks decided the house on Fernwood Terrace was the best buy.

13. After the school census had been taken the census-taker discovered twenty-four new families had moved into the town.

14. By noon we had all our work done.

15. Although we wanted desperately to go on a skiing trip we realized there was not enough snow on the mountain to make it safe for us beginners.

16. Leaving the house so early in the morning I never see my neighbors.

SUMMARY OF USES OF THE COMMA

17a. Use commas to separate words, phrases, and subordinate clauses written in series.

17b. Use commas to set off expressions which interrupt the sentence.

(1) Appositives

(2) Words in direct address

(3) Parenthetical expressions

(4) The words *now, well, yes, no, why,* etc., when used at the beginning of a sentence

(5) Items in dates and addresses

(6) Non-restrictive clauses
(7) Non-restrictive participial phrases

17c. Use commas to separate main clauses joined by *and, but, or, nor, for, yet,* unless the clauses are very short.

17d. Use a comma after an introductory adverb clause, an introductory participial phrase, or a succession of introductory prepositional phrases.

REVIEW EXERCISE A. *Comma Rules* **17a–17d.** Select from the following sentences all words which should be followed by a comma. List these words on your paper, placing a comma after each. Number your answers to accord with the numbers of the sentences.

EXAMPLE Yes the boys did a good job but the girls did a better one.

yes,
job,

1. We could we believed make it in an hour.
2. As long as we could see the liner from the pier we frantically waved our handkerchiefs.
3. Bayne ran across the deserted field and stooped so low on the other side of it that Sam couldn't see him at all.
4. Mother will you please pass the fruit?
5. At 212 Front Street Emporia stands an ancient jalopy advertised for $25.
6. Steve Mary and I were on the prom committee.
7. As we quickly backed out of the garage we heard an

ominous sound and we were afraid to get out to view the damage we knew we had done to Dad's car.

8. Although we realized we'd have to pay for it out of our allowances the prospect of ever borrowing the car again looked dim.

9. We screwed up our courage and timidly peering around the rear wheel we were delighted to find it was only the garbage pail caught on the bumper.

10. In a second our worries had disappeared.

11. You can imagine however how scared we'd been.

12. Betsy and Charlie and Tom and I ceremoniously carried the pail back to where it belonged.

13. After a thorough search to make certain the driveway yielded no more hazards we pulled out again.

14. Miss Jones this letter goes to Mr. A. R. Morton 113 Lake Shore Drive Chicago Illinois.

15. Doubleday Doran is a publishing company in Garden City Long Island New York.

REVIEW EXERCISE B: *Comma Rules* **17a– 17d.** Copy each of the following sentences, inserting commas. After each copied sentence, write the numbers of the comma rules you have followed. There are at least two rules (for commas or the omission of commas) involved in each sentence.

EXAMPLE 1. Yes, your mail has arrived, Abner. 17b (4), 17b (2)

1. When Arden came home from school her friends met her at the door and they led her into her own surprise birthday party.

2. Since everyone enjoys being fooled a magician I believe provides excellent entertainment.

3. A tall gaunt gentleman in black a scarecrow met us at the door.

4. No you will not be permitted to leave the house tonight nor can you stay up late.

5. Maps charts paintings and photographs covered the walls and in my opinion gave the classroom an interesting appearance.

6. He was born on January 24 1935 in Provincetown which is on Cape Cod.

7. His sister Frances an A+ student is always kidding him about his marks but he doesn't seem to let her worry him.

8. Do you remember George where you found the pamphlets books and other articles?

9. Miss Brown take a letter to Professor John Mills 221 W. Seventh Street Conniston North Carolina.

10. This school according to the principal provides expert instruction in the classrooms on the playing fields and in the gymnasiums.

11. Yes we have hotel reservations in Winter Park Florida from Friday February 1 to Saturday March 1.

12. A worker who is able to increase his output receives a special bonus but no one is charged for decreasing his output.

13. Cut off from us by the storm the animals in the barn whinnied and brayed and grunted all night.

14. When I sailed for Europe my friend Allan who is older than I gave me some valuable advice.

15. Jerry who won the contest last year is in the opinion of many one of the boys who will be chosen this year.

16. Well on the morning of our eighteenth day at sea we sighted the land and everyone rushed on deck.

17. Slowly silently the darkened vessel covered by a starless night slipped out to sea.

18. Mr. Adams who was recently elected to the City Council told parents teachers and taxpayers that he approved of a new school building.

19. Your letter reached me April 1 1948 and as you will recall gave me renewed hope.

20. Through the long hot lazy afternoon I watched the workmen in the old quarry where I used to work.

REVIEW EXERCISE C. Referring to the *Summary of Uses of the Comma* on page 418, write a sentence to illustrate each of the rules, including all seven of the interrupters.

REVIEW EXERCISE D. Spend half an hour going through a newspaper or magazine to find examples of as many *different* uses of the comma as you can. Cut out the examples — the entire sentence in each case — and paste them on paper to bring to class. Under each clipping write the rule which the sentence illustrates.

REVIEW EXERCISE E: *End Marks and Commas*. Copy the following sentences, inserting end marks and commas as needed.

1. "Good heavens" exclaimed Miss Ruley the new teacher
2. What I wondered do all these facts figures and experiences mean
3. For weeks I think we ate nothing but baked beans and salt pork and Harry Evans the cook became very unpopular
4. Jimmy rose to his feet was recognized by the chairman and asked what had happened to the treasury
5. "Why I never heard of such a thing John" exclaimed Mrs Bellis shaking her head in dismay
6. The boys who are on the baseball team will I understand be excused early on Friday May 4 and Wednesday May 9
7. On the contrary Mr Sanford the coach told us that our chances were good
8. The dinner that the girls served consisted of lentil soup baked ham and escalloped potatoes fresh peas a green salad and apple pie

9. Andy who is very particular about food asked for a second helping of ham and peas and pie

10. It was at the carnival in Youngstown Ohio that I saw that tall thin young man who had six fingers on each hand

11. Who will deny that shorter hours higher wages and better working conditions are desirable

12. Jane if you want to improve your marks you will have to do your English and science and social studies homework more carefully

13. He is I believe more capable than his brother Frank who has as far as I know shown very little aptitude for business

14. Although the meeting had been scheduled for September 23 1947 it was according to the book I read postponed until January 24 1948

15. I lived at 22 Clancy St Davenport Iowa for five years but I never knew who lived at No 23

18. PUNCTUATION

THE SEMICOLON

A semicolon [;], as you can see by looking at it, is part period and part comma. It is a very useful mark of punctuation. It says to the reader, "Stop here a little longer than you stop for a comma, but not so long as you stop for a period."

18a. Use a semicolon between main clauses not joined by *and, but, or, nor, for, yet*.

RIGHT The taxpayers voted in favor of a new school building; a site for the structure will be chosen next week.

In cold weather she spent her afternoons on the skating pond; on warmer days, she went to the indoor rink.

In this use the semicolon acts like a period, for each main clause is really a complete sentence. Where the thoughts of the clauses are very closely connected, as in the examples above, a semicolon is better than a period.

EXERCISE 1. Read the following and decide where semicolons may be used. Copy on your paper the word preceding each semicolon, and write the semicolon after it. In some sentences you may prefer to use a period. Be prepared to tell why.

1. Each boy in our shop class was making a piece of furniture everyone had common problems to solve everyone was interested in the others' work.
2. Plans were drawn up each boy worked out a drawing of his project.
3. Cutting the boards and planing them down required more brawn than brains the opposite was true of fitting the pieces together.
4. Joining boards together to make wider panels requires experience many of the boys had a hard time getting the boards to fit smoothly.
5. My project was a table on a pedestal turning out the pedestal on the lathe was a lot of fun the wood under the sharp chisel was easy to work.
6. My hardest job was finishing the wood so that it would look smooth and shining it seemed that I used reams of sandpaper my hands and arms were sore from the exercise.
7. When all was ready, I asked Mr. Lacey if I could stain the wood he told me to go ahead he showed me how to do it.
8. The staining was fun too I got more stain on myself than on the wood.
9. After staining the wood, I had to rub filler into it to bring out the grain this is done with hard woods like the walnut I was using.
10. Finally the job was done I assembled my table I carried it home very proudly.

18b. Use a semicolon between main clauses joined by the words *besides, accordingly, moreover, nevertheless, furthermore, otherwise, therefore, however, consequently, also, thus, instead, hence.*

NOTE: When preceded by a semicolon, these words are usually followed by a comma.

RIGHT He was a quiet boy who made friends rather slowly**;** *therefore,* I advised him to choose a small college.

RIGHT I thought the book much too long**;** *nevertheless,* I made up my mind to read it all.

18c. Use a semicolon between main clauses if there are commas within the clauses.

RIGHT This car, a revolutionary model, was invented by one of our engineers**;** but the high cost of manufacture prohibits large-scale production.

RIGHT Helen Burgess, the girl who is running for president of the senior class, has an excellent chance to win**;** and if she does win, she will be the first girl ever to achieve that position.

18d. Use a semicolon before *for example, namely, that is, for instance, in fact, on the contrary,* when they join main clauses.

NOTE: When preceded by a semicolon, these expressions are followed by a comma.

RIGHT He came to the meeting quite unprepared**;** *that is,* he had forgotten his notes.

EXERCISE 2. List on your paper, in the order in which they appear in the sentences below, all words which you think should be followed by a semicolon or a period. After each word place the mark you decide on. Be able to explain your decision. Number your list by sentences, keeping the words from each sentence together.

EXAMPLES 1. Someone left a coat in the locker room it was blue with white buttons.

2. Barbara had no room for us in her car however, we got a ride with Ethel there was plenty of room in her car.

    1. room;
    2. car;
       Ethel.

1. The first task was to decide what the class should make we found this a harder job than we had anticipated.
2. Our sewing class had only ten girls in it nevertheless, the teacher couldn't give any of us all the individual help we needed.
3. We had to choose our own materials furthermore, she insisted that we pick out our patterns ourselves.
4. When we had finally bought what we wanted, she let us lay the pattern on the cloth she said planning where a pattern should be put was the most important part of the job.
5. Cutting into our precious material was the first thing that really scared us Miss Ames watched us like a hawk as our scissors somewhat crookedly found their mark.
6. Making skirts, we discovered, was very complicated we soon learned the importance of accurate measurements.
7. After the cutting, we continued with the job of basting that is, we put the skirts together tentatively — very tentatively.
8. Apparently my measuring hadn't been too good for instance, I was very much surprised to find the pieces didn't quite match in places.
9. I became very much absorbed in cutting I was determined to achieve a good skirt out of this mess.
10. Finally the pieces all came out even I was at last making progress.

11. The machine sewing was easier than any step to date moreover, the work went very quickly from then on.

12. After the finishing touches, I proudly presented my masterpiece to Miss Ames I had actually made a skirt I could wear!

REVIEW EXERCISE: *Commas, Semicolons, and End Marks.* Copy the following sentences, inserting necessary punctuation.

1. How fascinating astrology is

2. Astrology which is the ancient art or science of predicting the fate of people from the positions of the stars is I understand widely practiced today

3. Most of us have heard of the word *astrology* but how many realize I wonder just what it can mean

4. People believed in astrology centuries before Christ the doctrine I think had spread from Babylonia to Greece before 400 B.C.

5. Famous and infamous people alike have believed in astrology however fearing the laughter of those who scoffed they did not always make their beliefs public

6. Hitler the Führer never acted until his astrologer had told him the signs were right nevertheless his belief in the art didn't do him much good did it

7. When we asked him about astrology Mr. Thomas our science teacher grinned he said it was too advanced for us were we insulted

8. My sister Eileen reads the daily column "Your Horoscope" in the paper hoping her horoscope will be given her birthday is in March and she says the predictions are already given for people born up to February 15 1935

9. "Eileen what's come over you" asked my mother one day "You surely don't believe these absurd ridiculous horoscopes"

10. Well I think we should try to control our own futures

by working first on the present for instance our job now is to get our lessons done properly

11. My birthday is July 13 1932 I was according to the astrologers born under the zodiac sign of Cancer the Crab

12. At 32 Reeves Street San Francisco California is an office sign reading *Know Your Future* do you think many people go there

13. The office which is a small room upstairs doesn't look very prosperous they'd probably like to know their own future

14. I know mine already in fact it's settled now I'm going to be an orthodontist a specialist in straightening teeth

15. Our Dr. Smith is one and he says the training is hard moreover you have to go to school for years even after college

16. I hope to be a veterinarian Mother says I'm awfully good at taking care of cats and dogs and horses

17. Your hours will be easy compared with those of most doctors no dog I think has ever gotten a vet out of bed in the middle of the night

18. Yes imagine us fifteen years from now having our own offices imagine hanging out our own shingles

19. I'd like to imagine our math homework was done but since it isn't let's get to work

20. Oh all right you win however I'd much rather talk wouldn't you

19. PUNCTUATION

COLONS, DASHES, PARENTHESES, ITALICS

THE COLON

The usual purpose of a colon is to call the reader's attention to what comes next. A colon means, "Notice the following."

19a. Use a colon after the salutation of a business letter.

RIGHT Dear Mr. Bernstein:
RIGHT Dear Sir:
RIGHT Gentlemen:

Do not use a colon after the salutation of a *friendly* letter. The salutation of a friendly letter is followed by a comma.

19b. Use a colon before a list of appositives or a list of items, especially when the list comes after expressions like *as follows* and *the following*.

RIGHT At our school we have all the spring sports: baseball, track, lacrosse, tennis, and golf. [appositives]
RIGHT Congress is considering several ways of raising money: a property tax, a sales tax, and an increased income tax. [appositives]
RIGHT In his pockets we found the following: a piece of string, a broken jackknife, six marbles, and several small sticks of wood.
RIGHT The five largest cities of the United States are

rated in size as follows: New York, Chicago, Philadelphia, Detroit, Los Angeles.

19c. Use a colon before a long and formal statement.

RIGHT The President summed up his remarks with the following words: "Never, in all our history, have Americans faced a job so well worth while. May it be said of us in the days to come that our children and our children's children rise up and call us blessed."

19d. Use a colon between the numbers when you are writing the time.

EXAMPLES 4:30 p.m.

3:00 a.m.

EXERCISE 1. Decide where colons may be used in the following sentences and be able to explain why.

1. We read the following poets last month Robert Frost, Carl Sandburg, Amy Lowell, and E. A. Robinson.
2. Many kinds of people jammed the trains at holiday time boys and girls going home from college, soldiers on a 72-hour pass, traveling salesmen hurrying to their families.
3. Essays have been handed in by the following students Mary Bohn, Eleanor Lord, Harold Weinberg, and Bill Mitchell.
4. The plane was due at 4 15, but it arrived at 4 30.
5. The box was filled with candy, nuts, fruit, and five-cent toys.
6. I should like to order the following articles a bicycle basket, a carrier for the rear fender, and a Super-ray lamp.
7. The principal began as follows "There are several important matters that must be discussed at this time....."

8. He offered the following excuses for his tardiness the poor condition of the roads, engine trouble, and his mother's illness.

9. At 11 00 p.m. the Weather Bureau issued this announcement Storm warnings are posted along the entire Atlantic seaboard, and all small vessels have been advised to seek port.

10. The following meats appeared on the menu roast beef, roast lamb, broiled steak, southern fried chicken, and lamb chops.

THE DASH

19e. Use the dash to indicate an important break in thought.

RIGHT I suddenly decided —— the decision still surprises me when I look back upon it —— to become an aviator.

RIGHT We ran toward the edge of the road —— the road was especially narrow at this point —— and looked with horror over the edge.

19f. Use the dash to mean *namely, in other words, that is,* and similar expressions which come before explanations.

RIGHT He showed himself to be one of the bravest of men —— he dared to stand up to the skipper and say exactly what he thought. [*that is*]

RIGHT These historical novels were more exciting reading than the other novels I read this year —— they had more action and more interesting characters. [*in other words*, or *that is*]

RIGHT The traffic policeman has many duties other than directing traffic —— he must watch people's faces, keeping an eye out for suspicious characters; he must watch for stolen cars; he must give information to strangers. [*namely*]

NOTE: The dash and the colon are frequently interchangeable.

PARENTHESES

19g. Use parentheses to enclose matter which is added to a sentence but is not of great importance.

The comma, the dash, and the parentheses may all be used in this way. It is good practice to use the dash and parentheses sparingly.

RIGHT I approached Mr. Sandle (I knew him by his long red nose) and asked for a word with him.

RIGHT Several of the new planes (they are not yet available to the public) have such excellent safety devices that almost anyone can fly them safely.

EXERCISE 2. Decide where in the following sentences colons, dashes, and parentheses should be used. You will find some places where any one will be acceptable.

1. There are many more people backstage than the average audience ever thinks about electricians, prop boys, scenery movers, prompters, wardrobe mistresses, and stand-ins.
2. Trotting merrily down the center of Main Street no one knew exactly where they all came from was an amazing collection of assorted dogs two purebred collies, all sorts of terriers, one Boston bull, one battered dachshund, and three obvious mutts.
3. Peter said and no one ever knew where he picked up these facts that the Senior Dance had been postponed on account of the flu epidemic.

4. At 4 31 we dashed headlong up the platform, hoping against hope the 4 30 train hadn't left an optimistic thought soon shattered.

5. Clearing his throat, the speaker began to quote "When in the course of human events . . . . ."

6. Ford was certainly the school's outstanding athlete captain of the football team, center on the basketball team, star hurler on the championship baseball team.

7. Mr. Shipman has many things on his mind the school enrollment, the schedules of several hundred students, and the sports program.

8. Mabel said she'd be glad if she had nothing more important to do to come over tomorrow.

9. Many new products pre-fabricated houses, private planes, illuminated road maps for night driving, etc., were released to the public the year after the war ended.

10. The list of sundaes looked tempting Forbidden Fruit, Hot Fudge with crushed walnuts, Pineapple and Marshmallow, and the old favorite Banana Split.

11. The Dean told us as though we didn't already know it that we'd be having many new subjects in college philosophy, psychology, anthropology, etc.

12. This year I'm taking the following subjects English, plane geometry, American history, French, and Latin.

13. Last year I took English, ancient history, general science, algebra, and Latin.

14. Barry wanted to invite Marcia she's the new girl from Hartford to go to the party with him, but he'd already asked another girl.

15. Trains leave here every night at 6 00, 8 42, and 11 30 p.m.

16. We grabbed our hats somebody had thoughtfully mixed them all up on the piano and flew out the door.

ITALICS

19h. Italics are printed letters which lean to the right.

EXAMPLE *This sentence is printed in italics.*

When you are writing or typing, indicate italics by underlining the words you want italicized. If your composition were to be printed, the typesetter would set the underlined words in italics.

The two Dickens books I have read are <u>David Copperfield</u> and <u>A Tale of Two Cities</u>.

Your sentence would then be printed like this:

The two Dickens books I have read are *David Copperfield* and *A Tale of Two Cities.*

(1) Use italics (underlining) for titles of books, works of art (pictures, musical compositions, statues, etc.), names of newspapers, magazines, and ships.

EXAMPLES　*The Adventures of Tom Sawyer*
　　　　　the Boston *Herald*
　　　　　the *American Boy*
　　　　　the *Queen Mary*

NOTE: In writing the name of a newspaper, it is customary to italicize only the name itself, not the city.

EXAMPLES　the Kalamazoo *Gazette*
　　　　　the New York *Sun*

ITALICS AND QUOTATION MARKS

In general, the use of quotation marks for titles is going out of practice; the tendency is toward italics. Magazine articles and chapter headings, when referred to in the course of a composition, may be placed in quotation marks. All other titles

(books, works of art, magazines, newspapers, ships)
are italicized (underlined).

EXAMPLE I studied Chapter IV, "Tom Comes Home," in
George Eliot's novel *The Mill on the Floss;* and
I read an article in *Cosmopolitan* entitled "They
Are a Funny Race."

**(2) Use italics (underlining) for foreign words, words referred
to as words, and letters referred to as letters.**

Picking your teeth at the table is not *comme il faut.*
There are four *and*'s in this sentence.
Dot the *i*'s and cross the *t*'s.

EXERCISE 3. List on your paper all words and
word groups in the following paragraph which should
be italicized. Underline each. List also those titles
which should be enclosed in quotation marks. Place
quotation marks around them.

1. Fourth period I went into the library to get an article
on modern gold mining. 2. It was in the Saturday Evening
Post and was entitled Canada's New Gold Boom. 3. While
I was looking for the Post, I saw the new Reader's Digest.
4. I picked it up, read Picturesque Speech and Patter, an
article on the superliner Queen Mary, and another on the
famous statue, the Venus de Milo. 5. Lying on the table
next to me were the New York Times and the home town
Herald. 6. I skimmed an editorial on scrapping old ships
such as the Aquitania and the Paris. 7. Jack came in and
asked me to help him with his book report on Craig's
Danger Is My Business, which I read last month.

8. "How many s's in business?" he asked.

9. "Three," I replied and, picking up Principles of Physics and my notebook, dashed off to class.

REVIEW EXERCISE A: *Commas, semicolons,
colons, dashes, parentheses, italics.* Copy the sentences below, inserting punctuation.

I

1. Beret a character in O. E. Rölvaag's novel Giants in the Earth was unable to endure the long lonely barren winters on the prairie.

2. The small sod huts which the settlers built were cold and ugly and hard to keep clean but the women managed to raise healthy children to keep their homes tidy and to make the huts livable.

3. Although their land cost the pioneers nothing the cost of lumber glass and other building materials was hard for them to meet they had almost no ready cash furthermore such things had to be brought in by wagon from distant towns.

4. A trip to town which took several days was a big event the pioneer could spare little time from his farming except in winter and then the snow made any journey hazardous.

5. Each settler had to be many things farmer blacksmith handyman doctor teacher and priest.

6. Entirely dependent on his crops the settler feared above all else drought locusts and hail against these he had no defense and they could destroy in days the labors of a year.

7. Their pleasures were simple but they were deep and lasting for example the pleasure of watching their farms grow the joy of creating something from nothing the satisfaction of harvest time.

8. Some settlers in fact preferred the rugged adventurous life as soon as civilization caught up with them they moved westward and opened more new land.

9. Daniel Boone according to S. E. White's book Daniel Boone Wilderness Scout was a man who disliked civilization that is he loved freedom which he said only the wilderness afforded.

10. Boone the most famous American backwoodsman was born November 2 1734 near Reading Pa. and

he died the exact date is not known in September 1820 already a legendary figure.

II

1. On July 20 1946 I remember the day perfectly Don Harry and I set out from Sudbury Ontario on a camping trip.
2. At Jamieson's a campers' supply store we had obtained our supplies canned goods fishing tackle extra blankets it was hard to think of blankets that hot day mosquito netting and a first-aid kit.
3. Don who was in charge of supplies almost forgot the matches and I much to the alarm of the others almost left our ax behind.
4. Our guide an experienced woodsman was recommended by my Uncle George who had been out with him several times twice last year and once this year Uncle George you see is crazy about fishing.
5. Since we didn't want to be kidded on our return we had never referred to our trip as a fishing trip we had merely said we were going camping.
6. In all our plans however fish played a big part we didn't take rods and flies and bait along for the fun of carrying them.
7. The long deep pine-bordered lake was beautiful the water was unbelievably clear and on bright days it was unbelievably blue.
8. Because the water was cold we did no voluntary swimming however Harry and I took an involuntary swim which scared us badly.
9. Early one morning Harry the proud fisherman went to sleep in the boat and while he was dozing a big fish started off with his line.
10. Harry grabbed for the rod but as he wasn't fully awake he reached a little too far lost his balance and fell overboard.

REVIEW EXERCISE B: *Commas, semicolons, colons, dashes, parentheses, italics, end marks.* Where there are quotation marks *in this exercise,* place other punctuation *inside* the quotation marks.

1. As we listened to the bad news the prospect of easy victory faded suddenly we were being told that the star hitter the catcher and the team captain were all too ill to play
2. The following equipment will be issued paper drawing boards pens ink textbooks and a T square
3. My friend Caroline who is always well dressed helped me pick out a new dress she did not realize however that I am not a millionaire
4. Those students who made the honor roll may be excused at 2 30 on Monday Wednesday and Friday all others must remain until 3 15
5. The school according to Mr Barnes has many needs a new field a new gym floor tennis and handball courts
6. If the weather changes Mr Sommers who has a new sailboat will take us sailing if it rains we will go to the Paramount my favorite theater
7. "Well you have certainly made a mess of the house" exclaimed Mother returning after her vacation
8. Mr Simpkins waiting uneasily for his turn to shoot grew more and more nervous finally when the gun was handed to him he pointed it at the target closed his eyes and pulled the trigger
9. "A bull's eye" exclaimed the proprietor then he handed Mr Simpkins the first prize a beautiful blanket
10. Although the train was not to leave until 4 30 everyone who was going on the excursion was on the platform at 4 15 therefore we were able to see who was going with us
11. The Boston Evening Transcript recommended Charles Evart's latest book The Man from Mars

20. PUNCTUATION

QUOTATION MARKS

20a. Use quotation marks to enclose a direct quotation — a person's exact words. Do not use quotation marks to enclose an indirect quotation — not a person's exact words.

DIRECT QUOTATION [the speaker's exact words]
Harry said, "I am going to ask Betty for a date."

INDIRECT QUOTATION [not the speaker's exact words]
Harry said that he was going to ask Betty for a date.

NOTE: *Enclose* means place quotation marks at both the beginning and the end of the quotation. Omission of quotation marks at the end of a quotation is a common error.

20b. A direct quotation begins with a capital letter.

RIGHT She said, "Ask your father."
RIGHT Father asked, "What did your mother say?"
RIGHT "She said I should ask you," I replied.

NOTE: If the quotation is only a fragment of a sentence, do not begin it with a capital letter.

RIGHT He denied the Senator's accusation that he was a "two-faced scoundrel."

20c. When a quoted sentence is divided into two parts by such interrupting expressions as *he said, she replied, Jack added,* etc., the second part begins with a small letter.

RIGHT   "I think," said Mary, "that you are mistaken."

RIGHT   "One afternoon last week," she explained, "our teacher kept us after school."

RIGHT   "We tried to do what was expected of us," he said; "however, the work was too hard."

If the second part of a broken quotation is a new sentence, it begins with a capital.

RIGHT   "The feature has just started," he said. "You will see almost all of it."

20d. A direct quotation is set off from the rest of the sentence by commas.

RIGHT   "You shouldn't have left school," said the principal, "without getting my permission."

20e. Other marks of punctuation when used with quotation marks are placed according to the following rules:

(1) Commas and periods are always placed inside the closing quotation marks.

RIGHT   "I know the right answer," he said, "but I don't know how to get it."

(2) Colons and semicolons are always placed outside the closing quotation marks.

RIGHT   Miss Crane said to us, "You are all in danger of failing"; what she said after that I was too dazed to hear.

RIGHT   The following students have, in the words of the superintendent, "surpassed all expectations": Homer Earll, Don McCurry, Jack Kenmore.

(3) Question marks and exclamation points are placed inside the closing quotation marks if they are a part of the quotation; otherwise they are placed outside.

RIGHT "What are your reasons?" challenged the speaker.

RIGHT Did he say, "Turn west" or "Turn left"?

RIGHT Never say, "It can't be done"!

20f. When you write dialogue (two or more persons carrying on a conversation) begin a new paragraph every time the speaker changes.

RIGHT "Hello, mates," said Captain Handy softly, "what can I do for you now?"

"You can turn over the ship to me," replied the first mate, his voice filled with tension. "I'll promise you fair treatment and a safe voyage home."

Handy looked with deliberation at the crowd of mutineers. "So it's mutiny, is it, you blackguards? You can't get away with it!" he roared.

"We have got away with it, sir," replied the mate, the automatic "sir" emerging in spite of himself.

"And we'll thank you for stepping down and turning over the ship at once," added Johnson, impatience in every word.

20g. Use quotation marks to enclose titles of chapters, articles, poems, and other parts of books or magazines.

For the correct way of indicating titles of books and magazines see page 435.

RIGHT Chapter II, "Capital Letters and Punctuation," is very valuable.

RIGHT The captain recommended an article in *Harper's*, "The Control of Science."

20h. Use *single* quotation marks to enclose a quotation within a quotation.

RIGHT George said, "As I remember, his exact words were, 'Meet me at the bank.'"
RIGHT Helen said, "I liked Henley's poem 'Invictus' very much."

EXERCISE 1. The following exercise is designed to test your ability to use quotation marks and the other marks of punctuation used with quotation marks. Copy it on your paper, inserting quotation marks and other necessary punctuation. Watch your paragraphing.

I don't care if I live to be a hundred said Pat I want an Easter basket every year. Why her mother asked you're too old for that. I still don't care replied Pat. Well said Mrs. Fletcher I suppose you may, if it amuses you to hard-boil eggs and dye them and then go out and buy yourself some candy and a chocolate Easter bunny, but it seems a little silly to me. The thrill is *supposed* to be in the surprise. Oh I'll be surprised all right answered Pat because when I wake up in the morning I'll be surprised that I really did all that work myself.

EXERCISE 2. The following exercise is designed to test your ability to use quotation marks and the other marks of punctuation used with quotation marks. Copy it on your paper, inserting quotation marks and other necessary punctuation. Watch your paragraphing.

A good secretary should anticipate her employer's needs Mr. Brown said, when I pinned him down to it.

She should know what he wants almost before he does
he took another turn around the room before he added
she shouldn't make him feel that she thinks she is smarter
than he is I'd never think I was smarter than my boss I
told him, rather scared. He continued you're new at the
game, aren't you the only trouble I've ever found with
secretaries is that when they become good ones, they know
it surely they'd not show they know it I put in hopefully.
He looked at me kindly as he explained that it took more
than ordinary tact to conceal that. I don't really mind
their thinking they're smarter than I he added. I often
get very good ideas from my good secretaries I'm glad to
give them credit more bewildered than ever, I made one
last attempt to find out what he was driving at do you
think I asked rather weakly I shall ever become a good
secretary it's quite possible, quite possible he beamed;
and I beat a hasty retreat.

EXERCISE 3. Try your hand at writing an interesting dialogue. Select two characters for your
conversation, put them in a special situation, and
make them talk. Two high school boys in the locker
room, two girls sitting next to each other in the
library or study hall, a student making thin excuses
for being an hour late to school, you and your father
after you have presented him with your report card.
These are suggestions. How can you work the
characters' actions into your dialogue? Remember
how to paragraph dialogue.

21. PUNCTUATION

THE APOSTROPHE

THE POSSESSIVE CASE

In the English language the possessive case of *nouns* is formed by adding an apostrophe and an *s* or, in some words, merely an apostrophe, to the noun.

RIGHT this man's coat
       Fred's bicycle
       both girls' hats

In forming the possessive of most nouns you will encounter no difficulty at all. Your problem, as you may already have discovered, will be *remembering* to put in the apostrophe. In other words, carelessness is responsible for most errors in omitting apostrophes.

NOUNS

21a. **To form the possessive case of a singular noun, add an apostrophe and an s.[1]**

RIGHT the boy's hat
RIGHT Bill's excuses
RIGHT Gus's baseball bat

21b. **To form the possessive case of a plural noun not ending in s, add an apostrophe and an s.**

[1] Many writers prefer to use only the apostrophe with words ending in *s*, but you will find the use of apostrophes easier if you always use the ' *and* s with any singular word, whether the word ends in *s* or not.

RIGHT men's club
RIGHT children's playground

21c. To form the possessive case of a plural noun ending in *s*, add the apostrophe only.

RIGHT ladies' handbags
RIGHT girls' sports

NOTE: Do not use an apostrophe to form the *plural* of a noun.

WRONG Three day's elapsed.
RIGHT Three *days* elapsed.
WRONG The plane's were left in hangar's.
RIGHT The *planes* were left in *hangars.*

Study the following examples of the application of these rules. Explain each.

SINGULAR	SINGULAR POSSESSIVE	PLURAL	PLURAL POSSESSIVE
car	car's bumper	cars	cars' bumpers
Mr. Barnes	Mr. Barnes's car	the Barneses	the Barneses' car
woman	woman's child	women	women's children
American	an American's pride	Americans	the Americans' pride
dog	dog's tail	dogs	dogs' tails
baby	baby's rattle	babies	babies' rattles
policeman	policeman's uniform	policemen	policemen's uniforms
book	book's cover	books	books' covers
army	army's equipment	armies	armies' equipment
doctor	doctor's prescription	doctors	doctors' prescriptions

PRONOUNS

21d. The possessive pronouns *his, hers, its, ours, yours, theirs,* and *whose* do not require an apostrophe.

The lists below show the nominative and possessive

forms of those pronouns. Note that there are *no* apostrophes.

NOMINATIVE CASE	POSSESSIVE CASE
you	yours
he	his
she	hers
it	its
we	ours
they	theirs
who	whose

21e. The pronouns *one, everyone, everybody,* etc., form their possessive case in the same way as nouns.

EXERCISE 1. On your paper make a 4-column chart like that on page 446, using these words: *enemy, laborer, coach, monkey, child, Mr. Jones, friend, teacher, fireman, clerk.* If you do not know how to spell the plural form of any of these words, look it up in the dictionary.

EXERCISE 2. List on your paper in the order in which they appear in the following paragraphs the words requiring apostrophes. After each word with an apostrophe write the thing possessed. Remember that the only nouns requiring just an apostrophe are plural words ending in *s*.

EXAMPLE 1. At Marians party the girls costumes were very funny.

  1. Marian's party
     girls' costumes

(The paragraphs are apostrophe exercises; they are not intended as models of good English.)

  1. At Walters suggestion our boys club decided to build

a club house in the Bergs back yard. 2. Everyones basement was searched, and Jimmys and ours yielded some useful crates. 3. (Jimmys uncle in Florida had been sending crates of Floridas best fruit to the Wrights all winter.) 4. The crates and some lumber from Fishers old fence were all we needed, according to our architects plans. 5. While we hunted, the other boys got shovels and spades from Mr. Greens tool shed and dug a hole for the foundation. 6. Then came the problem of nails and saws. 7. McGregors Department Store had plenty of nails, but the cost was a problem.

8. Someone remembered that Mrs. Longs lawn needed mowing, and everybodys lawn mower was rushed into action on the Longs yard. 9. Of course, Mrs. Long approved, and the mowers profits were soon turned over to our treasurers safekeeping. 10. Johns tool kit was raided for hammer and saw, and under Walters able direction, the house was begun. 11. By evening the neighborhoods interest was centered in the new project, and Franks father, together with Georges and mine, was out there helping.

12. In two days our clubs new house was finished.

EXERCISE 3. List in order on your paper the words requiring apostrophes. After each word with an apostrophe write the thing possessed. Remember that the only nouns requiring just an apostrophe are plural words ending in *s*.

1. Meanwhile Bills sister had brought several friends of hers to see our clubs new quarters. 2. Janes first idea was to have a house for their girls club too, but the boys spirit failed when they were asked to build another. 3. Helens suggestion that the girls could use the attic of her house seemed popular. 4. We all traipsed over to the Browns home and filed up the attic stairs. 5. The girls request that we boys put up a partition was granted;

and after getting Mrs. Browns consent, we set to work like experts. 6. With boards and old blankets the partition was built. 7. The new room was larger than our new house, and the girls originality in furnishing it far exceeded ours. 8. Our clubs furniture consisted of old boxes and crates, but theirs was old articles gathered from the girls homes. 9. They found an old rocker in Wrights attic, two porch chairs in Longs basement, and a folding cot. 10. The cots springs sagged pretty badly, and no ones home yielded a mattress. 11. The suns rays beating on the roof above the attic raised the temperature pretty high, and the girls decided their room would be used only on rainy days. 12. They said they would use ours on nice days!

21f. In compound words, names of business firms, and words showing joint possession, only the last word is possessive in form.

COMPOUND WORDS

   RIGHT brother-in-*law*'s home
   RIGHT sergeant-at-*arm*'s gun

NAMES OF BUSINESS FIRMS

   RIGHT Marble and *Wood*'s Furniture Store
   RIGHT Harcourt, Brace and *Company*'s office

JOINT POSSESSION

   RIGHT Ken and *Joe*'s jalopy
   RIGHT Alison and *Jean*'s room

21g. When two or more persons possess something individually, each of their names is possessive in form.

RIGHT *Ken*'s and *Joe*'s tennis rackets

21h. The words *minute, hour, day, week, month, year, etc.,* when used as possessive adjectives, require an apostrophe. Words indicating amount in *cents* or *dollars,* when used as possessive adjectives, require apostrophes.

RIGHT ten minutes' delay
RIGHT an hour's wait
RIGHT a month's vacation
RIGHT two cents' worth
RIGHT a dollar's worth

EXERCISE 4. Copy the following paragraph, inserting apostrophes where needed.

1. As it was an hours walk to Burgum and Barrs store we accepted my sister-in-laws offer of a ride. 2. Mothers and Dads cars were both in use. 3. After three days delay, Ruth and I were finally getting around to exchanging Ruths birthday present. 4. At her sisters suggestion I had bought her one of Burgum and Barrs teen-age handbags. 5. But good things, it seems, come in bunches, and Ruth got three of them. 6. Before her birthday Ruths junk was always cluttering up others handbags. 7. Mine was known as "Ruth and Marys bag"; no one knew really whose bag it was. 8. When my plans agreed with hers, our joint ownership of a bag worked out all right; however, if Ruths plans took her downtown and mine took me over to Andys, we didn't do so well. 9. Now that she had three bags and large gold *R*'s had been stamped on two of them, she had decided to exchange the one I gave her.

EXERCISE 5. Copy the following paragraph, inserting apostrophes where needed.

1. As we completed our ten minutes ride, I explained that she could exchange the bag for three dollars worth of

something.   2. She said she wanted a scarf like Jeans or a pair of gloves like her sisters.   3. Jeans and Barbaras scarves were alike, but that didn't bother Ruth, whose mind was made up.   4. "I never see Jean and her anyway," she argued.   5. We went straight to the girls sportswear counter, caught the clerks eye, and looked for a scarf.   6. To Ruths delight, we found what she wanted, a scarf like Jeans and Barbaras; then, to the clerks surprise, Ruth handed over the handbag as payment.   7. After about an hours delay, while the manager and everyone else struggled with red tape, we got the exchange straightened out.   8. Now that it was hers, she put the scarf on her head, and we went over to Klipps Drug Store for a coke.   9. The first people we saw there were Jean and Barbara, both wearing their scarves too!   10. Ruths face was red, but I grinned.

CONTRACTIONS

21i. Use an apostrophe to indicate where letters have been left out in a contraction.   A contraction is a word made up of two words combined into one by omitting one or more letters.

What words have been contracted and what letters have been omitted from the following?

We *can't* go.
It's going to rain.
They're staying at home.

EXERCISE 6.   Study the following contractions. Be able to write them when your teacher dictates to you the words in the numbered column.

1. should not	shouldn't	4. is not	isn't
2. they have	they've	5. they would	they'd
3. of the clock	o'clock	6. have not	haven't

7.	we are	we're	13.	I am	I'm
8.	were not	weren't	14.	they will	they'll
9.	that is	that's	15.	let us	let's
10.	has not	hasn't	16.	who is	who's
11.	she will	she'll	17.	he would	he'd
12.	he is	he's	18.	they had	they'd

19.	Bill is	Bill's
20.	does not	doesn't
21.	will not (other changes in the spelling here)	won't
22.	did not	didn't
23.	we would	we'd
24.	we should	we'd
25.	they are	they're

EXERCISE 7.   Copy the following sentences, inserting apostrophes wherever necessary.

1. Hed met radios greatest personalities.
2. Well get Mothers permission.
3. The boys bicycles werent all the same size.
4. The theaters policy wasnt clear.
5. Andersons Department Store announced that theyll be closed tomorrow.
6. Im sure hell accept Marys invitation.
7. Its three oclock according to Jacks watch.
8. Youll get a special price on the book because its cover isnt in good condition.
9. I havent met Annes brother.
10. Didnt you think wed be on time for Helens party?

"ITS" AND "IT'S"

The word *its* is the possessive form of the personal pronoun *it*. As you know, personal pronouns do not require an apostrophe in their possessive forms.

The word *it's* is a contraction of *it is*. The apostrophe takes the place of an omitted letter.

EXERCISE 8. This exercise is designed to give you practice in using *its* and *it's*. You should be able to do the exercise perfectly. Copy the sentences, inserting apostrophes where needed.

1. Its likely that the storm has already spent its fury.
2. If its lucky, the ship will make port without its rudder.
3. The box was in its proper place, but its contents were missing.
4. According to its author its a true story.
5. At its best its an exciting sport; at its worst its very dull.
6. Although its frame is too big, its a beautiful picture.
7. Its a letter for you even though its addressed to me.
8. The firm increased its salaries when its profits went up.
9. The team is doing its best, but its too late to win.
10. With its large print and many pictures, its an easy book to read.

21j. Use the apostrophe and *s* to form the plural of letters, numbers, and signs, and of words referred to as words.

RIGHT There are two *r*'s and two *s*'s in *embarrass*.
RIGHT He shot two *3*'s and two *2*'s in the first round.
RIGHT I had five *+*'s and seven *0*'s in this exercise.
RIGHT There are too many *and*'s in your sentence.

EXERCISE 9. Copy the following paragraphs, inserting apostrophes where needed.

1. Nancys a whirlwind. 2. Shes never idle. 3. Its not unusual when weve finished a hard days work to hear Nancys deep voice calling up someone to go swimming

at Morgans Pond or bowling at Johnson and Johnsons bowling alleys. 4. The chances are that shell be late for supper, argue her way out of doing the dishes, and be off again to Bettys or Joans or maybe out on the Wilsons lawn playing croquet. 5. Shes always borrowing her brothers things. 6. The other day she was wearing Harolds varsity sweater and Jims slacks, and riding Andys bike. 7. I guess youd say Nancys a tomboy.

8. Last spring Frank and Henry bought a little sailboat which they kept at Jessups Landing. 9. One day Nancy arrived, hopped aboard, untied the boat, and pushed off. 10. She knew whose boat it was, and in spite of Mr. Jessups warning that it was Frank and Henrys, she hoisted its sail and set out up Drakes Creek. 11. After three hours cruising, she came gaily back to find Frank and Henry waiting anxiously for her on the dock. 12. Theyd arrived a few minutes after shed left, and Jessup had told them whod taken their boat. 13. Its a wonder they didnt throw her into the river. 14. Nancys innocent air and laughing eyes only increased the owners rage as they pointed out that the boat was theirs, not hers; but she got them to drive her back to town in their car, and they even bought her a soda at Petes on the way. 15. Thats typical of Nancys power over males. 16. Now the boys keep the sail locked up in the boathouse — they alone have the key. 17. Theyd never trust anyone else, after having fallen victims to Nancys charm.

REVIEW EXERCISE A: *All Punctuation*. Copy the following sentences on your paper, inserting all necessary punctuation.

1. Saturdays game which was played at Baker Field was the last of the season

2. At six oclock in the morning Don plays his cornet and Lois practices her piano lessons

3. At 3 15 oclock school was dismissed and everyone went home

4. Where I asked have Billy Helen and Jane gone

5. Mr Hall the truant officer knew we had been to Kornfields Drug Store were we surprised

6. If the gloves are yours Mike youll have to identify them

7. Whose book is this Jean I asked its not mine

8. Barry on the contrary is a tall handsome young man

9. My friend Alex and Johns brother Jim are going to the movies with us however theres plenty of room in Freds station wagon for you and Hal and Jud

10. Gee I exclaimed leaping to the curb that was a close call

11. Dr Hardy who is our family doctor came here from Boise Idaho many years ago

12. The letter that I saw was addressed to Gerald Kahn 25 Cedar Lane Omaha Nebraska it was dated July 6 1948

13. Pupils who wish to take this test must bring the following articles drawing paper pencils and a compass

14. Well youd better hurry warned Miss Huss were late already

15. Its never too late George said his father when I was a boy I made many mistakes

REVIEW EXERCISE B: *All Punctuation.* Copy the following paragraphs, inserting all necessary punctuation.

1. School luckily for me was dismissed at 11 45 oclock this I thought was an undeserved break as English math and science are my afternoon classes the night before my sister Jane and I had asked Mary Sue and Evelyn to come over to do science and math with us they arrived right after the dishes were done it was Janes turn to wash and when they left at ten we hadnt even mentioned homework the books notebooks and pens which they had brought along lay untouched on the hall table with spring vacation less than one day away how could we think about school

2. Well it was a warm bright April day and as I walked home I could feel spring fever coming on I thought of things to do after lunch go over to Helens and play records go downtown shopping take a lazy sun bath I might even finish A Tale of Two Cities which I was supposed to have finished today yes it was going to be a wonderful afternoon

3. Mother however had another idea spring cleaning now dear she said in her customary businesslike tone Im going to need you this afternoon Aunt Alice is coming for the week end and the house has to be thoroughly cleaned furthermore Mrs. Lake our new neighbor and I are going shopping while were gone I want you and Jane to straighten up the house wash the living room windows and above all clean out your rooms Im putting Aunt Alice in yours Jane

4. Oh Mother I protested its such a nice day why do I have to stay indoors well be home all next week couldnt the cleaning wait besides I want to get that hat at Blumbergs yes I got nowhere I could see my own expression in Janes face

5. By five oclock when Mother returned the work was done and the best thought of the day occurred to me at least tomorrow we wont have to clean house

6. Hello girls Mothers cheerful voice came from the hall my how nice the windows look wed better do the rest of them tomorrow and by the way you can wash the living room curtains for me in the morning too Mrs. Lakes curtains are all done and ours look frightful

REVIEW EXERCISE C: *Capital Letters and Punctuation.* Copy the following sentences, inserting capital letters and punctuation.

1. My brother George who spent the summer at camp wildwood near burlington vermont likes new england summers

2. While Sally went shopping Mary set the table Helen dusted and I did the french homework for all of us

3. The mississippi river drains the middle west and its tributaries the ohio river and the missouri river reach as far into the northwest as montana and as far east as new york

4. The bergen electric company on market street had filled its showroom with new merchandise toasters irons washing machines lamps and a variety of radios

5. Yes I remember judge lamberts home said the old resident it was a big ugly brick house at the end of cherry street it stood where the first national bank now stands

6. On the southern shore of long island the surf is usually heavy on the northern side which is not on the atlantic ocean but on long island sound theres very little surf

7. You will Im sure be impressed by the beauty of yellowstone national park but nothing that youll see will surpass the grand canyon of the colorado

8. The sunnyside laundry on east state street advertised in the millville daily news for saturday march 3 that it would provide overnight service without extra cost

9. Come to my office at 3 45 said mr Atkins the mayor to patrolman Johnson so that I may hear your story of the robbery at the Hansen milling company

10. Its true said coach Horton that the team will do its best to win its last game against washington academy

11. Stewart Lister graduated from west high school in june and after studying at the university of chicago during the summer entered college in the fall as a sophomore

12. The players club of our high school rented the franklin theater for its production of Thornton Wilders play our town

22. SPELLING

LEARNING TO SPELL

By the time you reach high school you know whether or not you are a good speller. Really good spellers are rare people. If you are one of them, thank your lucky stars. If you are not, and you know you are not, you are like most of us who have to work at our spelling. You can improve your spelling if you want to, but you must make an effort. No one else can be of much help to you. *Learning to spell is your own personal responsibility.*

There is no one way to learn to spell. There are many ways, and you should learn what they are. By using a combination of several methods, you can in time become a good speller. Some of these ways which have helped many students are listed below. Read them over; put them into practice.

1. *In your notebook, keep a list of the words you misspell.*
2. *Get the dictionary habit.*
3. *Proofread your papers before handing them in.*
4. *Learn to spell words by syllables.*
5. *Learn to pronounce words correctly.*
6. *Use your ears, eyes, and pencil when learning to spell a word.*
7. *Learn lists of commonly misspelled words.*
8. *Learn a few helpful spelling rules and apply them.*

1. *In your notebook, keep a list of the words you misspell.* Set aside a few pages in your notebook

for listing words you have misspelled. This list, if kept up faithfully and reviewed frequently, will be the best means of removing your spelling errors. This method tests your will power. To copy down in your notebook all the misspelled words on your school papers *in all subjects* takes time and may seem a nuisance to you. But if you aren't willing to do that much to improve your spelling, you really don't have much desire to be a better speller.

2. *Get the dictionary habit.* The dictionary is the authority on correct spelling. Whenever you wish to write a word that you think you can't spell, you may try to solve your problem in several ways. You may simply take a chance and guess at the spelling. This has an element of sportiveness in it, keeps you in suspense until the teacher has corrected your paper. Besides, it is by far the easiest way — the easiest way to misspell a word!

You may ask someone how to spell the word you want. This method, like all methods which depend on others, has one big drawback. You have probably already discovered what the drawback is.

A third solution to your problem is to look up the word in a dictionary. You may quite reasonably wonder how you can look up the spelling of a word when you don't know how to spell it. This is sometimes an impossible task, but most of the time you can guess well enough to find the word; and once you have found it, you are really sure of the correct spelling, something you can never be sure of when you use the "guess" or "ask somebody" systems. Furthermore, the very experience of looking up the word helps you to fix the word in your mind so that you'll remember it longer.

3. *Proofread your papers before handing them in.*
"Proofreading" is the process of rereading carefully for errors whatever you have written. Proofreading is the best cure for carelessness in punctuation, using capital letters, spelling, etc. It takes only a few minutes, yet it makes a great difference in the correctness of your work.

4. *Learn to spell words by syllables.* A syllable is a word part which can be pronounced by itself. For instance, the word *af'ter* has two syllables; the word *bas'ket·ball* has three syllables; the word *an·ti·sep'tic* has four syllables. How many syllables has each of the following words? What are they?

1. apartment	4. America	7. information
2. friend	5. understand	8. break
3. jumper	6. villain	9. superintendent
	10. sacrifice	

When you divide a long word into its syllables, you are really making a number of shorter words out of it (these shorter words may have no meaning by themselves) and since short words are easy to spell, you make spelling easier. The word *congratulate*, for example, is a long word that may prove hard to spell unless you can divide it into syllables. Then it becomes much easier: *con·grat'u·late*. Dividing a word accurately into its syllables can be done only if you can pronounce the word correctly.

5. *Learn to pronounce words correctly.* Faulty pronunciation may lead to faulty spelling. The boy who says *ath·a·let'ics* for *athletics* will probably *spell* the word incorrectly. He will add an extra syllable. *Incorrect pronunciation* of *arctic* (as *artic*) will result in *incorrect spelling*, leaving out the first *c.* You

need to learn the correct pronunciation of a word in order to spell it correctly.

Study the pronunciation of the words in the following list. Notice how incorrect pronunciation could lead to incorrect spelling.

film	[**not** fil'*u*m]
library	[**not** lib*a*ry]
lightning	[**not** light*e*ning]
mis'chievous	[**not** mischiev'*i*ous]
probably	[**not** pro*bly* or pro*bally*]
surprise	[**not** *su*pprise]
privilege	[**not** priv*l*ege]
performance	[**not** *pre* formance]
perspiration	[**not** *pre*spiration]
boundary	[**not** bound*ry*]
candidate	[**not** can*i*date]
representatives	[**not** represen*tives*]

6. *Use your ears, eyes, and pencil when learning to spell a word.* When you undertake to master the correct spelling of a word, there are three steps you should take.

First, *pronounce the word*, noting its syllables. As you know, thinking of a word syllable by syllable makes the spelling easier.

Second, *study the word*, noting especially any letters which might make the spelling difficult. Notice, for instance, the two *c*'s and one *s* in occasion; the fact that there is no *e* after the *u* in argument; that there is an *e* in description, etc. After you have *seen and studied* the word, close your eyes and try to *visualize* it.

Third, *write the word*. Spelling is of use only in writing. The movement of your hand in making the letters will help to fix the spelling in your mind.

7. *Learn lists of commonly misspelled words.* The majority of the spelling errors made by students are made on a relatively few, frequently written words. Many of these words will appear easy to you. They should. But they *are*, nevertheless, so often misspelled that anyone wishing to improve his spelling should master them, and misspelling any of them should be counted as a serious error.

ONE HUNDRED SPELLING DEMONS [1]

ache
again
always
among
answer
any
been
beginning
believe
blue
break (to shatter)
built
business
busy
buy
can't
choose [present tense; *chose* is past tense]
color
coming
cough
could
country
dear
doctor

does
done
don't
early
easy
enough
every
February
forty
friend
grammar
guess
half
having
hear (ear)
heard
here (*there* — a place)
hoarse (frog in your throat)
hour
instead
just
knew
know
laid

loose (adjective and verb)
lose (verb — to *lose* money)
making
many
meant
minute
much
none
often
once
piece (a part of something)
raise
read [spelling is same for all tenses]
ready
said
says
seems
separate
shoes
since
some

[1] Reprinted from *Syllabus in English for Secondary Schools*, the University of the State of New York, 1945.

straight	tonight	where
sugar	too (too much;	whether (. . . or
sure	also)	not)
tear	trouble	which
their (ownership	truly	whole (sum of all
—*heir*)	Tuesday	parts)
there (*here* — a	two (2)	women
place)	used	won't
they	very	would
though	wear	write
through	Wednesday	writing
tired	week (52 in a year)	wrote

A list of other commonly misspelled words will be found on pages 479–81.

8. *Learn a few helpful spelling rules and apply them.* Once you have memorized some of the more useful spelling rules, you can "figure out" correct spelling. Most spelling, to be sure, is learned by memorizing, yet many people find rules helpful. The rules given below are the kind that will be of most help.

22a. Write *ie* when the sound is ēē, except after c.

EXAMPLES   believe, thief, fierce; ceiling, receive, deceive
EXCEPTIONS seize, either, weird, leisure, neither, financier

Write *ei* when the sound is *not* ēē, especially when the sound is ā.

EXAMPLES   freight, neighbor, weigh, height
EXCEPTIONS friend, mischief

EXERCISE 1. Write the following words, supplying the missing letters (*e* and *i*) in the correct order. Explain how the rule applies to each.

1. for...gn   4. conc...ve   7. c...ling
2. br...f   5. y...l   8. gr...f
3. rel...ve   6. n...ce   9. p...ce

10. rec...ve	15. perc...ve	20. s...ge
11. retr...ve	16. th...f	21. s...ze
12. sl...gh	17. bel...ve	22. bel...f
13. ach...ve	18. w...rd	23. f...nd
14. handkerch...f	19. rec...pt	24. l...sure

22b. When the prefixes [2] il–, in–, im–, un–, dis–, mis–, re–, and over– are added to a word, the spelling of the word itself remains the same.

il + legal = *il*legal

in + elegant = *in*elegant

im + movable = *im*movable

un + necessary = *un*necessary

un + excused = *un*excused

dis + appear = *dis*appear

dis + satisfied = *dis*satisfied

mis + understood = *mis*understood

mis + spell = *mis*spell

re + commend = *re*commend

over + run = *over*run

over + eat = *over*eat

22c. When the suffixes [3] -ness and -ly are added to a word, the spelling of the word itself remains the same.

EXAMPLES   mean + ness = mean*ness*; final + ly = final*ly*

EXCEPTIONS   Words ending in *y* change the *y* to *i* before a suffix: ready — read*ily*; heavy — heav*iness*; happy — happ*iness*.

EXERCISE 2. Spell correctly the words indicated.

1. *rate* with the prefix *over*
2. *usual* with the suffix *ly*
3. *agree* with the prefix *dis*

[2] A prefix is a letter or group of letters added to the *beginning* of a word to change its meaning.

[3] A suffix is a letter or group of letters added to the *end* of a word to change its meaning.

4. *green* with the suffix *ness*
5. *mature* with the prefix *im*
6. *approve* with the prefix *dis*
7. *used* with the prefix *mis*
8. *general* with the suffix *ly*
9. *natural* with the prefix *un*
10. *practical* with the suffix *ly*
11. *able* with the prefix *un*
12. *stubborn* with the suffix *ness*
13. *logical* with the prefix *il*
14. *accurate* with the prefix *in*
15. *able* with the prefix *dis*
16. *moral* with the prefix *im*
17. *construct* with the prefix *re*
18. *efficient* with the prefix *in*
19. *similar* with the prefix *dis*
20. *stern* with the suffix *ness*
21. *step* with the prefix *mis*
22. *use* with the prefix *mis*
23. *opened* with the prefix *un*
24. *brutal* with the suffix *ly*

22d. Drop the final *e* before a suffix beginning with a vowel.

EXAMPLES care + ing = car*ing*   use + able = us*able*
EXCEPTIONS Keep the final *e* before *a* or *o* if necessary to retain the soft sound of *c* or *g* preceding the *e*: noti*ce*able, coura*ge*ous.

22e. Keep the final *e* before a suffix beginning with a consonant.

EXAMPLES care + ful = care*ful*   care + less = care*less*
EXCEPTIONS true + ly = tru*ly*   argue + ment = argu*ment*

EXERCISE 3. Write correctly the words formed as follows:

1. cure + ing
2. hope + ing
3. fame + ous
4. approve + al
5. nine + ty
6. change + able
7. prepare + ing
8. name + less
9. write + ing
10. singe + ing
11. desire + able
12. love + ing
13. hope + less
14. move + ing
15. true + ly

THE PLURAL OF NOUNS

22f. Observe the rules for spelling the plural of nouns.

(1) The regular way to form the plural of a noun is to add an *s*.

EXAMPLES chair, chairs   book, books

(2) The plural of some nouns is formed by adding *es*.

The *e* is necessary to make the plural form pro-
nounceable in the case of words ending in *s*, *sh*, *ch*,
and *x*.

EXAMPLES dress, dresses   bush, bushes
            birch, birches   box, boxes

(3) The plural of nouns ending in *y* *following a consonant* is
formed by changing the *y* to *i* and adding *es*.

EXAMPLES fly, flies   lady, ladies
            enemy, enemies   salary, salaries

(4) The plural of nouns ending in *y* *following a vowel* is
formed in the usual way.

EXAMPLES monkey, monkeys   donkey, donkeys

(5) The plural of most nouns ending in *f* or *fe* is formed by
adding *s*. The plural of some nouns ending in *f* or *fe* is
formed by changing the *f* to *v* and adding *es*.

EXAMPLES Add *s*: roof, roofs   dwarf, dwarfs
            chief, chiefs

Change *f* to *v* and add *es*:

knife, knives	calf, calves
loaf, loaves	wharf, wharves
leaf, leaves	

(6) The plural of nouns ending in o *following a vowel* is formed by adding s. The plural of most nouns ending in o *following a consonant* is formed by adding es.

EXAMPLES *o* following a vowel:

rodeo, rodeos   radio, radios

o following a consonant:

hero, heroes   potato, potatoes
mosquito, mosquitoes

(7) The plural of most nouns ending in o and *referring to music* is formed by adding s.

EXAMPLES

piano, pianos   soprano, sopranos   solo, solos

(8) The plural of a few nouns is formed by irregular methods.

EXAMPLES

child, children	tooth, teeth	woman, women
mouse, mice	ox, oxen	goose, geese

(9) The plural of compound nouns (more than one word) is formed by making the *principal word* plural.

EXAMPLES mother-in-law, mothers-in-law
man-of-war, men-of-war
court martial, courts martial
lieutenant colonel, lieutenant colonels
passer-by, passers-by

(10) The plural of compound nouns ending in *-ful* is formed by adding s to the end of the word.

EXAMPLES cupful, cupfuls   handful, handfuls

(11) The plural of foreign words is sometimes formed as in the foreign language.

EXAMPLES alumnus (man), alumni (men)
alumna (woman), alumnae (women)
datum, data
analysis, analyses
bacillus, bacilli
crisis, crises

(12) The plural of other foreign words may be formed either as in the foreign language or by adding *s* or *es*.

EXAMPLES index, indices *or* indexes
appendix, appendices *or* appendixes

(13) The plural of numbers and letters is formed by adding an apostrophe and *s*.

EXAMPLES There are ten *5*'s in this column.
There are two *s*'s in *necessary*.

(14) Some nouns are the same in the singular and plural.

EXAMPLES sheep, deer, trout, species, Chinese

EXERCISE 4. Write the plural form of each of the following nouns. After each write the number of the rule that applies.

1. bench
2. boy
3. gas
4. potato
5. hoof
6. torch
7. cry
8. man
9. house
10. key
11. cargo
12. fox
13. brother-in-law
14. goose
15. radio
16. shelf
17. editor in chief
18. bacillus
19. wolf
20. spoonful

EXERCISE 5. Write the plural form of each of the following nouns. After each write the number of the rule that applies.

1. candy
2. sheep
3. piano
4. valley
5. alumnus
6. library
7. handkerchief
8. crisis
9. lady
10. tomato

11. fly
12. alto
13. appendix
14. calf
15. century
16. major general
17. mouthful
18. hero
19. knife
20. brush

EXERCISE 6. By referring to the rules you have learned, explain orally the spelling of each of the following:

1. receive
2. illegible
3. coming (e dropped)
4. niece
5. contraltos
6. misstate
7. drunkenness
8. peaceable
9. belief
10. ladies

11. unnoticed
12. alumnae
13. naturally
14. seize
15. writing (e dropped)
16. overrule
17. roofs
18. weigh
19. loaves
20. disappear

WORDS FREQUENTLY CONFUSED

Mastery of the words in the lists on the following pages — their meaning and their spelling — will greatly improve your spelling. Study only a few at a time, and really master them.

already   *previously*
     I had *already* finished my homework before you called.

all ready	*all are ready*
	We were *all ready* at the same time.
altogether	*entirely*
	He doesn't *altogether* approve of me.
all together	*everyone in the same place*
	We were *all together* at Christmas.
capital	*city*
	Washington is the *capital* of the United States.
capitol	*building*
	The *capitol* stands at the end of a broad avenue.
cloths	*pieces of cloth.*
	Try the new cleaning *cloths.*
clothes	*what you wear*
	She has a wardrobe full of expensive *clothes.*
course	*path of action*
	He followed a straight *course.*
	The golf *course* and the race *course* are outside of town.
	Soup was the first *course.*
	I am taking a *course* in cooking.
coarse	*rough, crude*
	He wore a suit of *coarse* cloth and used *coarse* language.
des'ert	*a dry region*
	We flew across the *desert.*
desert'	*to leave*
	He *deserted* his family.
dessert'	*what you eat last*
	The *dessert* was ice cream.

EXERCISE 7. Number on your paper from 1 to 15. Write after the proper number the correct one of the words given in parentheses in the sentences below.

1. The mail had (already, all ready) been collected.
2. You were (altogether, all together) in the gym when the alarm sounded.
3. What is the (capitol, capital) of Virginia?
4. This wood seems very (coarse, course) grained.
5. I expected a delicious (dessert, desert) after such a good dinner.
6. She spends her money on (cloths, clothes).
7. We had our picture taken on the steps of the (capital, capitol).
8. I wasn't (all together, altogether) sure of myself.
9. When you are (already, all ready) let me know.
10. The painters used these (cloths, clothes) for cleaning.
11. Henry is taking the commercial (course, coarse).
12. The (desert, dessert) was an almost impossible barrier to the pioneers.
13. We are (all ready, already) to begin.
14. He showed himself to be an (altogether, all together) disagreeable person.
15. The new golf (coarses, courses) will be laid out here.

EXERCISE 8. Write sentences in which you use correctly each of the words just studied.

hear	*using your ears*	
	I *hear* him coming.	
here	*this place*	
	He promised to wait *here*.	
its	*possessive*	
	The village is proud of *its* school.	

it's *it is*
It's a long way.

lead *present tense — to go first*
You *lead* us and we will follow.

led *past tense*
He *led* the army to victory.

lead [pronounced lĕd] *a heavy metal; also graphite in a pencil*
The industrial uses of *lead* are many.

loose *free, not close together*
The animals broke *loose*.
He stumbled in the *loose* sand.

lose [pronounced lōōz] *to suffer loss*
When did you *lose* your books?

moral *good; also a lesson of conduct*
His good conduct showed him to be a *moral* person.
The class understood the *moral* of the story.

morale *mental condition, spirit*
The *morale* of the army is high.

peace *opposite of strife*
Everyone prefers *peace* to war.

piece *a part of something*
They ate every *piece* of cake.

EXERCISE 9. Number on your paper from 1 to 15. Write after the proper number the correct one of the words given in parentheses in the sentences below.

1. They are all (here, hear) now.
2. He (led, lead) his horse into the clearing.

3. Did you (loose, lose) your bag?
4. Last year Captain Jones (lead, led) his men through maneuvers.
5. Our class (morale, moral) has been higher since the last class meeting.
6. A (peace, piece) of the kite was hanging from the telegraph pole.
7. At the first turn, Harry (lead, led) the field.
8. I (hear, here) you are going on a trip.
9. (It's, Its) a good day for a picnic.
10. The bolt is (lose, loose) on my wheel.
11. We hope (peace, piece) will last a long time.
12. As we approached the city, we noticed that (its, it's) skyscrapers could be seen for miles.
13. I'll give her a (piece, peace) of my mind.
14. If (its, it's) required, I'll take Latin next year.
15. Springfield held (its, it's) community parade on Memorial Day.

EXERCISE 10. Write sentences in which you use correctly each of the words just studied.

personal   *individual*
He gave his *personal* opinion.

personnel   *a group of people employed in the same place*
The *personnel* of the company ranged in age from 16 to 64.

plain   *not fancy;* also *a flat area of land;* also *clear*
She lives in a very *plain* home.
We crossed the *plains* in two days.
Our problem is quite *plain*.

plane   *a flat surface;* also *a tool;* also *an airplane*
Plane geometry is a study of imaginary flat surfaces.
The carpenter used a *plane*.
A *plane* circled the airport.

principal   *head of a school,* also *the main one of several things*

He was sent to the *principal's* office.

The *principal* cause of accidents is carelessness.

principle   *a rule of conduct;* also *a main fact or law*

The judge accused the criminal of having no *principles.*

He understands the *principles* of mathematics.

shone   past tense of *shine*

The sun *shone* all day.

shown   *revealed*

We were *shown* several unusual exhibits at the museum.

stationary   *in a fixed position*

The classroom desks are *stationary.*

stationery   *writing paper*

I received three boxes of *stationery* at Christmas.

there   *a place;* also *an expletive* (see page 44)

We were *there* at two o'clock.

There were four of us.

their   *possession*

The pupils bring *their* own lunches.

they're   *they are*

They're going with us.

EXERCISE 11. Number on your paper from 1 to 15. Write after the proper number the correct one of the words given in parentheses in the sentences below.

1. My (principle, principal) difficulty is learning irregular verbs.

2. The child's face (shown, shone) with delight.
3. The Indian remained (stationery, stationary) in his canoe.
4. (There, Their, They're) we were, standing in the pouring rain.
5. In geometry we're studying (planes, plains) and angles.
6. My (personal, personnel) opinion should not influence you.
7. The movies were (shown, shone) in the school auditorium.
8. If (their, they're, there) going with us, they had better hurry.
9. "It is a matter of (principle, principal)!" the judge declared.
10. The queen, according to her portraits, had a (plain, plane) face.
11. As usual, I have no (stationery, stationary) left.
12. (Their, They're, There) schoolbooks were strewn all over the floor.
13. The (personal, personnel) manager was very sympathetic with the employees.
14. The (principle, principal) of our school went to college in Ohio.
15. "(Their, They're, There) making an awful racket," complained Mother.

EXERCISE 12. Write sentences in which you use correctly each of the words just studied.

threw	*hurled*
	Somebody *threw* a stone at the dog.
through	*in at one side and out at the opposite side*
	The stone went *through* a window.
to	[preposition]; and part of the infinitive form of a verb

Give the book *to* me, please.
We will have *to* leave early.

too   [adverb] *also,* **too** *much*

I am a sophomore, and George is a sophomore *too.*

There were *too* many problems in one home-work assignment.

two   *one + one*

We had only *two* dollars.

weather   *conditions outdoors*

The *weather* was stormy all week end.

whether   (**whether** or not)

I don't know *whether* or not he meant what he said.

who's   *who is, who has*

Who's coming?
Who's been here?

whose   *possession*

Whose coat is this?

your   *possession*

Is this *your* coat?

you're   *you are*

You're out!

EXERCISE 13.   Number on your paper from 1 to 15.   Write after the proper number the correct one of the words given in parentheses in the sentences below.

1. Who (threw, through) that eraser?
2. (Your, You're) going to have to study hard tonight.
3. (Whether, Weather) you can go or not depends on your behavior this week.

4. (Too, Two, To) of us trailed out to the car together.
5. (Who's, Whose) going to go with us?
6. (You're, Your) father said we could drive over with him.
7. The boat shot (threw, through) the water at 60 knots.
8. "May I come (too, to, two)?" Marie asked.
9. (Whose, Who's) rubbers were left here in the hall?
10. We will be there (weather, whether) it rains or not.
11. The (weather, whether) has been fine this spring.
12. It's (your, you're) responsibility to pass the course.
13. I don't know (whose, who's) clothes these are.
14. (To, Two, Too) many of us tried out for football; we weren't all accepted.
15. I don't believe she knows (whose, who's) invited.

EXERCISE 14. Write sentences in which you use correctly each of the words just studied.

REVIEW EXERCISE. Number on your paper from 1 to 50. Select the correct one of the words in parentheses in each sentence and write it after the proper number.

1. Down the (Capitol, capital) steps came the President and his cabinet.
2. Red flags marked the race (course, coarse).
3. How long have you been (here, hear)?
4. When you are (all ready, already), let me know.
5. The fire may have started in a pile of oily dust (cloths, clothes).
6. (Its, It's) never too late to mend.
7. The navy found that good food was an excellent (morale, moral) builder.
8. When we were (altogether, all together) we had our picture taken.
9. I can't remember (whether, weather) John was here or not.

10. A country's largest city is not always its (capital, capitol).
11. The seats in this room are (stationery, stationary).
12. You are (all ready, already) late.
13. There were only twenty-one years of (peace, piece) between World Wars I and II.
14. He teaches two classes in (plain, plane) geometry.
15. Our guide (led, lead) us to the top of the monument.
16. (Their, They're, There) the best friends I have.
17. You will (lose, loose) your money if you are not careful.
18. You came (to, too, two) late for the show.
19. The sun had (shown, shone) all day.
20. How long were you (they're, their, there)?
21. Watch where (your, you're) going!
22. The (coarse, course) in physics nearly finished me.
23. Forgetting her weight, she devoured two rich (deserts, desserts).
24. He was wearing a (lose, loose) cape.
25. The (principal, principle) speaker was the Governor.
26. We couldn't tell (whether, weather) the ball was a foul or not.
27. Are there more than (too, to, two) of you?
28. When he (through, threw) the ball, everyone ducked.
29. He is liable to (lose, loose) his temper.
30. She has a wardrobe of the finest (clothes, cloths).
31. Buffalo Bill scoured the (plain, plane) for wild animals.
32. He is a man (whose, who's) friendships are few but lasting.
33. By ten o'clock we were (all ready, already).
34. If you start fast, (you're, your) sure to win.
35. The (desert, dessert) is no longer a serious obstacle to travel.
36. We studied the (principals, principles) of good writing.
37. The house sank as (its, it's) foundations gave way.
38. (Whose, Who's) in charge of the dance?
39. The peasants' coats were made of (coarse, course) material.

40. If you (desert, dessert) us now, we shall never forgive you.
41. He seemed (altogether, all together) sure of himself.
42. I gave him a (piece, peace) of cake.
43. Dr. Michael is (principal, principle) of our school.
44. Do you know (whose, who's) this is?
45. The judge accused his prisoner of low (morale, moral) standards.
46. We asked for information regarding the factory's (personnel, personal).
47. I thought I'd (lose, loose) my mind!
48. General Eisenhower (lead, led) us to victory.
49. The yearbook staff has (its, it's) own office.
50. Each officer in the company uses business (stationary, stationery).

THREE HUNDRED SPELLING WORDS [4]

absence	apologize	awfully
abundance	appearance	bachelor
accidentally	appetite	banana
accommodate		bargain
accurate	appreciate	basketball
acknowledgment	approaching	beautiful
acquaintance	appropriate	beginning
across	approval	
advice	argument	believe
advise	arrange	bicycle
	assistant	biscuit
aerial	association	bookkeeper
aisle	athletics	brake
all right	attach	break
almost		breathe
amateur	attacked	bruise
annual	attention	bulletin
anonymous	awful	bureau

[4] This list includes some but not all the spelling words taken up as individual problems elsewhere in this chapter.

buried
business
cafeteria
calendar
campaign
candidate
captain
caricature
cellophane
cemetery

certain
character
chauffeur
college
column
coming
commission
committee
comparatively
completely

complexion
conquer
conscience
conscious
convenience
copies
cordially
corps
correspondence
courageous
courteous
courtesy
criticism
customer
cylinder
defense
definitely

delivery
descent
description

despair
desperate
develop
dictionary
dining
diphtheria
dirigible
disappear
disappointment
discipline

disease
dissatisfied
doesn't
dutiful
earnest
economical
ecstasy
efficient
eighth
embarrass

endeavor
equipment
equipped
especially
etiquette
exaggerate
excellent
exercise
exhausted
existence
explanation
extraordinary
familiar
fascinating

fatigue
faucet
February
fierce
fiery
finally

foreign
forfeit
forty
fourth
fragile
gasoline
genius
government
governor
grammar

grateful
guarantee
guard
gymnasium
handkerchief
happened
haven't
height
heroes
hoping

horizon
hospital
humorous
imitation
immediately
indispensable
influence
initial
irresistible
kerosene

knowledge
laboratory
license
lightning
likelihood
loneliness
losing
luxurious
lying
maneuver

marriage
martyr
matinee
meant
medicine
medieval
mentioned
microphone
minimum
mischievous
misspelled
monotonous
mortgage
movable
municipal
necessarily
necessary
necessity
nickel
ninety

ninth
nuisance
occasionally
occurred
o'clock
omitted
opinion
opportunity

optimistic
orchestra

original
parachute
parallel
particularly
pastime
perhaps
permanent
personally
perspiration
picnic

picnicking
planning
pleasant
pneumonia
possess
possibility
practice
prejudice
prisoner
privilege

probably
procedure
professor
pronunciation
propeller
purpose
pursue
questionnaire
quiet
quite

realize
really
receive
recognize
recommend

referred
rehearse
reign
relief
repetition
representative
restaurant
rhythm
sandwich
satisfactorily
schedule
scissors
seize
semester
separate

sergeant
shining
similar
sincerely
sophomore
souvenir
specimen
speech
speedometer
strategy

stretch
subtle
success
sufficient
suggestion
superintendent
superior
surgeon
surprised
syllable

sympathy
symphony
synonym

tariff
television
temperament
thoroughly
tomorrow
tournament
traffic

tragedy
transferred

truly
twelfth
tying
tyranny
umbrella
undoubtedly
unnecessary
until

using

vacuum
vengeance
vicinity
villain
waist
waste
Wednesday
weird
writing

INDEX